Planning and Operating
Motels and Motor Hotels

Planning and Operating Motels and Motor Hotels

GEORGE O. PODD & JOHN D. LESURE
partners in the
firm of Horwath & Horwath

AHRENS BOOK COMPANY, INC., NEW YORK
a division of HAYDEN PUBLISHING COMPANY, INC.

Preface

If, after reading this book, you still want to go into the motel business, you will at least be entering the field knowing much more about it than the people who ventured that way in the 1940's and 1950's and whose experiences have been drawn on to make this book possible. Also, we expect that those experiences will continue to conform to the pattern of travel, which is still changing and probably always will be, presenting additional challenges and opportunities in the future for those interested in serving the traveling public.

The material in this book could not have been put together without the fine cooperation received from many persons, to whom we wish to express our sincere thanks. The partners of Horwath & Horwath were quite lenient about the time taken from other duties in helping with the book. They assisted the authors greatly with advice, research and review. Special thanks are due Mr. Henry W. Espersen, head of our Chicago Special Services Department, who prepared the original text and illustrations for the chapter on food and beverage facilities as well as in the preparation of the food and beverage cost control section, and many of the charts used in connection with other chapters in the text. The sections on the referral, franchise and trade associations could not have been as informative as they are without the complete cooperation of those organizations. The American Institute of Architects was most kind in allowing us to use their examples of guest room layouts and our clients and other friends in the business were liberal with photographs and data which assisted greatly in completing the book. We wish also to thank Richard Neuberger for his help in editing the manuscript and Mrs. Patricia Cihomski for the many hours she spent in manuscript preparation.

While motels and motor hotels are faced with certain problems at the present time, we believe that the long-term outlook is very bright. It is our hope that this book will play at least a small role in guiding the future growth and progress in this field of accommodations to a soundness and success that will enhance its reputation with the traveling public and its contribution to our general economy.

George O. Podd
and
John D. Lesure
January, 1964

Contents

Introduction

The last decade has seen vast and rapid changes in the accommodations and public hospitality business, during which time motels have become recognized as an established and important segment of the industry. In fact, written information and reference data are far outdistanced, mainly because of the speed with which new establishments have been built. As a result, the motel business has changed from an essentially amateur operation which once found its profit in the highway traveler to a complex operation that today demands a much more professional approach from those entering the field.

We believe this book to be especially timely and valuable for those who contemplate entering the business, either through investment or as a direct means of livelihood. We have outlined our views and what we know to be helpful advice on the many aspects of this field, trusting that the reader will be on much more solid ground after examining a reasonably full picture of the factors involved. To do this it has been necessary to go beyond the areas in which we ourselves have specialized and to cover such problems as choice of site, organization, financing, construction, furnishings and operation, as well as the hazards of changing times, competition, and human tastes. Naturally we do not cover all of these subjects in detail. Rather we plan this book as a preliminary approach from which the reader will be better able to decide his own plan of action and judge for himself the extent to which he will have to further supplement his own knowledge and experience.

This book also serves as a functional reference and guide for those already in the motel and motor hotel business. The text will be useful as a check on their own views, since it draws heavily from the judgment and experiences of the men in our own organization and of the operators who have been in the business long enough to offer their views on a sound professional basis. As in any field of endeavor, the axiom that "experience is the best teacher" applies to the motel business. Certainly the next best thing is to be in a position to profit from the experience of others. Therefore this text will be helpful in expanding the scope of knowledge of those engaged in the business beyond the limitations of their own experience.

Then there is the need for a general guide for those who are interested in the motel and motor hotel business because they gain their livelihood from related fields. These are the real estate men, architects, builders, suppliers, and decorators, as well as the lawyers, accountants, financial advisers and lending agencies, all of whom should benefit from a review of their particular function in relation to the entire project. A myriad of people less directly involved—such as those in the appraisal field, public officials, or civic-minded private citizens—will also find this a useful guide.

Strictly speaking, this is not a "textbook." But we have endeavored to make it as factual and authentic as possible in order that it be reliable for general reference, phrased in the language of the layman. Thus we also intend it as a helpful source of information for those to whom an overview of the nature of the business and the reasoning behind the development of the form and content of financial statements and related statistics will be particularly helpful.

The reader should bear in mind that in covering a field as wide and varied as this one we could not confine ourselves entirely to general terms which would apply to all sizes and types of establishments which comprise the motel and motor hotel field. Therefore the reader will, we hope, apply the text as it is written to his own circumstances in a way that will best fit his needs. In the interest of clarity, for instance, we have used the expanded staff to illustrate the functions connected with these positions. The jobs under these titles may, of course, be covered by one person in a smaller operation, in which case the reader should apply the functions outlined under these titles to the person to whom they are actually assigned. Nor could we hope to cover in detail all of the conveniences and niceties of service that might be found in a large motor hotel, in which case the reader may amplify the text with his own ideas and experience.

This book is intended primarily as an introduction to the business. Its main purpose is to assist in keeping the motel and motor hotel business on a sound basis, so that it will not only show solid growth and make a real contribution to the economy, but also that the people in it will be happy and thus better able to contribute to the comfort and enjoyment of the traveler who comes their way.

1

Brief History of the Accomodations Industry

The public hospitality business in this country has its roots in pre-Revolutionary times when the traveler, on horse or foot, journeyed from one community to another. Naturally, early establishments were placed at convenient resting spots along the road. They provided the traveler with food and drink, a bed and a place for his horse. Prior to and during the Revolution, establishments of any consequence might generally be categorized as the New England-type inn, the southern coffee house, the stagecoach way station and, in large cities, the tavern and the early hotel. Places doing the greatest volume of business at that time were located near water transportation.

The rapid development of the railroad had a pronounced effect on the mode of travel and resulted in a new and expanded field of public hospitality. Indeed, the hotel business as we knew it from the mid-nineteenth century through the 1920's grew apace in size and service with the railroads and soon dominated the field.

While many of the inns in the smaller towns continued to prosper during this transition period because of their fortunate proximity to main streams of travel, the way station and coffee house succumbed, along with a great many of the inns and taverns. Changes in the travel pattern increasingly favored the hotels accessible to the railroad station.

With the development of larger hotels in the metropolitan centers the personal touch of "Ye Host" greeting his guests and seeing personally to their comfort had to be delegated to a team consisting

4

of members of the expanded staff of front office employees. Hotels remained in the forefront in developing the tastes of the guest, with such items as the private bath, the room telephone, bellmen, porters and room service. Most of these conveniences, once regarded as luxuries, soon became accepted as necessities by the traveler. This period culminated in the development of larger hotels, many of five hundred rooms or more, and a few that could boast of over two thousand.

The feverish building of the 1920's included not only these larger transient and many residential hotels in major cities and towns, but also smaller town hotels developed by civic-minded groups and other promoters. The resort business grew up in that time too, supplemented to a small extent by what was known as the "tourist home."

The economic climate of the 1920's and the eagerness of the general public to invest in real estate bonds increased the supply of capital for these promotions to the point where equity money necessary to ownership and operation of these properties was often comparatively low in proportion to the total cost of the hotel. Nor was there a Securities & Exchange Commission devoted to the protection of the investing public, and the prosperity after World War I enabled many persons not familiar with investments to have funds available for what appeared to be a safe and highly profitable investment. Real estate has always been related to safety in the minds of investors, but the manipulations and distortions that took place in the type of securities involved in these ventures soon made it apparent that safety factors were spread too thin. During the early 1930's and the grave depression that set in, the financial structures of those properties financed through bond issues began to reflect their weaknesses. Receiverships and loss of properties took their toll among owners and investors in that reorganization period.

Foundations were laid at this time for several of the large hotel chains through the purchase of properties by group operators at prices far below replacement values. Shortly afterward came the conflict in Europe and our entry into World War II. Our involvement in war resulted in a wholesale shift of population that suddenly caused hotel occupancies to rise from 64 per cent in 1940 to 93 per cent in 1946, the highest level recorded in our statistics for hotels. People who traveled in this country during that time can well remember the difficulties encountered in finding a room in a hotel.

Hotels at that time operated under rent control regulations, which froze room rates at their 1942 level through 1946. Many of the residential properties converted space to transient occupancy during that period. Also, it was almost impossible to obtain materials and labor for improvements and additions because of wartime restrictions. These circumstances combined to bring the hotel business back to a period of comparative financial soundness which it continued to enjoy though the postwar period of the late 1940's and early 1950's. The chain operators swelled their holdings and built to their present status of dominance in the industry.

Few hotels were built in that decade, but hotelmen were busy rehabilitating, modernizing, and extending their existing properties to make up for the wear and tear of the war years and the immediate postwar period. It was not until the late 1950's and early 1960's that many new hotels of consequence were built. Principally additions to the larger chain operations, they included the Philadelphia-Sheraton, The Statler Hilton in Los Angeles, the Sheraton-Dallas and the Hilton hotels in Denver and Pittsburgh. The Americana, Hilton and Summit in New York City were built in the early 1960's. The Executive House, the newest large hotel in Chicago, became the headquarters property of its group. The construction of other new properties now in process indicates that the once often-quoted statement, "There have been no new hotels built in the past thirty years," is now far from the truth.

While the hotel business expanded rapidly from the 1920's, another major development was also taking place. With the advent of Henry Ford's mass-produced auto, the American traveler had opened to him a new, convenient means of transportation. The automobile freed him from his close dependency on railroads and soon the traveler was relying heavily on the highways once more, bringing full circle the modes of transportation in this country. This time we are going around on a much wider circle than was known or dreamed of by the New England or East Coast traveler of Revolutionary times. The increase in speed of travel, the growth in population and the improvement in the standard of living all contributed to rapid changes in travel patterns. Starting in the late 1930's and increasing steadily after World War II, the hotel guest was arriving by car, statistics of the American Automobile Association indicating that over 85 per cent of the arrivals in the 1950's used this means of transportation.

During this same decade hotel occupancy percentages showed a steady decline from the high eighties down to the mid-sixties by 1960 and to the low sixties in 1962. The hotels in metropolitan centers had benefited from massive convention business which grew up during this period and helped them to maintain their profit margins, but smaller hotels in the towns and villages around the country suffered more severely, their percentage of occupancy dropping into the fifties and below by 1960.

Almost without those in the hotel business realizing it, a whole new major segment of the accommodations industry was being developed by persons who were taking advantage of the changes in travel patterns brought about by the automobile.

It started in the early part of the century with the appearance of what were called tourist cabins, built along the road to provide only a place to sleep, with no such refinements as private bath or telephone, and no provision for food or other basic needs. Often crudely constructed and operated by farmers, these installations were not then regarded as serious competition by hotelmen. In fact, in the early days many of these tourist cabin operations were derided and reviled by hotelmen as being unsanitary and dilapidated, and were often described by them and by newspapers as being places of ill-repute. Cabins of this type, however, were appealing to some travelers by virtue of cheap rates made possible by low construction costs and simplicity of operation, which did not require any significant expenditure for payroll and only a modest amount for utilities and upkeep.

Then came the development of the tourist court, usually owned by individuals or families and operated under the supervision of a husband and wife team. These courts upgraded this section of the accommodations industry with guest units which were more substantially built and which eventually included tiled bath, wall-to-wall carpet, free radio and television, air conditioning, and room telephone. Because their location was adjacent to highways or on the outskirts of towns and cities they still presented no major threat to hotels, but did become annoying competition. The beginnings of the shift were on.

We do not know exactly when the term "motel" first came into use. General acceptance of it appears to date prior to 1940. The "Tourist Court Journal," which commenced publication in October 1937, was designated as the official publication of the International Motor Court Association, the name of which association had been changed from "National Tourist Lodge and Motor Court Association" in April of that year. United Motor Courts and the Tourist Court Owners Association had already been in existence four or five years by that time. The term "tourist cabins" had been discarded, and the terms "motor court" and "lodge" were in general use in 1937. The descriptive term "motel" was by then already used by such facilities in San Luis Obispo, Fresno, Bakersfield and Delano, California. Bakersfield also had a "California Motor Hotel" and Dallas, Texas boasted a "Motor Inn Hotel." The new facilities were making evident their important contribution to the comfort and convenience of the traveling public, and their owners were making evident their firm intention to maintain and improve their standing in the accommodations field through their own group efforts.

In 1937 the construction cost averaged from $1,100 to $1,500 for a unit 12 feet by 14 feet and bath 6 feet by 9 feet—wood frame, tile roof and no basement. The average size of an operation was then 20 units, small enough to remain a man and wife operation, with one or two maids added on days of full occupancy. The appeal was largely to the tourist and the major growth of these operations was in the South, Southwest and California. Then came the war control years, 1942-1944, with food and gasoline rationing, rent control, full employment and little time for vacation travel. During this period the tourist court business slumped, many of the operators feeling the pinch and needing financial assistance.

The postwar development of toll highways in Pennsylvania, New York, New Jersey and their extensions into Ohio, Indiana and Illinois, plus the plan for extending the federal highway system to cover the entire country, encouraged the very rapid progress that has led to the establishment of the motel and motor hotel as a major part of the accommodations business. Many of the postwar guest facilities were impressively large and had vastly increased their services to the traveling public. There were, by 1950, many motels and motor hotels ranging in size from 50 units to over 150 units. More were being built with increasingly elaborate facilities and services. Those in the smaller towns were serious competition to the existing hotels, which suffered by comparison with the newness, modern conveniences, recreational facilities and more informal atmosphere offered by the motor hotel. In many instances the motor hotel supplanted the town's hotel as the local stopping place.

As early as the mid-1950's motor hotel facilities were coming up north, their development as year-round operations being augmented by advances in construction and the inclusion of air conditioning, restaurant facilities and other services once confined to hotel operation. Meeting rooms and convention facilities were added to attract group business as well as regular commercial and tourist trade. Motor hotels also began entering the larger cities, some locating right in the heart of downtown business areas. Because of higher land costs and limited lot size within the city limits, facilities located there usually were multi-story structures, and the designation "horizontal hotels" or "vertical hotels" could no longer be used to differentiate between motor hotels and conventional hotels. Neither was the term "highway hotel" descriptive of the motor hotels in or near the center of town.

The Mead Inn, Wisconsin Rapids, Wisconsin, one of the early motels with complete hotel facilities, was built in 1951 to supplant the former hotel.
Courtesy: Mead Inn

The motor hotel had, in fact, now established itself as an important part of the hotel business of America, and for want of a better label we now refer to the "hospitality industry" or the "accommodations industry" as applying to both motels and hotels. Insofar as the increased travel was accommodated by motels and motor hotels, it is evident that the upsurge in the building of such facilities met a definite need and also that the competition from these operations was responsible for the then-puzzling decline in hotel occupancy during a travel boom.

Hotelmen, once they grasped the impact of the change in travel patterns on their businesses, devoted much effort to rehabilitation and improvement projects which would make their properties more acceptable, convenient and therefore competitive with the new motels and motor hotels. The American Hotel Association issued studies outlining the problem and offering suggestions for meeting it. Motor entrances, informal atmosphere, "come-as-you-are" advertisements, the "family plan," swimming pools, additions constructed along motel lines, conveniently located parking lots, guest-room television and air conditioning were some of the major items added to hotel facilities and operating policies during this period of adjustment. The hotelman was learning from the motel operator and giving evidence that the lesson was coming through to him. Hotel associations began to solicit the membership of motel and motor hotel operators, and by the late 1950's it was plain that motels were generally being accepted as a recognized part of the hotel business.

The Jayhawk Junior Highway Hotel, Topeka, was one of the first motels directly connected with a hotel operation. The long structure running parallel to the highway is typical of the early motel.

Courtesy: Alsonett Hotels

In the early 1960's many state and regional hotel associations changed their names to include the words "motel" or "inn" in recognotion of the fact that hotelmen and motel operators had a common interest in catering to the traveling public. As far back as 1948 a few hotelmen were getting into the motel and tourist court business; with the advent of such chain organizations as Holiday Inns, Ramada Inns, Marriott, Congress of Motor Inns, Superior and Howard Johnson's, hotel chains also entered the field. One now finds the names of Hilton, Sheraton, Albert Pick, Boss, Knott, Schimmel and many others long known in the hotel field attached to the motor hotels and inns constructed since the mid-1950's.

Another change in travel patterns that also became a factor in this field was the rapid growth of air transportation. Chain operators took the lead in developing facilities convenient to the busier airports, and today not a major airport in the country lacks motel, motor hotel or motor-inn facilities adjacent to it or within its property lines, not only for the traveler changing planes, as in New York, San Francisco and Miami, but also at terminal points where the development of outlying community centers has grown naturally with the increased convenience of automobile and airplane travel. Offices, industrial plants and shopping centers have sprung up in sections where land development included parking provisions for employees, customers and other visitors. This decentralization movement has been another factor favorable to the growth of motels. The car rental business, which has also flourished in this period, has combined with the convenience of air travel to make these locations easily accessible to visitors from near and far.

The Western Hills Hotel, Fort Worth, was one of the first deluxe resort-type motor hotels to be constructed on the outskirts of a city.

Courtesy: Western Hills Hotels

Promotion and feverish construction of motels and motor hotels in the past decade—particularly from 1958 to the present—have already resulted in some casualties due to overbuilding, changes in road patterns and airport facilities. Many projects promoted and built for sale have also suffered from cheap construction and the ravages of time and use. Motels and motor hotels in the area adjacent to Chicago's Midway Airport, for example, have gone begging since jet passenger service has moved nearly all of the traffic to O'Hare Field, almost 30 miles away. Motor hotels at O'Hare Field are also faced with problems stemming from the intense competition of many new motor hotel projects recently opened in that area.

The lesson learned in earlier days by hotelmen that new facilities do not in themselves create new business has yet to be learned by some motor hotel investors and promoters. New business is created by influences other than the mere availability of accommodations at a given point. The motel and motor hotel business is no longer new enough to warrant construction on any site that may be suitable to the facilities it might accommodate; a much more selective market is now in evidence, requiring considerable forethought and research into the problems of the patronage prospects and existing competition in the area. Naturally, as the field has grown the opportunities have narrowed, and the newcomer must recognize the risks involved in an indiscriminate plunge into the business.

MOTEL STATISTICS

Published statistics on the growth of the motel business are obtainable from several sources. Their reliability, of course, depends on who prepared them and for what purpose. The figures which we regard as the most reliable and indicative of the growth of this section of the accommodations industry are those published by the "Tourist Court Journal" of Temple, Texas. This publication was the first to make annual studies of motel operations, starting in 1937, and their research staff has established a sampling method that is scientifically sound.

The earliest statistics were guided estimates based on comparatively sketchy answers to questionnaires. But the interest of motelmen in this effort grew to the point where by 1950 the statistics showed trends that indicated greater reliability. Studies soon pointed out the need for a uniform classification of accounts similar to the one that hotels had been using since 1927, and a suggested uniform classification was published by the "Tourist Court Journal" in 1961. The American Hotel and Motel Association has also revised its booklet, "The Uniform System for Motels and Smaller Hotels," for the same reason.

The 1937 "Tourist Court Journal" study indicated the existence of about 12,000 establishments, averaging 20 units per court. The number of establishments rose to 30,000 in 1948 and to 53,000 in 1954, at which time these annual studies were amplified to their present format.

The following table summarizes the results of these annual studies.

Summary of Statistics—1950-1962

Year	Number of Establishments	Guest Units Per Establishment	Average Daily Rate Per Unit	Room Occupancy Ratio	Ratios To Room Sales						Cost of Land, Building and Equipment	
					Payroll	Other Direct Expenses	Total Operating Expenses	Rent, Financing and Depreciation	Profit Before Income Taxes	Profit Available for Financing	Per Establishment	Per Room Unit
1950		13	$4.35	71.93%	10.46%	35.63%	46.09%	28.34%	25.57%	48.01%	$57,716	$4,440
1951		17	4.46	75.09	11.47	31.26	42.73	26.19	31.08	51.55	67,149	3,950
1952		16	5.29	68.12	10.58	32.83	43.41	29.91	26.68	50.90	79,389	4,962
1953		17	5.63	70.61	12.11	32.97	45.08	28.53	26.39	49.78	80,818	4,754
1954	51,000	16.2	5.01	74.25	14.60	31.18	45.78	30.46	23.76	49.32	77,892	4,808
1955	53,000	18	6.14	70.72	13.77	28.99	42.76	33.27	23.97	52.45	93,784	5,210
1956	55,000	19	6.20	76.43	16.99	31.70	48.69	31.95	19.36	46.88	118,263	6,224
1957	57,000	21	6.71	69.93	16.72	32.89	49.61	31.41	18.98	45.28	121,017	5,763
1958	59,000	22.3	6.83	73.76	17.66	32.68	50.34	35.15	14.51	44.46	137,884	6,183
1959	60,500	25	7.65	70.67	18.37	31.97	50.34	37.03	12.63	44.02	156,774	6,271
1960	60,777	28	7.89	75.56	23.79	32.07	55.86	35.80	8.34	39.13	180,120	6,433
1961	60,951	30	8.40	69.91	19.50	32.21	51.71	38.74	9.55	42.17	199,385	6,646
1962	61,550	31	8.37	66.17	22.11	33.03	55.14	36.15	8.71	39.24	207,865	6,705

The reader will note the steady growth in size, the increase in average rate, the rise in operating costs (reflected especially in the payroll ratio) and the steady upward movement in capital expenses due mainly to increased interest on borrowed funds and depreciation. The increase in depreciation was due not only to higher costs of construction and furnishings but also to the more liberal accelerated depreciation rates allowed under current income tax regulations. Whereas one usually had expected about 50% of room sales to be available for rent, financing, return on investment and income taxes in earlier years, the increased load of payroll and fixed charges, particularly in the larger projects built in the past five years, has reduced these ratios materially, bringing the motel and motor hotel ratios closer to those of the hotel business.

In several of these annual studies the size of the establishments included in the total count was calculated, the 1959 distribution being as follows:

Size	Establishments Number	Percentage	Room Units Number	Percentage
10 units or under	14,088	23.29%	111,008	7.34%
11 to 20 units	22,839	37.75	381,775	25.24
21 to 40 units	16,217	26.80	472,629	31.25
41 to 60 units	4,362	7.21	228,256	15.09
61 to 100 units	2,058	3.40	170,342	11.26
Over 100 units	936	1.55	148,510	9.82
Totals	60,500	100.00%	1,512,520	100.00%
Franchise motels		.4%		1.5%
Chain motels		.5		1.9
		—		—
Total franchise and chain		.9%		3.4%

The average investment in land, building and equipment has also been included in this study since 1954. However, in comparing these averages with present-day costs the reader must bear in mind that costs have risen steadily since the majority of the projects included in these annual studies were put into operation and that this factor has been compounded by the need for increasingly elaborate accommodations. The figures on average investment, in themselves especially revealing to the newcomer in the business, are summarized as follows:

	Average Investment Per Establishment			Per Room Unit		
Year	Land	Building	Equipment	Land	Building	Equipment
1954	$10,755	$ 54,849	$12,288	$ 664	$3,386	$ 758
1955	12,225	66,809	14,750	679	3,712	819
1956	16,471	80,105	21,687	867	4,216	1,141
1957	24,974	77,599	18,444	1,189	3,696	878
1958	20,890	92,661	24,333	937	4,155	1,091
1959	29,973	103,640	23,161	1,199	4,146	926
1960	29,002	123,711	27,407	1,036	4,418	979
1961	24,800	136,625	37,960	826	4,555	1,265
1962	24,215	145,941	37,709	781	4,707	1,216

As might be expected during this period of rapid expansion, land costs have shown a general rise, tempered in recent years partly by changes in construction and design and partly by fluctuations in land values. Building and equipment costs have grown because of the installation of more complete facilities, rising wages and material costs.

The U. S. Department of Commerce, Bureau of Census, has published statistics on hotels, motels and tourist courts from time to time in its "Census of Business." Growth figures are summarized as follows:

	Number of Establishments	
Year	Motels	Hotels
1935	9,848	28,822
1939	13,521	27,987
1948	25,919	29,202
1954	29,432	24,778
1958	41,332	29,203

Some idea of how the business volumes of motels and tourist courts has compared with that of hotels is also provided by the following Census figures:

Year	Motels	Ratio to Total	Hotels	Ratio to Total
1935	$ 24,300,000	3.3%	$ 720,145,000	96.7%
1939	36,722,000	4.1	863,155,000	95.9
1948	193,505,000	8.1	2,172,410,000	91.9
1954	457,065,000	16.0	2,404,829,000	84.0
1958	850,381,000	23.3	2,794,055,000	76.7

The relative size of the hotel and motel fields is further illustrated by the following breakdowns based on comparative room units and sales reported in the 1958 Census:

Hotels	Establishments	Sales
No payroll or less than 25 rooms	18,062	$ 429,728,000
25-49 rooms	4,903	176,227,000
50-99 rooms	3,376	293,422,000
100-299 rooms	2,308	753,657,000
Over 300 rooms	554	1,141,021,000
Total	29,203	$2,794,055,000

Motels and Tourist Courts	Establishments	Sales
No payroll or not reporting size	20,886	$177,422,000
Less than 10 rooms	3,857	34,941,000
10-19 rooms	8,852	170,405,000
20-29 rooms	4,243	144,564,000
30-39 rooms	1,653	85,307,000
40-49 rooms	757	59,756,000
Over 50 rooms	1,084	177,986,000
Total	41,332	$850,381,000

The 1958 Census figures also provide geographical distribution of motels and tourist courts covering operations having a payroll and more than 10 rental units:

	Establishments		Sales	
Northeast	2,377	14.33%	$ 87,551,000	13.72%
North Central	3,418	20.60	116,741,000	18.30
South	6,287	37.90	263,048,000	41.23
West	4,507	27.17	170,678,000	26.75
Total	16,589	100.00%	$638,018,000	100.00%

As of 1958 the South and West together led the country with 65 per cent of the number of motel projects and 68 per cent of the sales. In the 1954 Census the leading states in number of establishments were California, Florida, and Texas, in that order. However, based on revenue, the leading states were New York, California and Illinois, which we believe is indicative of the impact of the motor hotel on the motel business.

Horwath & Horwath has prepared an annual study of motor hotels starting with the year 1956. Data for these studies are provided by the larger and more completely serviced projects in this section of the hospitality industry.

In our 1962 study, which is compiled from 100 carefully selected operations averaging 134 rooms and ranging in size from 33 to 402 rooms, the average investment for motor hotels with leased or operated restaurants was reported to be as follows:

	Cost Per Room
Land	$ 754
Building	8,083
Swimming pool	145
Furniture and fixtures	2,184
Total	$11,095

It has been our custom to divide the sampling for our motor hotel study into two groups: those which do not operate a restaurant on the premises, and those which do operate a restaurant. In 1962, the former category had an average daily rate per occupied room of $10.91 and a room occupancy of 72.03 per cent, while the corresponding figures for the latter category were $11.20 and 70.72 per cent, respectively.

For motor hotels with no operated restaurant, the ratio of payroll to room sales was 24.9 per cent; of other direct expenses to room sales, 32.2 per cent; of restaurant lease and other income to room sales, 4.3 per cent, leaving a profit ratio before the fixed charges of property taxes, interest, depreciation, etc., of 47.2 per cent. For those that operate their own restaurants, restaurant profit and other income amounted to 20.9 per cent of room sales; payroll was 27.1 per cent of room sales; and the ratio for other direct expenses, 38.3 per cent, leaving a profit, before fixed charges, of 55.5 per cent.

The differences in the statistics quoted from these three sources should establish for the reader that one must be familiar with the background of any statistical study in order to apply its findings meaningfully. The entire field of motels and motor hotels was the source of the "Tourist Court Journal" and Census statistics, whereas the Horwath & Horwath figures are based on a sampling of motor hotels, the latest development in the field. Taken together, the three sets of statistics will give the reader a good idea of the pace at which the motel and motor hotel industry is developing and the extent to which it has progressed thus far.

There will be further developments which will affect the hospitality business as it adjusts to the continuing changes in travel patterns. Although the motel field has reached a state of maturity, in which it has the benefits of experience and of guides developed thus far for successful operation, there will still be casualties caused by overbuilding, poor judgment, bad management and daring risks. It is important, however, that the negative factors which exist not be allowed to hide the opportunities. The construction of a network of national highways in the United States and Canada has only started. The airplane is steadily increasing the speed of travel, and the economy of the country is enabling more people to travel in the new patterns which have made the motel an important contribution to the comfort of the public. New express highways leading into downtown areas are again making hotel facilities located there convenient to the airplane and motor traveler, but at the same time the larger function, meeting-room and exhibit areas now being provided by motor hotels are capturing a significant share of the convention and party business.

The pattern of travel, whether in a city, a resort area or along the highways, is by no means static and the travel business apparently continues to expand.

In the earlier days of the hotel business much stress was laid on European experience, and managers, chefs and others with European training were in constant demand in many of the larger and finer houses in metropolitan centers. As the flow of this talent to our shores dwindled, more attention was centered on the training of executives and workers in this country. Many of the colleges and universities now offer this type of training, notably Cornell, Michigan State, Oklahoma State, and Denver, among several others. Vocational training in the secondary schools, short courses and correspondence courses are proving of value to many persons already employed in the accommodations field who desire to prepare themselves for advancement. Many hotel and motel staffs are now benefiting from the product of these educational efforts.

Just as the hotel business received a gift of experience from Europe, we might now say that the motel is the gift of the United States to the world, for motel-type accommodations are being copied in many countries. The hotel chains have already spread to distant parts of the Free World and it appears that motel chains will soon follow, for there are already several establishments in Europe.

The implications of the space age for the accommodations industry are many. Air speeds of several hundred hundred miles per hour are impressive when compared to automobile speeds, but within a decade both may be dwarfed by still further refinements and innovations in transportation. In the area of foods, the development of prefabricated products, concentrates, faster and more efficient methods of cooking, storage and service may soon help to bring about astonishing changes in the restaurant department. The application of plastics to many articles of furnishings, utensils, wall and floor coverings, the development of time-saving tools for maids, kitchen help and others is already a reality. The possibilities of using atomic energy to power engine room and utility services are not too far off. Machine operation in the front office and business office will probably soon be facilitated by the adaptations of electronic computers. Their use by smaller operations may be made practical as a result of research now being conducted by manufacturers of office equipment. These developments and many others too numerous to mention in a short chapter are challenges of the future, the future in which the accommodations industry will continue to play an important role; for as long as man finds reasons to travel, it will be necessary to furnish him with food and shelter.

2

The Nature of the Business

Just what does one see when he looks at a motel or motor hotel? It depends largely on one's viewpoint. The guest notices the conveniences and services that are available for his comfort and pleasure. The real estate owner or promoter sees the opportunity of compensation for his efforts and the possibilities of enhancing his professional reputation. The lawyer, financial agent, banker, accountant, interior decorator and others serving in an advisory capacity see a different picture. The same is true for staff members from the desk clerk to the maid, the chef to the bus boy, the engineer to the yardman, each of whose view is often confined to the horizons of his job.

It is highly probable that everyone concerned will improve his view and his chances of success in this field if he is exposed to aspects of the business beyond his immediate role. The intent of this chapter is to start with fundamentals on which we hope the reader will build a sound understanding of the business and insights into his position in it.

WHAT IS A MOTEL?

In attempting to define the term "motel" one is forced to take into account the many yardsticks that are used in measuring establishments of this sort. State and local statutes and ordinances have laid down widely diverse specifications as to number of rooms and types of facilities that must be met for the establishment to be included in a given category. State and local hotel and motel associations, as well as referral organizations and publishers of travel guide listings, also list specifications as to size, nature and quality of services offered.

In some instances these organizations have refused to accept an establishment because it failed to meet certain service standards.

Among other things considered, minimum number of guest units, restaurant facilities, phone service, availability of television, radio, air conditioning, wall-to-wall carpeting and tub and shower facilities figure in acceptance and definition of the motel and motor hotel. Hence, definitions depend on the circumstances at hand so far as facilities and services are concerned.

The Motel Investment

However, there are aspects beyond these which should be weighed in studying the business. Certainly of prime concern is the question of the fundamental purpose of a motel or motor hotel project as an investment. Basic to this consideration are the following three points:

1. A motel or motor hotel is real estate improvement. Moreover, it is a "special purpose" improvement which, once constructed, does not lend itself readily to conversion to other purposes without considerable cost. Therefore it is of paramount importance for the potential investor to first determine whether the project is best suited to the site involved and will make the most of the location.

2. Being a venture in real estate, the investment in a motel or motor hotel is necessarily long-term. The money involved in the cost of land, building and equipment must be recovered through operation of the facilities, unless the original promoter decides to sell the project. It was possible in earlier days, when motels were not as elaborate and costly, for the owner to recover his investment in a relatively short time, sometimes within five to ten years. But with recent trends toward costlier facilities, as well as growth of competition, the time of such recovery has lengthened to as much as twenty to thirty years or more.

3. Being a long-term investment, a motel or motor hotel project naturally seeks the aid of long-term financing. It is now quite common to find that the equity owner or the promoter cannot personally provide all the necessary funds to construct and furnish a motel and therefore must look for financial assistance, usually in the form of a loan or loans for which the property involved serves as collateral security. This long-term financing normally can be obtained for only part of the investment, usually from 50 per cent to about 66 per cent, with the owner taking a secondary or equity position with respect to whatever security the property can provide.

This financing also requires that a fixed amount be paid to the lending agency in the form of interest and that the principal sum be returned to it in accordance with a specified schedule of payments. Thus, the owner must defer his chances for a return until loan requirements are met and must take the primary risk on the possibilities of profitable operation.

These three points are recounted for the benefit of the individual who anticipates going into the motel or motor hotel business or who is considering it as a real estate investment. We realize that there are others, particularly real estate promoters and builders, who have in mind the development of motel and motor hotel projects primarily for sale over a short space of time. Their success, however, depends on convincing the buyer of the possibilities of recovery of principal and realization of a profit over a considerable period of time. Therefore, it is necessary to start with the realization that investment in a motel or motor hotel is truly a long-term investment in a real estate improvement designed for a particular purpose.

The Motel's Place in the Accommodations Industry

The development of the accommodations industry, summarized briefly in Chapter One, indicates clearly that motels and motor hotels form an increasingly important segment of the industry. It follows that as these establishments become larger and more complete in their services they also become more a part of what was once classified as the "hotel business." No longer considered the step-child of the business by hotelmen, the motel is now looked upon as a distinct asset which has enabled the accommodations industry to meet the changes in travel patterns and personal tastes.

As the interests of hotelmen and motel operators continue to merge, the need for mutual study of problems and experience grows apace. For anyone involved in the motel and motor hotel field there is much to be learned from close investigation of, and association with, the hotel industry. Most important is the realization that, having won the battle for recognition, the motel and motor hotel business must bear the responsibility that accompanies its prominence by keeping its reputation sound and worthy of public acceptance.

The Operation

The principal revenue source of a motel or motor hotel has always been room sales. At one time it was the only source, but the demands of the guest and increasing competition have forced the addition of more and more services that are of a low-profit nature.

The first such service to be added was the guest-room telephone which required a centrally-manned switchboard. Restaurants and bars were added to existing motels or became standard facilities in new operations; now, relatively few motels are constructed without room telephones, restaurant, bar, swimming pool and, of course, television in each guest room.

Locally owned and operated, The Winding Brook Lodge, Keene, New Hampshire, is typical of a community effort to improve transient accommodations.
Courtesy: Winding Brook Lodge

The addition of new facilities and services tended to make what had been a relatively simple operation a very complex one. The role of the owner-operator gave way to a separation of owner and manager, and the duties and responsibilities of each became segregated. Generally speaking, the manager is responsible for the successful operation of the guest service facilities which are departmentalized for better adminis-trative control. These are: rooms, food, beverages, telephone and such other special services as may be required. The supervision and control of guest service personnel and the upkeep of plant and equipment are also a function of management. The owners, on the other hand, are responsible for providing adequate working capital and financing the

The motel addition to the Hotel Curtis, Mount Vernon, Ohio, is an example of
the adjustment made by hotel operators in order to cater to the motorist.
Courtesy: Packard Hotel Company

operation, and in some cases for the rental of the stores and ancillary
facilities not connected with transient guest service.

This division of operation into two distinct areas is reflected in the
typical motel operating statements that are presented and discussed
in a later chapter. The revenue-producing departments are considered
separately and departmental results are charged with overhead costs in
arriving at the figure for which management is directly responsible.
This "house profit" is then reduced by the charges for municipal taxes,
fire insurance, interest on long-term debt and depreciation, those "fixed
costs" being controllable by the owners and dependent upon the structure of the owning organization. "House profit" becomes an extremely
important measure of the efficiency of management, and in some cases,
the basis for rental when the operation is leased.

Thus the typical operating statement is designed to show a clear
picture of the operating result and how it meets the financial burden,
or the "nut," that must be earned before any net profit is realized.

The Composition of Sales

The nature of the business changes as facilities and services are added. The smaller motel with only room facilities very likely earns relatively little income from telephone, commissions on valet and laundry, vending machines, or similar sources. As other facilities are added the ratio of room sales to total sales decreases materially and the business becomes, in effect, a combination of many businesses, almost endless in their variety, under one roof. These added facilities bring the motel business closer in function to the hotel business, making the operating problems, accounting statements and public appeal of motels and motor hotels more nearly the same as those of conventional hotels.

In the 1961 Horwath & Horwath study of hotel operations the sales figures of 50 transient hotels of fewer than 500 rooms were distributed as follows:

	Per Cent of Sales
Rooms	43.16%
Food	37.12
Beverages	13.38
Telephone	2.68
Store rentals	1.55
Commissions, concessions and all other income	2.11
Total	100.00%

Naturally the breakdown of total sales will change with the size and complexity of the operation. For example, the ratio of room sales to total sales ranges from about 95 per cent in the smaller hotel with no major source of income beyond room rental to only 43 per cent for the larger, more complex hotels. The composition of sales in the modern motor hotel is quite similar to that of the large, complex hotel.

The Balance Sheet

The balance sheet of a motel is dominated by major investments in land, buildings and equipment. Illustrations of this statement in later chapters will substantiate that these assets comprise from 80 per cent to 90 per cent of total assets.

The working capital, that is, the funds necessary to operate the business, is consequently small in comparison to the total investment.

The carrying of large sums tied up in receivables and inventories is not usually a requirement in the motel business. Because motel sales are largely on a cash basis, especially in smaller operations, it is possible to use daily income to pay bills, payroll and other operating costs, thereby maintaining a good credit standing with comparatively little working capital. Although we do not advocate following such a policy, we often find that a motel has maintained its standing with creditors even at a time when the total of current bills and unpaid expenses equaled the funds represented in current assets. It is highly advisable in this business to be provided with sufficient funds to meet current obligations on time and to maintain a top credit rating.

The picture portrayed by a statement of financial condition further indicates that the business is a long-term investment in real estate. The depreciation reserve, based primarily on rates of depreciation used for income tax purposes, when deducted from the cost of the property represents the "book value" at the time the statement is prepared. This value is often regarded by a person not familiar with financial statements as the real or salable value of the property. In reality these depreciation charges are at best a guess based on the estimated useful life of the assets involved, their possible salvage value when no longer useful to the operation, and the desire of the owner to keep his income taxes at a reasonable figure. This situation soon reaches the point where there is no relationship between the book value and the actual value of the fixed assets. When the property is appraised at book value, or cost less depreciation to date, the figure actually represents the value that has not yet been recovered by charges to operating income.

The Guest Room as a Product

To adapt a maxim often used in the hotel business, "A motel or motor hotel is a business and not a building." Actually, in this business the primary product is the guest room and the service that goes toward making it a comfortable and attractive abode for the traveler. In other words, the operator is selling the building piecemeal. But in comparing his wares with those of a merchant he must also take into account the element of time; figuratively speaking, he has on his shelves for sale so many room-days per year. This points up the fact that his commodity is also a highly perishable product, for the room that is not sold today is forever gone without profit.

Another way of looking at it is to consider that the guest room units are not flexible and adaptable to fluctuations in demand. Once the number of rooms is established and built, it cannot be expanded or contracted like most inventories, but remains the same regardless of the extent to which the rooms are occupied. Therefore, it is most important that the rooms be of the kind that are most in demand by the type of guest making up the market for the facilities. Because the supply of rooms is inflexible it is unusual to find very high annual occupancies and it is advisable to make some allowance for vacancies when projecting the potential of an operation.

The statistics on room business are important guides for planning projections. They are based primarily on:

1. The percentage of occupancy, normally figured as the ratio of rooms occupied by paying guests to the number of rooms available for sale. Guest rooms permanently assigned as quarters for the manager and others of the staff or converted for use as offices, storage space or working quarters do not figure in the ratio.

In most transient operations the occupancy fluctuates daily during the week and with the seasons of the year. Although motels, with their attraction for tourist trade, do not ordinarily suffer the severe weekend drops in occupancy experienced by downtown hotels when there are no special events in town, they do experience some fluctuations because the inflexibility of the supply of rooms requires that occasional peak loads be accommodated in order to maintain a steady repeat business and good standing with respect to referrals. An annual occupancy of about 70 per cent is usually considered probable for a projected motel, but the economic feasibility of a project will be increased if the break-even point can be reached at an occupancy level lower than 70 per cent.

2. The average rate per occupied room, figured by dividing the room sales by the number of rooms occupied by paying guests.

The two foregoing factors indicate the major elements in room sales and thus become valuable indicators of the trend that the business is taking. They are also helpful guides for determining policies, showing the operator of a motel how to realize as fully as possible the potential of the facilities. Lastly, they form an excellent barometer for measuring the soundness of the room rate schedule. It is always surprising to us that so many of the smaller operators fail to maintain these simple statistics. Such data form a basic operational tool and no establishment should be without them.

A second set of room statistics is based on what is called the "house count," which is the number of paying guests housed overnight. By dividing the number of guests by the number of rooms occupied, one gets what is known as the "double occupancy" percentage. Although this figure does not indicate the exact number of rooms occupied by more than one person, since some rooms may have families or other groups of three or more in them, it is a practical indicator of the extent to which bed capacity is used. The average rate per guest is in turn figured by dividing the guest-room sales by the count of guests housed.

The statistics on sales and profits of other income-producing departments and of operating expenses are based primarily on their ratios to room sales. These percentages are the ones most often used in comparing one operation with another and in annual studies of the business. The Horwath & Horwath studies of motor hotels show annual sales and expenses per available room as well as the ratios of each item to total room sales. In this way it is possible to express in the more readily understood language of dollars and cents the sales and costs experience of the establishments included in the studies. The major purpose of the studies is to illustrate the actual sales and cost experience, the current trends and the effects of changes in sales volume and price structures.

Evaluating a Motel

Being a business, the motel is judged by its profit potential as soon as it is put into operation and its value is no longer based on "brick and mortar," or replacement cost. The profit potential is what most interests a purchaser, prospective investor or lending agency, while the "brick and mortar" appraisal is of interest primarily for insurance purposes.

For those who contemplate the purchase or leasing of an establishment there are many ways of calculating value, all based upon capitalization of earnings. Ordinarily one would take the earnings available for financing as the figure to be capitalized, that being the amount left after deducting operating expenses, property taxes and insurance and a reasonable provision for property replacements and renewals from the total income. Although past operating statements are often used in order to determine the earnings potential, they should be regarded merely as a guide for a projection of future earnings which should then be used as a basis for arriving at the amount to be capitalized. Of course, in addition to reviewing carefully the earning experience, the purchaser should make an inspection of the property to determine how well it has been maintained and to what extent improvement may be required. He should also study the general development of the area in which the motel is located and the competition that exists or is contemplated and have some knowledge of the staff—particularly the personalities and abilities of key employees. As well, he should be aware of the community's and traveler's opinions of the establishment.

A general method often used in making a preliminary estimate of the value of a motel or hotel property based on earnings is to multiply the earnings by 7.5. This figure is subject to wide variation, however, and is used primarily to indicate whether the value arrived at comes within the range where reasonable negotiations can be worked out.

Because of the risk factors involved, the purchaser will probably feel that he should anticipate a high return on his equity money, a pay-out in relatively few years. For example, a fifteen-year loan for 60 per cent of the necessary amount at 6 per cent interest might be obtained. This, plus the 40 per cent equity money, must earn a total of 8.5 per cent in order to pay 12 per cent earnings on the equity and 6 per cent interest on the loan. However, the owner will desire to liquidate the loan and recover his capital in addition. Therefore, a total return, before interest and depreciation, of 13.33 per cent (which is 7.5 times available earnings) should not appear to be an unreasonable expectation, provided that the property is considered to have a remaining useful life of 15 years or more.

Another method of capitalizing earnings, a bit more complicated, bases the value on a sinking fund theoretically provided at current interest rates over the expected remaining useful life of the project plus the anticipated residual value of the property (mainly land). The foregoing amounts would then be capitalized on an expected average total earning on the investment of 8.5 per cent, which will cover the amounts involved both in borrowed and equity capital.

In any event, when a motel or motor hotel is to be purchased, it would be advisable to have someone familiar with the business make a thorough appraisal of its value based on the earnings potential. In that way the purchaser would be considering the project as a running business, not as a building, which is the sensible approach to a deal for any existing motel property.

Leasing

In making a lease the owner of a motel property will want an income sufficiently large to cover his financial obligations and provide a return on the amount he has invested. There is no fixed formula to be followed since leasing negotiations are between an owner who wants as much as he can get and a tenant who wants to pay as little as is necessary to obtain the right to operate the property. The rental agreement also depends on how expenses are to be divided between landlord and tenant. The landlord, if he is to be relieved of all the worries of operation, must have a satisfied tenant. Therefore the landlord must expect that the tenant should be put into a position to realize adequate compensation for his investment, managerial effort and risks of operation.

The questions of who is to pay property taxes and insurance; who is to pay for the maintenance and upkeep of the property; who is to own the furniture, furnishings and equipment, are usually major items of negotiation and in practice lead to a wide variety of lease agreements. The assumption of existing loan requirements, the cost of contemplated improvements, the amount and kind of security to be provided on the rental and many other items covered in individual lease arrangements complicate the pattern and make the questions "What rent should I pay?" and "What rent can I expect?" impossible to answer except in very general terms.

The most common leasing agreement is one where the tenant owns the furniture, fixtures and equipment, receives all of the operating income of the property and pays all of the operating costs and expense, including maintenance, property taxes and insurance. It is commonly called a "net lease," in that the owner is faced only with the obligations of his own financial structure which are to be paid from the rental he receives. Often there is a basic or minimum rental, with additional rent based either on gross receipts or income or on a division of profits. We have seen recent leases where the rental is based on 20 per cent to 35 per cent of room sales, zero to 8 per cent of food sales and 8 per cent to 15 per cent of beverage sales. Store rentals may go directly to the landlord or be part of the percentage rental.

While no set guide exists for determining a leasing agreement, the terms should reflect what seems a reasonable division of income between landlord and tenant for their respective contributions to the success of the enterprise. In any rental based on a division of income or profit the landlord and tenant become partners in the business. The landlord thus loses a part of his position as a real estate investor and takes on some of the worry of maintaining an efficient operation. The tenant also sacrifices some of his opportunity for fully realizing the fruits of his efforts and should therefore expect that the basic or minimum rental will be at a level that can be met in poorer periods to compensate for the division of his profit with the landlord in good times.

Again, the individual is advised to seek out the advice and guidance of someone experienced in this phase of the business. For a person entering the motel or motor hotel field, good legal advice, although necessary, is not in itself sufficient. It takes more than a knowledge of law or ordinary real estate transactions to arrive at reasonable lease terms for a motel transaction. It is suggested that the services of an accountant experienced in the field also be obtained.

The Retail and Service Aspect

Motels and motor hotels are classified in the U. S. Census studies as a part of the service industries in that what is provided to the traveler is primarily for his comfort and convenience. Furthermore, because income is derived directly from the consumer the business should probably be classified as part of the retail trade. While it is true that in the past ten years the public's education in the use of credit cards has resulted in an increase in bookkeeping and investment in receivables, there has not been a sufficiently material change to increase greatly the need for working capital, especially in the smaller establishments which still deal largely in cash sales.

The Guest and Host Relationship

Five words are especially significant in describing the nature of the motel business. The first is "guest." The definition that "a guest is anyone away from home, receiving accommodations at an inn as a traveler" seems wholly inadequate for the modern accommodations industry. First of all, a warmer relationship should be implied to indicate that the traveler is in the house upon invitation, expecting the same courtesies and treatment that he would receive in the home of a friend. The second word is "host." In the old days "Ye Host" personally greeted his guests and saw to it that they were afforded the best his house could offer. In later years, as hotels became larger and more elaborate in their services, it was not always possible for the owners to maintain this direct contact; it had to be delegated to others on the staff. The direct guest-host relationship is an advantage that the smaller motels have over their larger competitors. However, it takes a little experience and effort to get full benefit from this contact and use it to make the guest a repeat customer and a booster of the establishment.

The third word is "courtesy." This aspect of the business starts with the host or manager, whose attitude toward his guests is often reflected down the line by his staff. A smile and warm greeting can do much to start the guest's stay off right. A solicitous attitude in satisfying the guests needs and desires, a polite "thank you" for any return courtesey or gratuity on the guest's part and a prompt reply to his inquiries are all a part of courteous treatment which costs little and means much in creating an atmosphere that attracts and satisfies patrons.

The fourth word is "comfort." Having the facilities that will give the guest real relaxation and rest, food and drink that will not only satisfy his appetite but give him real pleasure, service that tends to his wants primarily without the need of his asking for it, conveniences such as valet, laundry and telephone service—these facilities should total more than the comforts of home. A plentiful supply of towels and other bathroom accessories, ash trays and matches, glasses and convenient ice chests, sufficient lighting for reading and sufficient electrical outlets for shaving, pleasant decoration and ample living room space all contribute to the guest's favorable impression of the motel.

The fifth, but by no means least important, word is "cleanliness." Good housekeeping is surely the top essential in efficient operation. This is the responsibility not only of the housekeeper but of all the staff, for the guest will be exposed to all parts of the motel during his stay. Maintenance is as important as daily cleaning, for a spotted wall, a worn, torn or broken piece of furniture, a soiled lampshade or missing lamp bulb are factors in creating a bad impression. One of the reasons the new motel is attractive to the traveler is that he feels he will find everything fresh and clean. The older establishment must then strive to maintain its prestige by having facilities as comparable as possible to those of the newer operations, with stress on good housekeeping and maintenance.

The Staff

Essential to the motel or motor hotel are the people who work there, the staff that services facilities and guests. The relationship of staff member to guest is by no means that of servant and master, but the guest usually does expect to have his requests honored cordially and quickly.

"The guest is always right" was one of the famous quotations translated into operating policy by the late E. M. Statler. The guest is not always right, of course, but it should be the desire of anyone serving the traveler to cater to his wishes in all ways possible. Therefore, as the staff grows each person added must be trained to fit in with the policies and methods of operation desired by the management. This is best accomplished through instruction and example. It is almost axiomatic that the personality of the head of any organization is reflected to some extent in the attitudes and behavior of those under him, which means that he must take the lead in typifying the courtesy and cooperation he expects from his staff. He must also show his staff that they have his faith and respect. It is most important to realize that a happy, loyal staff makes for satisfied guests.

3

Types

The motel industry has in its development produced a wide variety of establishments designed to attract the entire spectrum of travelers. All income brackets are represented by today's guest, who may be tourist, traveling salesman, business executive or convention delegate. A look at the different classifications of accommodations will point up the diversities of the facilities now in existence.

Tourist Cabins or Camps

This type was the earliest forerunner of the modern motel. The typical tourist camp consisted of frame cottages renting at low rates and ranging in size from five to twelve units. The cabins provided little more than a bed and shelter from the elements. These installations, operated mainly as a sideline by farmers, date from the first decade of the century.

Tourist Courts

From the tourist cabin to the tourist court was a small but significant step in the development of the industry. Many courts are still in operation, consisting of detached frame cottages, now furnished more amply than formerly and offering private bath, carports or shelters and sometimes kitchenette facilities. They are almost always at the sides of highways, on the outskirts of town or in resort areas, their primary market being the tourist trade. However, growing in size and sharing a larger part of the travel market, their continued presence indicates that their business is bolstered by the continued

33

growth of travel in the middle-income groups. In fact, their adapta-
tion in many instances to the changes in travel patterns and guests'
tastes makes it difficult to continue to classify many of them as purely
"tourist courts." Improvements and added services have made a
number of them quite comparable to the modern motel. Many of
them now have restaurant facilities, swimming pools, television and
air conditioning.

Motels and Motor Hotels

The word "motel" was a fortunate label, for it quickly came into
general use and continues to be the most widely applied term for
for this type of facility. It is generally conceded that the motel grew
out of the tourist court. Early motels were also located in resort
areas, mostly in the southern and western parts of the country.
Their guest units were housed under one roof and in some cases the
buildings were two stories high. Swimming pools were beginning to
make their appearance on motel grounds prior to World War II,
but most operators remained reluctant to add restaurant facilities or
other services that might discourage patronage by threatening a tipping
problem.

This view from a guest-room unit in the Del Webb Towne Touse, San Francisco, is proof of the motel movement into the downtown section of the city.
Courtesy: Del E. Webb Motor Hotel Corp.

After the war came more rapid development of larger motels with extensive service facilities. These were initially called "de-luxe" motels and gradually became known as "motor hotels" because of the completeness of their facilities and services. They were also sometimes referred to as "horizontal hotels" as compared to the vertical or multiple-story structure of most existing hotels, but this attempt at classification soon lost its meaning as motels built in congested areas with higher land costs first rose to three stories and then as high as ten to fifteen stories as they moved into the downtown sections of larger cities.

As motels grew larger and more elaborate, operators recognized that they could not continue to delegate the catering operation to an adjacent or nearby restaurant, and to lease this department was to lose control over it to some extent, sometimes with the result that standards of service and menu offerings adversely affected the reputation of the motel. Nor could they largely offset the lack of full restaurant facilities by providing a free Continental breakfast as smaller operators did, for their guests no longer consisted only of tourists anxious for an early morning start. Thus, in order to expand their market to assure full use of their room facilities, motel operators saw the need for a good restaurant on the premises. Soon to follow were meeting rooms, private dining rooms and even large ballrooms and exhibition space in some instances. Some operators have even gone so far as to feature extensive entertainment or cabaret operations.

Roadside Motels or Highway Motels. Probably the earliest development in the business, the "roadside" or "highway" type of motel seems destined to continue its growth as super highways lace the country. However, changes in road networks which speed up or divert traffic and may bypass cities and towns are also responsible for casualties among motels. Some operators no longer find themselves in the path of traffic or even in the right part of town to make their establishments easily accessible to traffic. Many of the new toll roads and major arteries may not only prohibit direct access to motel projects but also may grant concessions to larger chain restaurants, gasoline stations and motels, thereby giving the concessionaire exclusive rights to highway traffic.

While smaller motels are not doomed to extinction by changing traffic patterns and indeed have profited from them, it is certain that the new highway systems are gradually concentrating traffic flow in many areas to the advantage of larger and newer establishments.

Resort Properties. The growth in popularity of this type of motel or motor hotel has been helped by the vast highway construction programs which have enabled many more travelers than formerly to reach resort areas by motor car. Florida, California, Arizona, Michigan, Wisconsin, Maine, the Carolinas and other popular resort states now have a wide variety of such accommodations. The Williamsburg Inn, for instance, is now supplemented by the 200-room Williamsburg Lodge and the 200-room Motor House, both designed primarily for the motor traveler, charging rates attractive to the middle-income group. The same Rockefeller interests have built like

The resort atmosphere is enhanced by the approach to the guest rooms of the Motor House in Colonial Williamsburg, Virginia. Note the spread of the buildings overlooking a landscaped vista.

Courtesy: Williamsburg Restoration, Inc.

accommodations in Grand Teton National Park, Wyoming. Other national parks around the country have also experienced a considerable growth in the supply of accommodations, supplementing and to some extent supplanting the lodges and hotels constructed some years ago by the railroads or with public funds. The development of deluxe resort motels in the Scottsdale, Arizona area near Phoenix is a good example of how this field has taken up the slack in providing accommodations for the vacation traveler. The state of Florida is another case in point. In fact, many of the motels in resort areas now offer such completeness of service and so many conveniences that they compare favorably with the original resort hotels and are more in the hotel than the motel field.

The pool and court area of the Executive House, Scottsdale, Arizona, conforms to the resort atmosphere of the area in which this motor hotel is located.
Courtesy: Executive House, Inc.

Because recreation is an essential part of the full services of a resort project, a swimming pool, or access to a beach, boating and water sports, a golf course on the grounds or arrangements for guest privileges at an adjacent or nearby course, tennis and badminton courts, shuffleboard, riding stables, fishing, hunting and similar attractions are important considerations in a resort property.

Suburban or Perimeter Motels and Motor Hotels. This type of motel or motor hotel facility combines the advantages of the roadside type with the convenience of proximity to a city or town. Located on the outskirts or suburban areas of the community and usually on a main road leading into the city as well as to the airport, the suburban motel is really a vestige of the decentralization trend in urban areas. These motels are more directly competitive with hotels in a community than are the other types mentioned thus far and are responsible for making the hotelmen aware of the necessity for adjusting their facilities to new travel patterns created by the automobile. Since there had been very little construction in the hotel field for almost 25 years these new motel facilities, which boomed in the 1950's, actually took over the former place of existing hotels in many of the smaller towns and villages.

This architect's rendering of the San Francisco Hilton Inn shows an example of an airport motel facility. The dining room and cocktail areas are located in the circular building to the right of the center for easy access by the general public as well as room patrons.

Courtesy: Hilton Inns

The growing importance of automobile transportation and the accompanying necessity for providing parking space resulted not only in the development of perimeter motels but also of outlying restaurants, which soon were a part of the trend away from the congestion of downtown traffic. These restaurants quickly established their popularity; it was a natural step for a motel to combine the appeal of a fine restaurant catering to the community with room facilities for the transient guest. In the 1962 Horwath & Horwath study of 100 motor hotels several establishments reported that restaurant sales exceeded room sales. The average ratio of food and beverage sales to room sales for the group included in that study was 97 per cent.

As a result of the impact of the perimeter motel, hotelmen became interested and were soon participating in the construction of motel and motor hotel projects. It was not long before many of the hotel chain operations had perimeter-type motel units. The growth of airplane passenger traffic furthered the impetus, with areas near the busier airfields acting as natural magnets. The newer facilities of the major chains now tend to be located in areas on the outskirts of towns and convenient to airports. The increasing scarcity of prime property has meant that many of the perimeter establishments are multiple-story. The first so-called "deluxe" motels are an outgrowth of this category.

City Motels and Motor Hotels. It was inevitable that motels would eventually invade the city itself. Soon all metropolitan centers throughout the country had new motor hotels constructed within the city limits, often even in the downtown sections. Naturally the limitations

The Executive House, Washington, D.C., is indicative of the construction of high-rise motor hotels in town. Note the sun umbrellas around the swimming pool area on the sixth floor.

Courtesy: Executive House, Inc.

of suitable land area and the increased land values made it more and more difficult to provide parking areas. The De Ville Hotel in New Orleans, about a mile from the famous French Quarter and downtown area, solved this problem by using the ground floor for parking, building its guest units on the second and third floors. For other projects, such as the Lake Tower Motel, Water Tower Inn, Ascot Motel, Essex Inn and proposed McCormick Inn in Chicago, the answer was to build structures up to fifteen floors in height, with ground floor auto entrances and basement, ground floor and adjacent lot parking for their guests and patrons.

It is in this group that one is most apt to find operations which can offer all of the facilities of a downtown hotel in addition to convenient parking. They are in direct competition with the downtown hotel, of course, and although their convenient parking facilities give them an edge which is reflected in relatively higher occupancies than are experienced by many of the older hotels, they are more subject to the fluctuations in occupancies caused by the typical weekend exodus than are motels located elsewhere. They do benefit from convention promotions of the cities in which they are located and are a bit more active in the hotel associations than the other types of motels. Nevertheless, they tend to retain some of the wariness that keeps motels and hotels apart to some extent in association activities. Their room rate structures are usually found to be quite comparable to those of major downtown hotels. In some instances, however, they show a higher average sale per occupied room unit.

4

Development of Services

The growth of the motel and motor hotel industry to its present status is as evident in the extension of services to the guest as it is in the number and size of the buildings that house these services. Once it has been determined which type of motel is best able to serve the market in mind it is possible to plan those services that will attract patronage and will most fully realize the potential of the business. These services can be divided generally into two groups, one being the equipment and comfort of the guest; and the second consisting of management and staff who will see that the facilities are efficiently operated and will complement them with the personal attention necessary to good service. Both of these elements are vitally important to a successful operation. Their extent is largely determined by the type of guest that is to be accommodated. This chapter presents a review of the major service factors.

Parking

The one service that is common to all motels and motor hotels is the provision of convenient parking facilities for the guest's automobile. This service plays a large role in setting motels apart from hotels in the public mind, for at a motel the guest expects to have easy access to his car at all times. Therefore it is not necessary that he unload all of his belongings. Instead, he can take only the articles that he needs for his stay, leaving the balance of his luggage easily available to him. This arrangement also gives him the advantage of

41

using the automobile trunk as a storage place for items he might not otherwise bring along on his trip. Close proximity to the car additionally gives the guest a feeling of freedom and mobility during his stay, inasmuch as he is only seconds away from a source of private transportation.

The Philadelphia Marriott Motor Hotel has a vast expanse of space available for parking, which includes especially convenient areas for house-guest parking and for patrons of restaurant facilities.

Courtesy: Marriott Motor Hotels

For these reasons the parking place for the automobile should be as convenient to the guest's room as possible. At the same time, the car's location should not interfere with the other features of the motel, such as the view from the guest room, patio, recreational area or restaurant section. The ideal arrangement is to have a parking space at every guest-room door and additional parking provisions for patrons of dining rooms, meeting rooms and entertainment facilities located elsewhere on the property. Many hotels have for a long time had convenient garage accommodations for their guests, but in most instances the stay still involved unloading bags and personal effects, obtaining the service of a car-hop to take the car at the door, notifying the garage when it was wanted, often waiting for its delivery and paying a storage charge.

A number of motels include in their transportation-related services shelter for the automobile adjacent to the guest's room or cottage, largely in the style of a carport. This facility is especially common with motor court establishments. Some motels have extended their services to include a gasoline station and garage facilities, with provisions for tire changes and minor repairs. Because of the growing number of travelers arriving by plane, motels have supplemented their service by furnishing courtesy transportation to the airport or to special points of interest or events in the area. In many instances they offer car-rental services, which business has been a natural supplement to air travel throughout the country.

Self-Service Versus Staff Service

The extent to which the guest is left to his own devices from the time of registration to departure depends, of course, upon the policy of the establishment. This in turn is dependent on the type of guest to be served. One aspect of motel operations in earlier days was the avoidance of services that involved tipping and minor service charges.

The compact layout of the Cherry Tree Coffee Shop of the Executive House, Washington, D.C., contributes to employee efficiency and facilitates fast service.

Courtesy: Executive House, Inc.

Instead, it was made convenient for the guest to serve himself. The absence of bellmen and porters was capitalized on by motel operators.

The self-service feature was extended by providing such things as ice chests and soft-drink vending machines in locations handy to the guest-room area. Some of the later motor hotels located small refrigeration and ice units in the guest rooms. Many hotels followed suit, installing similar features to satisfy the guests' desire for self-service.

However, as motels grew larger and their facilities became more elaborate they added bellmen and porters to the service staff. As the distance from the automobile to the room increased, the transportation of baggage again became a service opportunity. Provision for a bellman to run errands, escort guests to their rooms and give directions for operating various types of equipment has been a growing trend.

In many places doormen and parking attendants are now in evidence. Although the need for these positions was originally occasioned by the public dining facilities, it has become common practice to extend such service to the rooms department.

By and large, however, personal services are not yet offered to any great extent in motels, mainly because of the continued preference of motel guests for self-service made convenient by the nature of the facilities. Furthermore, motel operators desire to retain, insofar as possible, the competitive advantage of the "no-tipping" feature of the business.

Informality

One reason for the popularity of motels has been the desire of guests, particularly those who are traveling by automobile, for the comfort that accompanies informal dress and attire. In the motel the guest may go directly from his car into his room and relax. While it has taken time for the people themselves to become accustomed to this trend toward informality, hotels very quickly reacted to the motel's competitive advantage by building motor entrances which made it possible for the motor traveler to escape a trip through the lobby. By advertising "come as you are," hotelmen have attempted to make it clear that the motorist is very welcome even if he plainly shows the effects of a long day on the road.

The early motels did not have lobby or public lounge space, and such space as was later made available has maintained for the most part the informal atmosphere that typifies this segment of the industry. The same is true of the restaurant and other motel facilities, their addition coming at a time when the desire for informality was beginning to be a well-recognized trend in public tastes. Hotels, in attempting to adjust to the trend, have encountered difficulty and expense, both growing out of the inflexibility of existing structures.

Restaurant Facilities

Informality has extended itself to the restaurant area, coffee shops and specialty rooms taking the place of formal dining facilities. Sports attire is now acceptable in most motel restaurants, and in resort areas patrons in shorts and sometimes even bathing suits are no longer frowned upon in the dining rooms.

The Red Lion Cocktail Lounge in the Albert Pick Motel, St. Louis, offers a comfortable informality which goes well with beverage service.

Courtesy: Albert Pick Motels

We have mentioned that smaller motels have usually avoided offering food service beyond a Continental breakfast, which may be served either in the guest units or at the motel office. Those operators of small establishments who have felt it necessary to go beyond this have either leased out the food operation or have depended on their proximity to nearby restaurants. As larger motels were built, however, restaurant facilities were included on the premises and service was then extended to the community as well as the guest. It has become apparent to the motor hotel operator that direct control over food and beverage facilities is important in creating and maintaining the reputation of the house. Although a number of large operations continue to lease out this part of the business, many motel operators find it to their best interests to run the restaurant themselves.

The degree and nature of services combine to form what is usually labelled "atmosphere." Certainly informality is one aspect of atmosphere; luxury is another. For the motel or motor hotel that offers extensive services, it is not enough that guest units be clean and attractively furnished. Equally important is the atmosphere created by the decorations, tableware, uniforms and standards of service in the dining areas and bar. There is no better way to ensure the fullest possible use of facilities.

The interior of the Red Surrey Restaurant of the Hotel Syracuse Country House, Syracuse, provides an example of how decor can enhance the specialty-room type of dining facility.

Courtesy: Hotel Syracuse Country House

Catering to Groups

If a motel books business meetings, conferences and conventions, it should make sure that the public space used for these events is adequate, flexible enough to accommodate groups of various sizes and furnished with the equipment necessary to provide speaker's table, lecture platform, podium and such other items as may be required by the group. These public areas may also serve community needs for party and function facilities. Normally, the private dining area will suffice, but it is not unusual to find a motor hotel with a ballroom seating from 300 persons upward for luncheons and banquets.

Often there is need for entertainment in connection with these public or group affairs. The extent to which the motel operator provides entertainment in his cocktail lounge and dining area depends on the nature of the affair, the impression he wants to make and, naturally, the costs involved. Entertainment may range from "piped-in" music for the rooms and public areas to complete restaurant entertainment, including a cabaret-type operation with floor show. One will usually find in the motel and motor hotel field, however, that the expenditure for entertainment is quite modest, since the "nightclub" operation is generally regarded as a business in itself which does not blend well with other facilities.

Recreation

The motel business, influenced by its extension into the resort areas, has been the industry leader in providing recreational facilities to the traveling public. The swimming pool is a notable example. Although use of the pool is usually free to the guest, it has been a source of revenue in a few instances through membership arrangements and admission charges. Attempts to gain substantial revenue from this source have often been disappointing, however. The pool promotes informality, of course, and does present opportunities for obtaining additional income from the rental of cabanas, extension of the restaurant facilities to the poolside and the sale of food and beverages at snack bars. Therefore, the activity around the pool is often much more important than its actual use for swimming. A pool does add much to the atmosphere of leisure and has become to an extent a "status symbol" for motels.

Shuffleboard, putting greens, a children's playground, and similar facilities are also common recreational features of motels. Less common are bowling alleys, golf course, and private beach or boat docks, although they too are offered by some elaborate establishments. In some instances motels which do not furnish these recreational facilities themselves are sometimes able to make arrangements for guest privileges at nearby clubs.

Shops and Auxiliary Services

Motel guest services have been amplified to a considerable extent through the provision of shopping and auxiliary retail services. Most common are the cigar, news and gift counters often found in the lobby area of the motel. Many motels also have barber, beauty, drug, haberdashery, dress and gift shops on the premises. The larger motor hotels may offer a travel bureau, brokerage offices, medical and dental services and public stenographer. Also provided are guest laundry and valet services, often handled through a local plant or shop on a commission basis.

A heliport facility is now one of the services being provided on the grounds of the Western Hills Hotel, Forth Worth.

Courtesy: Western Hills Hotel

The Guest Room

Early in the development of the motel industry a significant departure was made from standard guest-room accommodations. Because motels once catered almost exclusively to tourists, double beds were substituted for twin beds, thereby making it possible to put family groups in one room. The increased size and comfort of the double bed is looked upon as an added luxury by guests and continues to be a standard feature in almost all motels. Of course motels offer other types of facilities too, including studio arrangements, twin beds or one double bed.

Most noticeable is the trend toward more living space, which has extended the function of the guest room considerably. Thus it is now a place for relaxation as well as rest, providing space for reading, writing and visiting. Space is often ample enough for setting up a card table without disturbing the sleeping area. In some motels the rooms open onto a patio, substantially enlarging the living area.

Modern motel furnishings should provide convenience and pleasure for the guest. The old-fashioned dresser, for instance, is being replaced by a dressing area with furnishings designed to reduce the amount of unpacking and storage of clothing and other personal effects. The modern bath offers plenty of counter and shelf space on which to place toilet articles. Bureau tops are also generous, as are closets. Convenience and luxury are further enhanced by such items as bathroom scales, heaters, sun lamps, a plentiful supply of towels, soap, tissue, shoe cloths, and related articles.

The motel operator pioneered in promoting television in the guest rooms. Not long ago this feature was stressed in motel advertising, but today the traveler expects to find a television set in his room. When this service was relatively new to the industry it was regarded as an extra and charged for separately; its impact has been so widespread, however, that it is now figured into the room cost structure.

Miscellaneous Services

As competition grows among motels and motor hotels other services continue to be added, such as the provision of baby sitters, special kennel accommodations for pets, lounge space for visiting and card parties. Various guest activities, often under the supervision and guidance of a hostess, may include special parties, lectures, and movies designed to take up leisure time.

5

Selecting The Site

Mr. Statler stated during an earlier hotel building boom that the three most important factors for success in the business were *location, location* and *location*. His theory applies equally to the motel or motor hotel of today. The motel must be in a convenient position to attract the type of guest it is designed for. And as competition for the traveler's patronage becomes more intense, location becomes increasingly important.

In order to choose a site one must, of course, first select the area. This in turn will largely determine the nature of the anticipated patronage. For the operator interested in a purely transient-type motel, a site on one of the major highways leading to resort areas or connecting high concentrations of urban population is desirable. His establishment must be in the flow of guest traffic at a point where the guest is most likely to stop overnight. The accompanying map shows the proposed network of federal highways, many portions of which are presently completed or in the primary planning stage.

Various studies indicate that today about 85 per cent of all travel in this country is by automobile. The motorist prefers to travel long distances on limited-access dual highways, and both en route and at his destination he will seek out easily accessible accommodations. Starting with these observations it becomes fairly easy to establish basic criteria for analyzing both the transient and terminal guest.

Characteristically, the transient guest will seek accommodations that precede some natural obstacle, such as a major city, a large mountain range or river, since it is normally easier to confront these obstacles early in the day. He will also look for accommodations at a major interchange or junction of highways when he is considering a route change near the end of the day. Although many motorists drive all day on high-speed highways and can cover 500 to 600 miles, the average day's journey is about eight hours at an average speed of 45 to 50 miles per hour, the distance generally covered being between 300 and 400 miles. It is obvious therefore that the most sought-after transient accommodations would be on the highways or at junctions within a normal day's drive from the traveler's logical starting point.

The terminal guest has somewhat different characteristics. His reasons for seeking accommodations are related not to the distance he has traveled as much as to attractions in the immediate area. This visit may be personal, in a resort area, or it may be connected with business. It may even be a combination of both. The operator selecting a site should therefore acquaint himself with the attractions that may make an area a terminal point. These are: (a) location of large branch plants of major firms frequently visited by executives from the home office, or of commercial and business establishments visited by both executives and salesmen; (b) a university, hospital or other institution that attracts visitors from a distance; (c) a tourist location offering recreation, natural phenomena, or historical attractions; (d) a seat of government, drawing tourists or visitors on government business; (e) a popular retirement area sought by persons on vacation, investigating retirement locations, or visiting retired friends and relatives; (f) a center for scientific research and development, attracting a wide variety of scientific and professional persons as well as some tourists.

Often the attraction of an area is emphasized and augmented by local promotion. Special tours are built around events such as the Kentucky Derby in Louisville, the Mardi Gras in New Orleans, and the Rose Bowl in Pasadena. Exhibitions, trade shows, sporting events, and celebrations are usually encouraged by chambers of commerce and other interested groups. The competition for large national conventions evidenced by the building of convention and exhibit halls in many of the metropolitan centers is a prime example of the manner in which modern travel has resulted in the creation of facilities intended to influence that travel market and capitalize on it.

These are only a few of the characteristics of a terminal area. Almost all major population centers fall into this category, many

of them such as New York City, Chicago, New Orleans, San Francisco, Washington, D. C., and others serving as tourist attractions as well as centers of culture, commerce and industry. Thus, they attract large numbers of visitors whose reasons for staying in the area are multiple.

CRITERIA FOR SITE SELECTION

Once the area has been selected and the types of prospective guests determined, attention is turned to finding the site within the area that is most suitable. The three principal factors in a good motel or motor hotel location are: (a) excellent visibility; (b) ready accessibility; and (c) adaptability to the proposed facility. If a site is seriously lacking in one or more of these three, development will be extremely difficult, and the operation has little chance for even modest success. There are, of course, exceptions to this rule; motels have been successful that are not readily visible or are relatively inaccessible to the traveling motorist. However, investigation of these establishments shows that they have unusual features that far outweigh the lack of one or more of the basic criteria. Generally, it would be best for the average operator to leave the development of the exceptional to those who have the talent and means for such experimentation and to concentrate his efforts upon a location that has natural advantages.

Visibility

People in search of accommodations are greatly influenced by their first impression. If the motel can be seen from the highway for a good distance in both directions it has a considerable edge on the one that must resort to other means of attracting the guest. At high speeds normally used on today's limited-access dual highways, the first impression is likely to be a fleeting one. At 60 miles an hour an automobile is traveling nearly 90 feet per second. Therefore, if a motel is readily visible from as much as a quarter of a mile away the car will cover that distance in somewhat less than 15 seconds. Even if the motorist is actively seeking accommodations, this brief interval will barely be adequate for him to determine whether he should stop and to give him the opportunity to find the turn-off and enter the property.

Easy visibility is much more critical to the motel that caters primarily to the transient guest than it is to the operation sought by the traveler who desires terminal accommodations. In city locations or in a tourist area, the factor of visibility from the road may not be as important. Nevertheless it is desirable to afford some ready means of directing the prospective guest, such as road signs near the turn-off point. Highway road signs are a valuable advertising influence, especially where competition is keen.

Accessibility

The desirable location will offer easy arrival and departure access. Traffic flow in and around the site should be studied carefully to determine the effects of left-turn restrictions, interchanges and turn-off points, connecting routes and projected plans for the present road pattern. Many a motel has suffered severely when a new cutoff or major highway change has diverted traffic, even when the change is miles away from the site.

This view of the Cherry Hill Inn, Haddonfield, New Jersey, illustrates the location of the facilities with respect to a highway interchange in the Philadelphia area.

Courtesy: Cherry Hill Inn

The transient traveler on a limited-access highway will not be likely to seek accommodations on a secondary road unless he knows he will have to leave the highway to find a place to stay. The terminal guest, however, will tend to avoid the highway location if he can find a spot closer to his destination. Exceptions to these general rules exist, of course, but if there is a choice between sites equally adaptable to the project, it is best to choose the more accessible one.

Accessibility can be enhanced by providing an inviting as well as adequate entrance to the property. Attractive signs often help. The Quality Courts organization has placed considerable emphasis on their eye-catching entrance sign and consider it one of the major factors in bringing business to their establishments. A good campaign of advertising and choice highway sign locations may encourage a guest to seek out a relatively inaccessible motel. It should be added, however, that unless the accommodations are very much above average for the area, it is not likely that he will return a second time to an inconvenient location.

Entrances and exits from both a freeway and a major highway are shown in this aerial view of a Howard Johnson's Motor Lodge, Hamden, New Jersey.
Courtesy: Howard Johnson's Motor Lodges

The terrain must also be considered. A level site would ordinarily be preferred to a steep hill. Moreover, property which slopes up from the road would be preferable to that which drops below road level.

Adaptability

Size is a primary consideration in choice of site. The land must be large enough to accommodate not only buildings, but also parking space for overnight guests adjacent to guest rooms and parking space for restaurant patrons and employees. There should also be ample room for proper placement of the swimming pool and other recreational facilities as well as for attractive landscaping to provide pleasant views from all guest and public areas.

The terrain should be studied critically to determine the amount of work necessary to level the space required for the facilities. A location that will require a great deal of fill or one on a hill, bluff or mountainside where extremes of leveling and grading are involved, may be impractical. The type of soil is a consideration, since it must offer a good base for building foundations, parking area and pool. Test borings should be made to estimate the amount of subsurface rock to be removed for placing footings, or the cost of added supports in sandy or loose soils. If heavy concentrations of either rock or sand are encountered, the cost of preparing the site could easily exceed the initial investment in the property. On the other hand, the terrain may have some natural advantages in its contour that can and should be exploited.

The land area required will depend upon the type and size of the buildings and other facilities to be constructed. A rough guide for a single-story motel with moderate restaurant and bar facilities is 1,000 square feet per unit. In other words, an acre (43,560 square feet) provides sufficient space for a 40- to 45-unit motor including parking area, bar and dining area. If the overnight accommodations are to be placed in a two-story structure, approximately 700 square feet should be figured for each unit.

Like all rules of thumb, these should be used with caution. It might be possible to construct more room units on a given site, but normally it would mean a sacrifice in room size, service space, storage and administrative areas. Non-income-producing areas such as these are often found to be lacking in size, the tendency being to sacrifice them in favor of earning space. Because later correction of these inadequacies is usually very expensive, it is wise when planning space needs to allow an additional 10 per cent margin of error.

It is also advisable to consider providing space for future expansion. Prospective investors are often well-advised to start with a moderate facility and then to add to it as the business warrants it. To do this, it is necessary to have a convenient area adjacent to the original facilities and a plan which will make it possible to integrate the added facilities with those already in operation.

Before assuming that a site is readily adaptable to the type of operation planned, it is best to familiarize oneself with the local

zoning restrictions, building codes, fire regulations and other laws
that might hamper or influence construction. It is always advisable
to seek professional advice at an early stage to be certain all contingencies are covered and that the best use is made of the site selected.
(A subsequent chapter is devoted to the subject of professional advisors.)

This aerial view of the Golden Triangle Motor Hotel, Norfolk, shows the
complete layout of the facilities and parking area of a high-rise building.
Courtesy: Golden Triangle Motor Hotel

Cost

Once the site has passed the test of the three general criteria,
it is time to consider more specific factors. Foremost among these is
the cost of the land itself. Inexpensive land is becoming increasingly
difficult to find, especially in areas sufficiently developed to offer motels
and motor hotels a reasonable chance for success. The only general
rule available for measuring cost is a negative one—that the total
cost of land and of site development should not exceed 20 per cent of
the overall cost of the project. This rule, which has been based on
a study of hotels, is frequently broken, particularly when a site is
considered to be highly desirable. It is generally feasible where land
prices are particularly high to increase the density of guest-room
units on the property by building a multiple-story structure. This is
especially true for the motor hotel located in or near the center

of a metropolitan area. The original advantages of low land cost and lower taxes outside the city limits were potent factors in the development of the earlier roadside motel, but have been diminished as motor hotel investors have found metropolitan area sites to be more desirable and suitable for their extensive facilities and service.

One fallacy that frequently attends the planning of multiple-story units is that increasing the number of guest rooms and thereby reducing the per unit cost of land is an answer to the basic problem of high initial property costs. Realistically, the number of units placed on a site should be based on the findings of market studies as to the local need, not on the cost of land.

Relation to Area Development

Another measure of the merit of a specific location is its relation to urban and area development. Ideally, a site should be located in an area or section of a city where the growth in activity that will increase guest potential is real and dynamic. The relation to area development must also be considered in light of activities or events that may occur several hundred miles from the site. It is entirely possible, for instance, that the construction of a new bridge or a new turnpike will change local traffic patterns to the extent that today's location may be completely isolated tomorrow. On the other hand, the building of a new hospital or other major institution, a contemplated shopping or recreational facility nearby may enhance the market possibilities for the motel site.

Some areas of the United States, expanding in their economy, have experienced steady increases in population and travel activity; other areas, contracting economically, present a much less optimistic picture to the prospective motel or motor hotel investor. Travel business is not unlike most other businesses which rise or fall with the general economy, and the potential of a given motel depends on the trends of the economy in its locale. Before a final decision is reached with respect to a motel project, representatives of municipal or local government should be questioned, for they often can give the best information on changing local traffic patterns and the future urban development in the vicinity of the motel site.

Supply and Demand

While it is not advisable to build a new motel in an area where the total number of available guest units already exceeds the demand, neither is it good policy, generally speaking, to be completely isolated. Other motels of good reputation in the immediate area often help to generate additional business through their combined efforts. The motorist frequently seeks out an area in which he knows there are several motels so that he will have ample choice of facilities. However, the construction of a new guest facility in an area already saturated with such establishments results only in a further division of the existing demand for overnight occommodations, with all the motels in the area consequently experiencing lower levels of occupancy.

The study of competing facilities should include an analysis of their rate and price structures, patronage and facilities. The prices obtained by the competition will to a great extent determine the prices that can be charged by the new facility.

Influence of Nearby Industry and Commerce

One important criterion used in judging the suitability of a site for a terminal operation is the degree of concentration of local commerce and industry. Industry is generally described as being either basic or sustaining. Basic industries are those which produce goods that are usually sold elsewhere. Sustaining industries are those such as laundries, bakeries and other service establishments producing goods or providing services that sustain the local population. Of the two, sustaining industries attract considerably fewer travelers.

An analysis of questionnaires returned by industrial firms shows that the following industries normally have the greatest need for overnight accommodations for visitors, provided the company employs over 100 persons and its business is national in scope:

Rank   *Standard Industrial Classification*
   1. Research, development and testing laboratories.
   2. Professional, scientific and controlling instruments.
   3. Chemicals and allied products.
   4. Electrical machinery, equipment and supplies.
   5. Petroleum refining and related industries.
   6. Fabricated metal products except ordnance, machinery and transportation equipment.
   7. Rubber and miscellaneous products.
   8. Machinery, except electrical.
   9. Primary metal industries.
  10. Transportation equipment.

Very little demand for overnight room accommodations is contributed by wholesale distribution plants, auto assembly plants, auto or machinery distributors and plants engaged in textile production. Companies engaged in these activities frequently have their administrative and sales offices in urban centers, and visitors to the production departments are not frequent. Commercial centers, rail and port facilities create a good demand for overnight accommodations, but that market is probably already largely absorbed by existing hotels.

In the metropolitan centers new motels and motor hotels have been built mostly in what is termed "the peripheral areas," and are thus in a position to attract the motorist as he approaches town. The general trend toward construction of neighborhood shopping centers and decentralization of commercial and industrial activities has augmented the markets of motels in peripheral locations.

6

Determining the Improvements

Once the site has been selected, it is important that the prospective investor take a fresh and detached look at the venture to further establish its feasibility. Two key factors in appraisal are the community and the guest.

NEEDS OF THE COMMUNITY

The type and extent of the facilities that will best answer the community needs can be determined only after an exhaustive study of the area. This is usually the starting point of what is commonly called a "feasibility study."

The attractions in the vicinity that would occasion the guest's visit should be listed and analyzed to determine those already established and well-known and those that must be further promoted to attract visitors. While almost every area has a number of attractions, each must be coldly evaluated in relation to the motel venture in order to be put in proper perspective.

The possible attractions are too numerous to be described here in detail, nor would an exhaustive listing have equal application across the country. Most attractions may be generally classified as either business or recreational, institutional or industrial, seasonal or year-round, natural or man-made. Some may be augmented at certain times of the year by special events such as state fairs, sporting events or activities associated with historical celebrations. Or they may be nationally known events, like the Indianapolis race or the Kentucky Derby.

An investor may be tempted to rely on the potential of an attraction that has been hitherto neglected. However, it is seldom advisable to construct guest facilities on the hopes of a possible awakening or rekindling of public interest in an attraction. In most cases the investment in promotion is expensive and relatively unrewarding. In other words, in the list there should be several established attractions that bring a large number of visitors into the area each year.

It is also important to determine the vitality and potential of the community in terms of economic growth. This may be indicated by such statistics as may available on population figures, building permits, new construction, bank clearings and deposits, postal receipts, telephone installations, services of other utilities and retail sales. Data of this nature will give some measure of population expansion, which in turn usually reflects a growing number of visitors.

Competing Facilities

An analysis of the size and type of competing facilities in the immediate area and the approaches to it is imperative. If existing facilities are adequately handling the needs of the local populace and visitors, a new establishment is faced with the difficult job of bringing new business to an area. Otherwise the operation can only hope to further divide existing business.

It is advisable to spend several days studying the community, staying in different facilities and analyzing their operations critically. Careful observations can yield many valuable facts. For example, the difficulties encountered in obtaining reservations for room accommodations would be an indication of the present demand for existing facilities. However, the relationship between supply and demand cannot be judged over a short period but must be weighed with respect to the possible effect of seasonal travel and also to the possible variations in demand during the week. (Don't forget that a 70 per cent occupancy average can result from 100 per cent occupancy three days of the week and 50 per cent occupancy over the weekend, and that major expenses of operation continue during slack periods.)

Spending a small amount of time in the registration lobby during the busiest periods of the day will enable the observer to determine any resistance to rates, the type of facility most sought after and the problems encountered by the visitor in obtaining the desired accommodations. It may be possible to take or obtain reliable traffic counts on automobile travel, paying particular attention to the percentage of out-of-state licenses as a gauge of the number of visitors in the area. Eating in the existing restaurants is normally an excellent way to obtain firsthand knowledge of the need for food facilities and the problems that will be encountered in competing for this trade. Room rates, menu prices and other charges can be obtained from printed pamphlets and from motel personnel.

Frequently one is able to obtain a very close approximation of the average occupancy of competing facilities merely by counting cars and vacant parking spaces late at night, and relating this count to the number of room units available. Another measure of tourist demand is the number of families that can be observed using the available facilities. Since the greatest commercial demand for overnight accommodations usually occurs on Tuesdays and Wednesdays and tourist or pleasure travel is more prevalent on weekends, it is best to continue the sampling throughout the week.

Food and Beverage Facilities

The community need for food and beverage facilities is somewhat more difficult to determine than the need for room accommodations since it is based on both the requirements of visitors to the area and the needs of local patronage. These facilities in competing hotels and motels should be studied, along with the activity in local restaurants, taverns and private clubs in the immediate vicinity. The availability of function rooms in local hotels and motels should also be determined. Very often all that is required is a visit or telephone call to the sales or catering manager, who is usually happy to discuss his wares. A list of local business and social organizations should be obtained, and these groups should be approached to determine the frequency and size of their meetings and their function activities. A visit to nearby industrial plants and business offices will enable the analyst to determine the type and extent of food and beverage facilities required by these companies, many of which may provide their own dining and meeting facilities.

Use of Questionnaires

The expert market analyst will use one or more questionnaires to obtain supporting data concerning the needs of the community for additional accommodations. The following questionnaire, with its covering letter, is directed to those local individuals and companies who would logically make use of the intended facilities.

Mr. John Doe
Acme Instrument Company
22 James Street
Center City, Oregon

Dear Mr. Doe:

We have been engaged to study the guest accommodations in Blank County in order to determine the need and feasibility of a proposed new 150-room motor hotel in Center City. In the course of our survey we have inspected and investigated the existing hotel and motel properties in Blank County. We are now in the process of trying to determine as factually as possible the adequacy of these facilities in meeting the current day-to-day needs and also the peak-load demand for them. We would appreciate your cooperation and assistance in this phase of our study whereby we hope to get the expressions and opinions of local individuals and companies that are interested in the use of such facilities, and we are enclosing a two-part questionnaire for your convenience which we would like you to complete and return to us.

We want your honest opinion only and your answers will not be considered as a commitment of any kind. This request is not in any way a forerunner of investment solicitation and will be considered a confidential matter as far as you or your organization is concerned. We are seeking the same information from others in the area, and the results of this inquiry will be combined and made known to authorized contributors in summary form only.

If you are willing, we would like to interview you or one of your representatives briefly in order to obtain information supplemental to the facts we hope to establish through use of the enclosed form. If an appointment is possible please advise as to whom we should contact.

The first part of the questionnaire concerns your use of existing hotel and motor hotel facilities; the second section concerns your potential use of the new property. Please do not feel limited to answering only the questions asked, for we are definitely interested in any additional comments which relate to the guest accommodations in Blank County.

We shall certainly appreciate your assistance and cooperation. A self-addressed envelope is enclosed for your convenience in replying.

Very sincerely yours,
(Signature and company affiliation of
market analyst.)

BLANK COUNTY GUEST FACILITIES

(Insert name and address of market analyst here.)

PART I

A. *Transient Guests*

1. In finding accommodations for your visitors from other areas, how does the percentage of motor hotel facilities used compare with the percentage of hotel facilities?

	Percentages
Motor hotels	——%
Hotels	——%
Total	100%

2. Approximately how many of your guests use these facilities in the course of a year?
    a) Average number of persons per visit ————
    b) Number of visits per year ————
3. What is the average duration of each visit? ————
4. Do your visitors have difficulty in obtaining accommodations during any part of the week? *Yes* ———— *No* ————
    If so, on what days usually? ————
5. Do your visitors seem to be satisfied with the types of room and service they receive? *Yes* ———— *No* ————
6. Do you or your visitors have any preference as to which existing hotel or motor hotel to use? *Yes* ———— *No* ————
    If so, would you care to state which one and why? ————

7. Do many of your visitors prefer motels to hotels? *Yes* ———— *No* ————
8. Are your guests generally satisfied with restaurant facilities offered at existing hotels and motor hotels? *Yes* ———— *No* ————
    Is there any preference as to restaurant facilities in the area? *Yes* ———— *No* ————
    If so, would you care to state which one is preferred and why?

9. Is there any serious resistance to the room rates and menu prices asked by existing hostelries? *Yes* ———— *No* ————

B. *Meetings and Functions*

1. Please comment on whether or not your needs or the needs of your firm for meeting and function facilities are met by existing hotels and motor hotels.
    a) Group Meetings ————
    b) Banquets ————
    c) Conventions ————
    d) Social Events ————
2. In order to get a firm commitment for a meeting or function is it necessary to make reservations so far in advance as to be inconvenient for you? *Yes* ———— *No* ————
    Does this happen frequently? *Yes* ———— *No* ————

PART II

Assuming that a modern first-class 150-room motor hotel were opened in Blank County and located on Route #1 north of Sunrise Highway and south of Sunset Road, what estimates would you make of the use of its facilities by you or your firm?

A. *Sleeping Facilities for Visitors*

	Number of Persons Per Year	Average Length of Stay
1. Company personnel on regular trips	————	————
2. Salesmen and buyers	————	————
3. Workshops and conferences	————	————
4. Other (professional, government, friends, etc.)	————	————

B. *Meetings and Conference Rooms*

	Number of Times Per Year	Average Attendance
1. Company meetings, local	————	————
2. Sales or other business conferences	————	————
3. Training groups or workshops	————	————
4. Professional or civic clubs	————	————
5. Other	————	————

C. *Banquet and Private Dining Rooms*

1. Company—Luncheons		
Dinners	————	————
2. Conferences	————	————
3. Training groups and workshops	————	————
4. Local staff parties (holiday, retirement, anniversaries, etc.)	————	————
5. Dances	————	————
6. Social events—banquets	————	————
7. Other	————	————

Submitted by:

Firm Name ————————————————————

By: ————————————————

Title ————————————————
(End of Questionnaire)

The main object of a questionnaire is to get prompt, accurate answers. It is therefore suggested that questions be limited in number and complexity so that answering the questionnaire will not overburden the person to whom it is addressed. Furthermore, it should be made clear that answers will be kept confidential and will not be considered a commitment in any way. Experience has indicated that the chances of a questionnaire being answered depend to a large extent on its source; if it is sent out by a responsible firm it is more likely to be regarded as unbiased and respectful of confidences. Of course many local citizens and firms will have strong loyalties to the operators of existing establishments. A reputable firm making a feasibility study will realize that these ties must be respected and taken into account in this phase of the study.

One advantage of engaging a professional analyst is therefore readily apparent. He can write a letter clearly setting forth his independence of financial interest in the project, and the person receiving the questionnaire will quickly realize that the answers do not commit him to any future actions.

It is worthy of note that a properly designed questionnaire will bring at least a 50 per cent return, and in many cases 75 per cent or more of the letters will bring usable answers. The percentage of response will, in itself, will be an indication of local interest in the proposed venture.

Personal Interviews

It is best to follow up a number of the questionnaires with personal interviews. Usually, when a business firm receives a questionnaire, an employee of the firm will pass the form on to the person who has the responsibility for obtaining accommodations for visitors. Frequently, however, there are others in the company and in the community who have definite ideas concerning the community needs and some whose interest may spring from a desire for civic improvement or from personal motives. Although their interest in the project may therefore be prejudiced, it is usually good practice to try to get them to express their thoughts. Local bankers, businessmen, government officials, civic leaders, club officers and other interested individuals definitely respond better to questions asked in a personal interview than to those on a questionnaire. It is wise to give such people this personal attention because they may later be important to the success of the project.

In conducting a personal interview, the interviewer becomes accustomed to learning as much from the way the questions are answered as from the answers themselves. In no circumstances should the interviewer argue with the person questioned. The purpose of the discussion is to tap the subject's personal thoughts, not to convey the thoughts of the interviewer.

It is a good idea to consult with representatives of the chamber of commerce or other local community organizations in determining which persons should be interviewed personally and which should be sent a questionnaire. Those who respond to the questionnaire by asking for an interview should not be neglected. In fact, at this point in the study it is best not to neglect anyone who may at some time have something to say about the completion of the project.

NEEDS OF THE GUEST

Once the needs of the community have been determined and the reasons for visiting the area have been listed, the next step is to analyze the sources of business. By listing the reasons for a visit to the community in order of importance based on the number of persons motivated, it is frequently possible to determine the probable percentage of guests who will be traveling for business and the probable percentage who will be traveling for pleasure or for personal reasons. Interviews, answers to questionnaires and personal observations should by this time have given some indication of the percentage of transients in need of overnight accommodations. Personal observations. should also have provided a basis for estimating the number of tourists or vacationers that are in the area at any given time.

A major determination as to the possible sources of business is the type of guest that will be accommodated. As we have established, it is important to know whether the majority of guests will be transient or tourist, for the accommodations to be offered depend not only on the number of visitors but also on length of stay. Accommodations also depend on the guests' tastes and their ability to pay for the conveniences offered. This can be determined only by finding out who they are, where they come from, and why they are stopping in the area.

Transportation

Passenger traffic from the local airport and train and bus stations should be investigated and, if possible, figures should be obtained on arriving and departing passengers. The State Highway Department is usually an excellent source of information on the number of automobiles leaving the major expressways in a given area and often can provide data on their states of origin.

Experience has shown that traffic counts are of value mainly in a negative way. A very low traffic count would probably indicate that the highway in question is a poor location for a motel. An extremely high count of traffic, however, might indicate the presence of sufficient congestion to motivate the prospective guest to continue to a less busy area. A very high traffic count would also indicate the need for a new route bypassing the existing highway. Traffic observers have stated that unless a count can be taken for almost every hour of the day, every day of the week through the year, the results can be very misleading. Added to this is the factor of change in local traffic patterns. Changes in highways have been responsible for many failures in motels in past years and established traffic patterns must be carefully reviewed to determine their permanence.

Need for Additional Facilities

With some knowledge of the type of guest in mind, one can determine the advisability of providing services beyond overnight accommodations. Such additional facilities will often be required to attract guests to the establishment. Later chapters are devoted to food and beverage facilities, minor services such as cigar and newsstand, valet and laundry, shops, parking and garage service. All of these features are now commonly found in both hotels and motor hotels. Whether they should be made part of a particular project depends on the tastes and desires of the types of guest to be served, a subject also examined in detail in subsequent chapters.

"Free services" are offered as an inducement to the guest in meeting competitive conditions. Each service or convenience contributes to the cost of operation, however, and there is a limit to what can be offered without charge. It is best to follow the policy that if the guest really appreciates the service and convenience he should be willing to pay for it.

Entertainment and Recreational Facilities

One of the direct results of the guest profile analysis would be a determination of the extent to which recreational and entertainment facilities should be provided. Installation of television, radio and piped-in music in guest rooms, the lobby and some of the public dining and meeting rooms has become commonplace in motels. Most guests now have the first two items in their own homes and expect them on the road. As a result, motels and motor hotels now include these items in their regular room rate structures.

However, there are a number of other forms of recreation and entertainment not as common to motels and motor hotels that often have been instrumental in attracting guests. The swimming pool has

The pool and patio area of the Marriott Motor Hotel, Philadelphia, provides a pleasant and interesting outlook for occupants of the guest rooms in this high-rise building.

Courtesy: Marriott Motor Hotels

become the most popular of these features. In fact, it is almost indispensable to motels in some areas. A majority of motel owners and many hotelmen who have added swimming pools to existing operations have said that they are a definite business attraction. The frequent highway traveler will soon note that motels with swimming pools seem to fill up earlier, especially during the normal swimming season.

Facilities for shuffleboard, badminton, tennis and table tennis are found only infrequently, mostly in resort areas. A short-hole or "pitch-and-putt" golf course may be a desirable feature in some areas. If the motel is located near a bowling alley, golf course or tennis courts, the advertising and promotion of these nearby attractions may help to bring guests to the motel's door.

The extent to which these recreational and entertainment facilities should be incorporated in plans for the site can be determined only after a careful analysis of the guests' needs and demands. It is important, however, that these points be decided before final planning, for all of them require an allotment of space and must be coordinated in the plan so that a complete layout of the site can be made. Many of the facilities for minor sports take up considerable space, require reasonably level terrain and, to have value as an attraction, de-

Architect's rendering of Hilton Inn, Kansas City, Missouri, shows the placement of guest rooms, restaurant, recreation and parking facilities, using the contour of land to best advantage for visibility on approach and an appealing view for guests and patrons.

Courtesy: Hilton Inns

mand more than a modest investment. Frequently it is best to allot a portion of the site to the future development of such minor sports as may seem to be necessary to retain patronage.

ECONOMIC FACTORS

Once the needs of the community and the guest have been determined to the best of the analyst's ability, it is time to undertake the planning of the overall site layout. Frequently at this point many of the highly desirable features proposed as a result of previous analysis must be discarded because the site is not readily adaptable to them. It is at this stage that the following questions must be answered:

1. How many buildings are to be constructed on the site?

2. Should they be one-story, two-story or multiple-story structures?

3. If more than one building, how should they be placed on the plot and how will they be connected?

4. What view will provide the most pleasing outlook for the guest units, the restaurants?

5. Must parking space be allotted directly adjacent to each room

unit? Based upon the guest's probable length of stay, the expected local traffic in the restaurant and bars and the more popular means of arriving at the destination, what is the amount of parking space required?

6. Should buildings be constructed with all guest rooms opening on an inside corridor, or should outside corridors, porches and central-core construction be used?

7. What are the noise and dirt factors? To what extent can highway noises and the noise of nearby industries be detected at various points on the site? How far from the highway should the buildings be placed and at what angle to decrease the noise and dirt factors? Are there any nearby factory odors or other pollution problems?

8. How should the entrance be designed and the entire project laid out to be most attractive upon approach? How can maximum income be obtained from recreational areas without sacrificing guest privacy?

9. What types of lighting should be used to enhance the motel's appearance without annoying the guests?

10. What signs are necessary and where should they be placed?

This view of the Holiday Inn from the grounds of the Dallas Airport presents a complete portrayal of the entrance sign, restaurant and recreational facilities, parking area and the arrangement of the room facilities of this motor hotel located in the outlying section of a highly populated area.
Courtesy: Alsonett Hotels

The cost of grading, leveling and generally adapting the site to the operation can be unduly expensive without proper planning. Costs can be cut, for example, if the buildings are so located that blank walls will provide sound buffers or deflectors and thereby eliminate the need for expensive soundproofing. The question of inside versus outside corridors is one that must be considered both in terms of climate and comparison of the additional initial investment with long-term services and maintenance costs.

The construction of a central core provides an area in which all utilities are placed centrally, with the guest rooms on both sides. This arrangement provides access to the guest rooms from outside entrances.

The full development of the available land and the layout of the facilities of the Continental-Denver Motor Hotel are two outstanding features of this establishment.

Courtesy: Continental-Denver Motor Hotel

Such a layout is generally less expensive, but ways of muffling room-to-room noises must also be considered in planning plumbing and inter-room walls. More maids may be required to service rooms not connected by a central corridor, since in bad weather it is often difficult to reach the rooms from outside. In an area where extensive winter heating and summer air conditioning are required, an inside corridor arrangement reduces utility costs. It is important to measure both the short- and long-term advantages of various styles of construction to determine the wisest expenditure.

Use of Schematic Drawings

Professional advice on building layout and design should be sought before the planning progresses very far. However, it is possible for the owner to analyze and outline his own ideas on improvements and

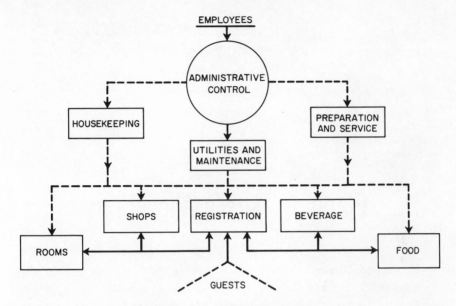

Schematic Design of Motel Operation

to assist the architect in grasping them by making simple rough drawings or schematic designs prior to calling on professional assistance.
The schematic drawing is the simplest form of diagram of the flow of
guests, service personnel and supplies through the proposed operation.
Such a diagram may answer many of the architect's questions in preparing more detailed plans.

7

Planning: Space Allocations

Professional help is a must at this point. We again urge that the services of a capable architect be obtained, preferably one who has already had experience in the field of hotels, motor hotels and motels. The owner should know by now the number and size of the buildings he plans to erect on the property and the desired capacity of the facilities. He can now decide together with the architect the layout of these structures as well as the parking and service areas. When this has been done, preparation of a general scheme can begin.

A significant consideration that is frequently overlooked is the importance of providing for future expansion. In a community where economic growth has been dynamic and is expected to continue, it is almost certain that competing ventures will be proposed. Therefore it is advisable to provide adjacent space, set aside for the eventual construction of additional guest units or improvements that will keep the motel up to date. Since it probably won't be necessary to provide for additional public facilities and service space in the overall operation, the square footage per living unit projected for future guest rooms can be modified somewhat from the general guide quoted earlier. If a single story extension is desired, an allowance of 700 square feet per unit should be sufficient. If it is to be a two-story structure, an allowance of 400 to 500 square feet per unit should be adequate. Once this expansion area has been set aside, the schematic drawings indicating the overall improvement plan should be further translated into a definite program for the best utilization of land space available for immediate development.

THE GUEST ROOMS

Although it remains a fact that there is room in the business for establishments that offer only guest-room accommodations, we are concerned in this discussion with those larger facilities that provide reasonably complete services to the traveling public.

Normally between 60 per cent and 90 per cent of the motel building's total square footage will be devoted to guest rooms and adjoining corridors, stairs and elevators. This ratio fluctuates widely, of course, because of the variations in the need for public space, such as lobby, dining rooms, meeting rooms, recreational facilities, stores and work areas. For many years the goal of successful hotel operators has been a hotel in which the guest-room area, including related service space, equaled 50 per cent of the total square footage of the building. Because motels and motor hotels usually have a smaller area devoted to public facilities, the ratio of guest-room space to the total area is consequently higher. Since the greatest contribution to net profits is almost always made on the sale of guest-room space, this factor of space allocation is obviously responsible for the financial success of many motel projects in past years.

Motels offering only guest-room accommodations can show a better profit ratio than hotels or motor hotels with more diversified facilities. The rooms department normally shows a profit of 60 per cent to 80 per cent, whereas the food and beverage departmental profit ranges from 5 per cent to 25 per cent, depending on the amount of beverage sales and banquet and party business. The difference between these ratios can be attributed to the greater direct costs and expenses involved in restaurant operation. One should not be swayed by ratios alone, however, inasmuch as the guest may demand additional facilities, and cutting back on other departments may be fatal to the project as a whole.

Room Apportionment

The total square footage of the guest-room area can be determined only after establishing the total number of each type of room. Therefore it is best at the start to give some consideration to how many different types of rooms and how many rooms of each type will be included. It is most difficult to set up any general rules applicable to all motels for determining the apportionment of guest-room space. This is a matter which depends entirely on an evaluation of the guest, his probable tastes and requirements. An analysis of a large number of motel plans reveals the following range of ratios for each of four popular types of guest room to the total number of rooms:

Room Type	Ratio To Total Available Rooms
Single	10% to 30%
Double	20% to 50%
Twin	30% to 60%
Twin Double	10% to 20%

The foregoing ratios have a very wide range, indicating much variation in the types of guest-room facilities desired in different communities. The proportion of rooms to be allocated for single occupancy is much higher in those motels located near urban centers or in industrial or downtown centers. The proportion of twin or large bedrooms is greater in resort areas. The range of room rates also has some bearing on the proportion of rooms of each type. For example, it may be desirable in a certain area to offer rooms for a very modest price during certain seasons of the year. In that case a greater number of smaller single or double rooms would be advisable. Many businessmen traveling alone prefer to occupy a larger room with a double bed even

This twin-bedded room in the Motor House in Colonial Williamsburg, Virginia, effectively combines living and sleeping areas by efficient spacing of furniture.

Courtesy: Williamsburg Restoration, Inc.

if it costs more than a single. It is customary and advisable to install at least a few adjoining rooms directly connected by double doors. These may be converted to suites when the demand warrants. In larger communities and in some resort areas it is particularly advisable to provide this type of accommodation.

Standard Guest-Room Sizes

Because the greatest proportion of total building area is devoted to guest-room space it is best to plan the space requirements for these facilities first. Serious consideration should be given to standardization of room sizes. A limited number of standard room types can be incorporated more easily in the layout than rooms with a wide variety of specifications. Standardization further offers distinct advantages in construction costs.

A typical room in Schimmel's Indian Hills Inn, Omaha, shows the combination of an extra-large double bed with additional studio lounge and efficient placement of living area, an arrangement which appeals particularly to the family trade as well as regular transient patronage.

Courtesy: Schimmel Hotels Corporation

It is possible by varying the furniture arrangement in a limited number of standard-sized rooms to provide a generous variety of accommodations in many price ranges. For example, a single room may contain a regular single bed or a studio-type bed. A room normally large enough to contain twin beds might accommodate a standard single plus a double bed or perhaps two to three studio beds. Twin double beds have found popular acceptance, especially with families.

The bed is not the only consideration in a modern guest room; the trend has been toward the provision of more living room space. It should therefore be determined whether areas for lounging will be provided in the guest room or in public space. If private patios or porches are to be a feature of the project, space must be allocated in the ground plot. In some instances, guest-room space must be set aside for kitchenettes, refrigerators and other added conveniences. The extent of closet space or drawer space depends on the profile of the guest. People are becoming more accustomed to "living out a suitcase" in transient facilities, and modern developments in furnishings and room arrangements have adapted to this trend.

It would be impossible to cover all combinations of ideas developed in guest-room accommodations, and this section must be confined to a review of the more usual or "standard" types, leaving decisions with respect to the need for refinements and embellishments to the reader's judgment. It should be realized, however, that each luxury adds to the cost of operation and to the investment.

In order to give some idea of the approximate square footage required for the desired number of units, the following tabulation has been prepared, showing room sizes fairly standard in motel and motor hotel operations:

Room Type	Square Foot Areas Including Bath and Closet
Single	180 to 220 square feet
Double	190 to 240 square feet
Twin	240 to 360 square feet
Twin Double	250 to 380 square feet

Corridor widths are generally 5 to 6 feet, 6 feet being the standard. Space will be required on each floor for fire exits, elevators, linen rooms and maids' or janitors' closets. A general rule is that a single room requires about 250 feet of space, including corridors and working areas, and a twin-bedded room may require as much as 450 square feet.

LOBBY AND LOUNGE

No set standards or patterns exist for lobbies and lounges. The large lobbies of the older hotels, often featuring mezzanine balconies and high ceilings, have become outdated because of the trend toward more living space in the guest rooms. Moreover, air conditioning has made high ceilings unnecessary. A measure often used in planning public lobby and lounge space is that between 15 and 20 square feet should

be provided per guest-room unit. Many motels have only a small office
lobby and a few have relatively large areas devoted to public space.
In a resort area a larger lounge space may be required to accommodate
card parties, general visiting among guests and other activities.

The guest-lounge area and the approach from the street to the elevators and
stairways are examples of the good planning that went into the Aristocrat Inn,
Chicago.

Courtesy: Aristocrat Inns of America

In addition to a lounge area, such space usually includes the front
office or registration, mail and information desk; the news and cigar
stand and direct access to the restaurant. Public toilets for men and
women should be convenient to this space as should guest elevators,
which are usually entered from the lobby. If retail shops, barber or
beauty shops are included in the plans, they should be accessible from
the lobby.

FOOD AND BEVERAGE FACILITIES

Very little relationship exists between the number of restaurant
seats in a motor hotel and the number of guest-room units. The
motor hotels that have contributed food and beverage figures to the

Horwath & Horwath annual studies over the past several years contain restaurant facilities varying in size from a coffee shop seating 40 persons to a tremendous complex of dining rooms and function areas seating nearly 2,000 people. If a restaurant is planned, it should contain as a minimum the number of seats that might be required for breakfast service at normal room occupancy. A rough rule would be one seat for two guest spaces. For this purpose one considers the number of beds available, counting a double-bedded room as two guest spaces, but not counting twin double beds as four guest spaces.

The International Room of the Albert Pick Motel, St. Louis, Missouri, is an example of the efficient layout of meeting and banquet facilities.

Courtesy: Albert Pick Motels

The amount of seating space in the dining rooms depends on the type of food and beverage service to be offered. For banquet seating, 10 square feet per person is normally adequate. For popularly priced table service, 15 square feet is considered sufficient, and for counter service in a lunch room or coffee shop, 20 square feet should be allowed, including counter and back service area. Similarly, space amounting to 18 to 20 square feet per person should be allocated for the bar or cocktail lounge.

These figures do not include space necessary for kitchen, pantry, warewashing and storage. The preparation, service, storage and employee facility areas that must be provided with any food and beverage operation should roughly equal the amount of space in the dining area. In other words, for each square foot of dining area another square foot should be added for non-selling area. Too frequently it is found that motel restaurants have not been provided with adequate space for preparation, storage and employee facility areas. The result is that service is hampered and unnecessary operating costs are added.

GENERAL SERVICE AND STORAGE AREAS

We have often heard the remark made by hotel and motel operators that there is never enough storage space. The general service and storage areas are often fitted into the plan, if at all, after the space allotment for the income-producing area has been decided. Thus they are often inadequate and sometimes require space that was originally devoted to guest rooms or public area, as many motel owners discover unhappily at some later date. The manager, auditor, housekeeper and engineer are usually the ones to suffer from this lack of planning.

About 100 square feet of space will usually be required for the work and storage space of each administrative or clerical employee. The space required for the laundry, linen room and maid's closet approximates 10 to 15 square feet per guest room, but may have to be expanded if the restaurant facilities are extensive. It is advisable that such space be located as close as possible to the areas to be served. The amount of other necessary service, storage, repair and utility space can be estimated at from 25 to 30 square feet per unit, and additional space will have to be provided for storage of tables, chairs, etc., if the motel or motor hotel has a catering department.

The size of the area to be allotted for employees' lockers, dressing. rooms and living quarters depends, of course, on the number of persons included in the service staff and on the amount of time the employees spend on the premises. In larger operations the manager will expect to have adequate quarters available to him, and usually the housekeeper and chef will expect to be provided with a room to be used for resting during off-hours even if they do not live on the premises.

In normal practice it can be estimated that for each guest unit constructed, an additional 425 to 450 square feet of floor area are required in the overall project. The foregoing figure allows for minimum restaurant requirements of one restaurant seat for each three room units. Each additional restaurant seat will add about 30 square feet to the floor area requirement. If the approximate local building construction cost per square foot is known, it is possible to determine roughly the construction cost of the buildings. Experience has shown that one should be liberal in making preliminary estimates of costs on the basis first described and that therefore it may be best not to divulge your estimate to the architect or building contractor. Such estimates are usually approximate in nature and cannot by any means be considered as suitable for use in a budget until they have been checked against the estimate of the architect and builder.

PARKING, DRIVEWAYS AND ENTRANCE

The major advantage a motel has over a hotel is that convenient parking is provided. Therefore proper planning of the parking space is of the utmost importance. Parking requirements vary, depending on the location of the project and the types of guests served. In instances where a substantial number of guests may arrive by taxi or be met by the motel station wagon or limousine at airports, train or bus station, fewer parking spaces will be needed. Also, if other off-street parking is available in the immediate area fewer parking spaces will be required for patrons of the restaurant and public-room facilities. Generally, however, requirements for parking space are as follows:

1 parking space for each guest unit.
1 parking space for each five restaurant seats.
1 parking space for every three employees.
2 additional parking spaces for service trucks.
1 unobstructed loading space.

An automobile itself takes up 120-150 square feet when parked and requires a total of between 300 and 400 square feet of parking area including driveways but excluding the entranceways. Driveways must be designed to allow adequate space for maneuvering. There must also be unblocked space for entrances and exits. If possible, a special area should be provided for temporary parking convenient to the front office.

Space requirements vary with the parking pattern. For example, curb parking requires more square footage per car but much less driveway width. Ninety-degree angle parking requires the widest driveway but the smallest square footage per car. Most guests find 45-degree angle parking to be the easiest. In a lot where parking is supervised or handled by employees the parking area can be much smaller than if it is left entirely up to the guest to maneuver his car into place. The entranceways to the parking spaces should be 20 to 25 feet wide for two-way traffic and 12 to 14 feet wide for one-way traffic. If parking is to be provided adjacent to the guest units it is well to remember that almost all cars have an overhang beyond the wheels. Thus when a car is pulled up or backed up so that the wheels touch the curb a large portion of the walk will be covered by the car itself. When that would leave insufficient sidewalk area for guests, it is advisable to provide a buffer to keep the wheels a proper distance from the walk. It is also helpful to mark clearly an outline of each space on the surface of the parking area.

Where the size of a site is so limited that a large area cannot be devoted to guest parking it may be wise to consider excavating for basement parking. An alternative involves elevating the rooms section one story above street level which then allows for parking directly beneath.

LANDSCAPING

Because first impressions have a considerable influence, the entranceway of a motel or motor hotel should be designed to make the proper impact upon the approaching traveler. Considerable attention should be paid to creating an inviting atmosphere from the start, with special emphasis on the appearance of building exteriors, signs and landscaping.

Thus landscaping, too, becomes an important consideration and as much space and effort as possible should be devoted to it. An unsightly view can often be screened by shrubs or trees, and a well-tended expanse of green lawn is a good advertisement for restful accommodations. A pleasant landscape makes a good impression on the guest for the length of his stay.

Local landscape architects should be consulted to determine the most hardy and adaptable plantings. Professional guidance in planting is advisable because trees and shrubs frequently require more space when fully grown than may be generally realized. It must be kept in mind that lawns and gardens require care in order to maintain their pleasing aspect and their full contribution to atmosphere. Grounds maintenance requires labor and supplies that must be included in the operating budget. This is an item often forgotten in figuring preliminary estimates of expenses. Not only must there be an investment in the necessary equipment for mowing, cleaning, pruning and general outside maintenance, but provision must also be made for tool storage.

RECREATION

We have touched upon the place of swimming pools as a feature of most motor hotels. They may vary in size from a small pool 15 by 35 feet to a large Olympic-size pool. In addition to the area required for the pool itself, provision must be made for the equipment needed to service the pool with filtered and sometimes heated water. The pool should vary in depth so that non-swimmers can have an area in which to play and better swimmers can reach a sufficient depth to swim and dive freely. Often the pool area includes a shallow wading pool for children and a patio for lounging and food and beverage service. In-door pools do not have the flexibility of outdoor pools and have failed to win sufficient guest acceptance to warrant their cost, except in rare instances. However, an increasing number of pools are being covered in some fashion to allow use during inclement weather.

The view of the pool and patio area from the dining room of the Cherry Hill Inn, Haddonfield, New Jersey, suggests the possibility of combining an informal atmosphere with gracious decor.

Courtesy: Cherry Hill Inn

Many motor hotels have added to their incomes by permitting local residents use of the pool on a limited basis. To accommodate day guests, dressing rooms and lockers may be installed at poolside or guest-room units may be offered for rent on a part-day basis for use as dressing rooms. Many hotels and motor hotels offer poolside cabanas or a pool club plan to augment income and add community appeal.

Many other minor outdoor sports may prove appealing to guests, and space, if available, can be allotted to them. However, it is not suggested that additional property be purchased for such activities unless a clearly defined need is found. A saying that should be applied is, "If it needs promotion and selling to create the demand, forget it!"

Estimates of the square footage required for various minor sports follow:

	Square Feet
Shuffleboard	600
Putting Green or Clock Golf	1,500 to 2,000
Horseshoes	750
Table Tennis	250
Tennis	7,500

A careful analysis of local attitudes and needs should be made before deciding whether to feature a cocktail room or bar with entertainment or a nightclub operation as part of the food and beverage operation. This is a venture entirely separate from catering to the normal wants of the traveler and requires investigation of community and guest acceptance as well as separate estimates of income and expenses. Such activity would not be directly related to the operation of the overnight accommodations but might tend to attract patronage for all the facilities of the motel or motor hotel.

8

Planning: Control, Storage and Utility Areas

The floor space required for adequate control, storage and utility areas does not produce direct revenue in the operation of a motel or motor hotel, but making proper provision for it in the planning and construction stages does save expense throughout the life of the project.

It is not possible to cover all contingencies with a check list because of the wide variety of services tailored to meet the needs of the local community and the guest and determined to a large extent by the individual tastes and ideas of owner, architect and operator. This discussion is limited to general guides, therefore, which must be amplified and patterned to fit specific situations.

As a general rule, each guest unit requires the following additional working space for service areas: (a) 10 to 15 square feet for control areas to be used for registration, management, accounting and general supervision; (b) 10 to 15 square feet for storage, including space for furniture, supplies and equipment; (c) 25 to 30 square feet for utilities; to be used for heating, air conditioning, plumbing, electricity, gas, and sewage-disposal equipment.

It is wise to use the best construction materials and to buy the best equipment available. Many earlier motels and motor hotels have suffered severely from problems of maintenance and loss of guest acceptance because of cheap construction, equipment and furnishings. Materials should be selected on the basis of their ability to serve beyond estimated maximum requirements. For example, when purchasing heating and ventilating equipment it is a mistake to select that which will perform satisfactorily only within the limits of average weather conditions. Extremes of humidity and temperature should be studied to determine maximum requirements.

Although selection of the best construction materials, equipment and furnishings available increases the initial investment, the probable result will be substantial savings in lower labor and maintenance costs over the life of the operation, which is an important consideration in a commitment of a long-term nature. Savings based on cheaper substitutes should be left to promoters and builders who intend to make a quick profit on the sale of a motel.

CONTROL AREAS

The space in which control functions are performed includes the front office, the manager's office, the accounting office, the housekeeping and maintenance areas. Although similar functions of control are performed by the department heads in the restaurant department, those areas are dealt with in a later chapter pertaining to that phase of operation. The primary concern of this section is with the needs of guest rooms and related services.

In addition to these specific areas are general sections of the buildings in which controls are carried out. For example, it is advisable for a motel to have a service entrance with a time clock if the size of the staff warrants it. This entrance should be located near the employees' lockers, dressing rooms and rest rooms. It might also be advisable to have available to the employees such conveniences as vending machines for cigarettes and soft drinks and a room in which to relax or have their meals. For protection, clock stations may be provided for the night watchman. Master light switches and control panels should be installed at strategic points, and much attention should be given to the proper location of fire walls and exits. Exterior and interior protective devices such as locks and bolts, fire alarm and sprinkler systems, are additionally considered to be part of the overall control area.

The Front Desk

The front desk space must be arranged for ease of registration and check-out as well as for provision of information, mail and message service to the guest. The work area should also contain space for either manual or machine control of the guests' charges and accounts, a money drawer for the cashier's functions, and, particularly in smaller operations, space for the telephone switchboard. Open floor space behind the front desk must be large enough to house the employees regularly assigned so that they may work without interfering with each other. The layout and functions of the front desk are outlined in Chapter Twenty.

Elevators and the main stairway can be controlled from the front desk of the Executive House, Washington, D.C., because of the carefully planned layout of the guest lounge.

Courtesy: Executive House, Inc.

Executive Offices

The manager's office should be located in or near the lobby. It should be sufficiently large to contain the manager's desk and work space plus accommodations for private consultations with guests, employees, salesmen and sundry others whom the manager will see in the course of the day. Depending on the size of the operation, this space may also need to house a secretary. Since the manager is also usually the motel's top salesman and will be required on many occasions to discuss the facilities of the operation with prospective guests and patrons, his office should be pleasing in decor as well as functional.

The auditing and accounting office should be located centrally, with easy access to the front desk. It would be advisable to place that office adjacent to the manager's office as well, since many of its functions require direct contact with the manager. In a small operation the daily bookkeeping functions would be performed either at the front desk or by the manager. However, if the establishment is large enough to warrant a full-time accounting staff, the space allotted to the auditing office should be capable of housing desks, work areas and office machinery required for proper accounting control and operational information.

Since there are many legal requirements pertaining to the retention of records, a separate chapter will touch upon these problems. It suffices at this point to realize that many records must be kept for extended periods of time and must be readily accessible. Storage space is therefore needed for that purpose as well as for stationery and office-supply inventory which is usually kept in or adjacent to the auditor's office.

Housekeeping and Laundry

In any operation, large or small, sufficient space should be allotted for proper care and control of linens. If the operation is large enough to require a housekeeper she must also be provided with desk space and other facilities related to control of maid assignments and the preparation of her reports on rooms occupied, changes, inspections and similar functions. Some space in the linen room should also be devoted to storing cleaning materials and equipment necessary to the servicing of guest rooms and other areas. That space should be convenient to the room sections and will, of course, be supplemented by maids' closets in those sections. It is also suggested that the linen room be near the laundry or the laundry delivery point, since the housekeeper is primarily responsible for linen control.

The question of whether or not to provide space for a laundry operation is one that must be carefully considered. Although it stands to reason that direct control of the linens and laundry operation should produce better service and savings in cost, these advantages must be weighed against the requirements of space, investment in equipment and time for supervision. The answer can best be arrived at by budgeting the house laundry operation and comparing the estimated costs with the charges of an outside laundry.

Rental of linens and similar items is sometimes adopted as a means of conserving capital. Inasmuch as this practice delegates an aspect of the guest's comfort to outsiders, particular attention must be paid to specifying proper quality and quantities for efficient service. A list of reasons favoring outside linen rental and laundry service follows:

1. The initial investment in floor space and equipment is higher in an operation that does its own laundry.

2. The investment in linen supplies is avoided if linens are rented.

3. Repairs to both equipment and linens can be avoided or minimized by renting linens.

4. Outside laundry service simplifies to some extent the control that must be exercised over the linen stock by the housekeeping office.

5. Outside laundry service eliminates one more department that may require time and effort for proper supervision.

Outlined below are the advantages of owning the linens and laundering them on the premises.

1. The operator is completely independent of outside services, thus reducing emergency situations that might arise through strikes, breakdowns, bad weather, etc.

2. The control of quality and quantity is directly in the hands of the operator.

3. More direct care and attention can be paid to the laundering processes, and formulas can be used which result in a longer life for linens and a less coarse product.

4. Linen inventory can be kept to a minimum since small quantities can readily be laundered for emergency use.

5. Direct laundry costs are frequently less than either rental fees or outside laundering fees.

A comparison of house laundry costs with the cost of local commercial laundry and linen rental services is necessary before a decision can be reached. Basic to the problem is the need for providing the space and investment for laundry equipment in the project. Laundry areas require good ventilation and adequate working and storage space for efficient operation. The spread of the initial cost of space and investment in equipment must also be considered together with the day-to-day operating cost of the house laundry in drawing a comparison.

A compromise idea is a partial laundry with equipment sufficient to do rags, bath towels and similar items not requiring ironing. Some motels also have facilities for doing maids' and housemen's uniforms.

Arrangements for the handling of guests' laundry and valet needs are essential to most operations and can provide a small additional income. In some instances motels have provided coin-operated washers and driers for use by guests.

Helpful information on both the installation and operation of laundries can be obtained from the American Hotel and Motel Association, New York City, and the American Laundry Institute, Joliet, Illinois.

Utilities and Maintenance

Few people realize the extent of cost control exercised by the engineer and maintenance superintendent in an operation large enough to hire people to supervise these functions. Space provided for their requirements should include the necessary work areas plus storage facilities for the following items:

1. Up-to-date working drawings, wiring and plumbing diagrams revised from the original construction. Very frequently this updating is sadly neglected or the continuity is lost through changes of ownership.

2. All information pertaining to the physical operation, the parts and maintenance contracts for mechanical equipment in the hotel. Often as a practical matter the file on contracts is kept in the auditor's office, but it should also be available to the engineer and maintenance man.

3. A maintenance log setting forth jobs performed, time spent and work required in maintaining the plant.

4. A proper place for the storage of repair parts, tools and supplies.

If the operation is not of sufficient size to require the services of a full-time engineer, the manager of the motel or someone on his staff will have to assume responsibility for the control functions normally handled by an engineer. If the manager does assume the responsibility, the files mentioned should be kept in his office. But in any event, the proper shop and storage space for these functions should be included in the plans.

Space requirements for utilities include allotments for: heating, lighting, ventilating, plumbing, air conditioning, waste disposal, building and equipment maintenance, grounds and landscaping upkeep. To some extent this department will also be responsible for phone, television and radio, internal communicating systems, public-address apparatus, and sprinkler system. Most of the work connected with these items will be under the direct supervision of the engineer or maintenance man.

One of the most frequent complaints of engineers after operations have commenced is that heating, ventilating, plumbing and other building equipment has been placed in almost inaccessible areas. All too frequently space consideration for extremely important pieces of equipment is an afterthought. Here again the recommendations and advice of professional persons should be sought and heeded.

A checklist of items frequently neglected or slighted in outlining specifications for the architect or engineer follows:

1. Adequate floor space and ceiling height for all utility elements: boilers, compressors, pumps, tanks, etc.

2. Adequate fire-protection devices: sprinkler systems, fire walls, fire hoses and extinguishers. In this regard it is best to consult local fire codes and fire department inspectors to make certain that adequate provision is made for these items, as well as for proper fire exits and other fire regulations.

3. A central music system, both in guest rooms and public space, or at least an internal communications system for prompt location of utility and service personnel.

4. Direct-dial telephones in the guest rooms. Their installation may result in far better service to the guest and reduce the switchboard traffic. However, the rental cost of such equipment may not be justified by any consequent savings in payroll cost. The appeal of modernization and more convenient service is the major consideration with respect to installing this equipment.

5. Adequate temporary storage areas and facilities for the disposal of waste matter: incinerators, garbage-disposal units, refrigerated garbage storage units, etc.

6. Readily accessible plumbing, heating, ventilating and electrical lines. It is advisable in certain areas to tag and color-code utility lines throughout the premises. Also, electrical outlets should be provided at logical points for outside lighting and equipment, for function-room public-address systems and spotlights, for vending and ice machines in halls and corridors and, of course, for guest convenience in the guest rooms and baths.

7. Well-equipped maintenance shops for furniture repair, painting, etc.

It goes without saying that adequate heat, light and ventilating systems will be required in any motel or motor hotel operation. Air conditioning has also become a must in most instances, not necessarily because of extremes in weather but because those who cater to the traveling public have made it a standard feature of first-class accommodations. Central air conditioning systems which combine with heating systems and can be controlled individually from the guest room have experienced popular acceptance in recent years.

The need for durable materials in the initial installation is again stressed. The replacement of fuel, water, air, plumbing or electrical lines after operations have commenced will be much more expensive than the installation of quality material in the first place. Advice of the architect and engineer should be heeded even if it means an increase in the initial investment. In the selection and installation of this equipment the architect, builder and owner should work in close harmony. Guest comfort and protection should be the foremost considerations in making a choice among the types and brands available, but ease of maintenance and the cost of servicing the installed equipment are factors which will be reflected in net profits throughout the useful life of the project. A good architect will also keep abreast of new and less expensive materials that offer durability.

A word of caution, however, should be injected regarding the use of newly developed materials that will influence decor: Many operators have found that innovations popular at the moment may prove temporary fads. Drastic departures from accepted forms may attract notice but also run the risk of clashing with the traditional tastes of the guest and eventually becoming tiresome.

It is always surprising to the operator how much storage space is needed once the motel commences operation. In storage areas the floor space should be sufficient and the ceiling height adequate to provide proper shelving and other facilities for the items to be stored and also to provide quick access to them. It is advisable to make sure that the storage rooms can be reached easily by wide corridors and to provide oversized doors to accommodate the various trucking and other labor-saving devices used in transporting materials and supplies. Odd-sized space is needed for storage of certain items. For example, many types of wall coverings come in 4- by 8-foot sheets. Ladders of adequate length to service some parts of the building may frequently be difficult to store. Some plumbing supplies, particularly pipe, come in lengths of up to 20 feet. In all storage rooms where employees will spend time, proper ventilation is important.

A check list of some of the storage areas most frequently neglected in planning a motel or motor hotel follows:

1. Space near the lobby for temporary storage or checking of guest's baggage, packages, guest's laundry or valet.

2. Storage space for outside furniture or seasonal equipment items during the off-season period.

3. Space for banquet tables and chairs, public-address equipment, rostrum and speaker's stand, movie screens and equipment, spotlights and other fixtures normally used in connection with function rooms.

4. Space for card tables and chairs in the lounge areas.

5. Space for storage of mattresses, springs, guest furniture, radio and television sets not in use or awaiting repair.

6. Convenient and readily accessible space for storage of outside and inside maintenance supplies and equipment, such as lawn mowers, rakes; salt or other supplies for walks and driveways; tools of all kinds; paint and other inflammable materials; oils; fireplace wood; housekeeping supplies; maids' carts and baggage trucks; small room supplies such as china, glassware, ash trays, lamps and light bulbs.

The linen room should have sufficient counter and shelf space for easy control of linen. In normal circumstances at least three complete changes of room linen should be planned: one for the guest room while the second is being laundered and the third is on the shelf. Frequently a fourth change is held in reserve for emergencies or for weekends. Many housekeepers and laundrymen believe that giving linens a rest between use and laundering adds to their life. The route of clean and soiled linen should be a logical one from laundry to linen room to floor closet to guest room and back to linen room and laundry. In a multiple-story operation it will usually save time and labor to install linen chutes leading directly to the linen room.

Maids' or janitors' closets should be conveniently located and readily accessible to the guest-room section and have facilities or chutes for disposal of waste matter and soiled linen. They should also contain emergency linen, cleaning and guest-room supplies, storage space for vacuum cleaners, brooms, pails and other maids' utensils.

Local fire laws should be investigated when planning storage space for paints and other inflammable materials. Inadequate space which results in cluttered hallways and working areas not only leaves a poor impression but also may constitute a fire hazard.

The Guest's Impression

The "home-away-from-home" concept generated by the modern motel or motor hotel has particular importance in the planning stages. During his stay the guest can be expected to make the same critical observations of housekeeping and service that he makes at home. Therefore, the efficiency and orderliness of the various working and control areas will be subjected to the guest's scrutiny. It is vital, if the guest is to return for another stay or to recommend the place to others, that these areas be run neatly and efficiently.

While the operator must cater to the guest's tastes and expectations in order to prosper, it is equally important that the layout and design of the entire plant be such that the cost of operation will be kept within the bounds of the guest's ability to pay.

9

Planning: Shops, Stores and Similar Guest Services

The advisability of allocating a portion of the project to retail shops and stores will depend on the location of the motel and in most instances the nature of the immediate area. If the site is within easy walking distances of a shopping center, either in a suburban location or in the center of an urban community, it may not be wise to plan to provide for shops. Conversely, the nearness of a shopping center may result in the rental of motel space to shops, thereby augmenting the appeal of the project to guests and local trade. In this case, shops on the premises might logically supplement rather than compete with those operating in the vicinity. In a resort area shops may be desirable not only because they will provide rental income but also because shopping can be a form of recreation for guests.

The annual Horwath & Horwath study of motel and motor hotel operations reveals that less than one per cent of their total revenue, on the average, comes from rentals and concessions. However, like all averages this one must be considered in light of known facts about the specific situation.

Again it is a question that involves knowledge of the type of guest to be served. If a major portion of the motel's business is to come from transient guests there is little need for shops in the motel, beyond facilities for the sale of articles to meet emergency requirements or for small gifts and souvenirs. However, the guest who has reached his destination and will be staying in the area for several days may desire convenient shops in which to buy personal items and will frequently purchase gifts for those at home. The extent to which this guest trade can be supplemented by local patronage depends largely on the same factors that determine the desirability of a retail store or shop in any type of building.

A guide used in hotel construction is that store rental space should be sufficient to provide the rental income necessary to cover the carrying charges on the land. In the hotel business the land cost generally amounts to between 10 per cent and 15 per cent of the total investment. Unless a motel is located in a busy shopping area, it is doubtful that store space on the premises will provide nearly that return. Generally, it is safest to provide in the plans only that retail shop space required to offer the services normally supplied in hotels and motels and to consider further ventures into the retail store market only if the location of the project is deemed particularly promising for retail trade and the necessary space, including direct street and lobby entrances, is available.

Even if the location of the project, local conditions and guest needs argue for some form of retail shopping facility, a careful study of space requirements as related to potential return on the additional investment should be made. In resort areas or other isolated locations the most frequent demand is for the variety of supplies ordinarily found in the modern drugstore. In addition, some sales potential may be present for a shop selling sport or play clothes and recreation equipment. Barber shops and beauty parlors are seldom found in motor hotels except in resort areas where the average length of stay exceeds four or five days. Since each barber or beautician requires about 200 square feet of floor space, the need for these services should be very real. It should be added that the success of these operations depends largely on the personality and ability of the barbers and beauticians.

The further amplification of retail services to include shops selling ladies' wear, sporting goods, haberdashery, etc., is unusual in the motel and motor hotel field, although it is often considered because of the specific location of a project.

Tenants of retail shops usually require, in addition to sales space, storage areas for merchandise, supplies and records. Sometimes these items can be placed in basement or other areas, but more frequently they are part of the store and must be on the same level as the selling area. Each store would, of course, be expected to pay rent for the storage space, but before space allocation is made, the amount of storage area needed and the requirements for delivery and movement of merchandise should be determined. It is important that there be complete agreement on these matters before any leases are signed.

Rather than construct store space, most operators find it simpler and less expensive to work out arrangements with nearby merchants to provide delivery service to guests of the motel. Local retailers often arrange to have display cases on the motel premises or to distribute lists of available merchandise and services so that guests may shop by telephone or be directed to their establishments. A directory of the shops located in the immediate vicinity is a definite convenience to the guest and can be a good public relations medium as well.

Among the shops most frequently found in motor hotels is the novelty or gift store. This is often operated by the owner but may be run on a subrental or concession basis, depending on the extent of service rendered and the floor space devoted to it. The merchandise most frequenty offered includes specialty items such as locally produced ceramics, carvings and other art objects; jewelry; candies, locally prepared preserves or other food products; small antiques

The gift shop at Schimmel's Indian Hills Inn, Omaha, has an entrance from the main lobby. Here also is an entrance to a retail liquor store and snack shop.

Courtesy: Schimmel Hotels Corporation

The Bridge Lounge of the Hotel Syracuse Country House, Syracuse, has a restful atmosphere conducive to the entertainment of the guest during his stay.

Courtesy: Hotel Syracuse Country House

having some connection with local history; and souvenirs. Maps, guide books, pamphlets and books covering local history or special events are also frequently displayed.

If an entire store space is not required, a portion of the lobby or lounge space is commonly devoted to a showcase and shelves for the display of gift shop merchandise. To save on payroll, the news and cigar stand is often combined with the gift shop, and sometimes all such merchandise is sold from the front desk. The important consideration in locating a retail shop in a motel is that it must be in the stream of guest traffic and be easy for the shopper to find and patronize.

PRIVATE OFFICE SPACE

When a motel or motor hotel is located in a downtown area or in the center of a suburban community, it might be well to consider the possibility of renting office space to doctors, lawyers and dentists. The current movement of some business offices to outlying areas also makes it possible to draw a variety of other desirable tenants such as real estate or insurance company offices, a bank, a brokerage firm, a local business club or civic organization.

The availability during daytime office hours of a large parking area, the ready access to major highways and through streets offered by a good motel location are distinct advantages to a professional or business man in a suburban area. Naturally, there are problems connected with such rentals, involving the control of parking spaces and the use of the motel facilities themselves. For example, the professional person must not expect to use the lobby of the motel as his waiting room, and he must make provision for accepting calls at his office without placing an undue burden on the motel personnel. It would be best to provide for a separate or outside entrance to the professional offices so that the traffic will not interfere with the normal operating routine.

A study of community needs for office space and current rental rates will yield indications of the potential market for these additional facilities. This study should be part of the preliminary survey made by a professional market analyst. The information gathered should be checked by a reliable local real estate man. In addition, the owner himself should question the operators of local office buildings to determine whether provision for office space rentals should be included in the project. It is generally recommended that the owner of the project meet other real estate holders in the area, for their good will and support can contribute much to the success of the proposed motel.

Another factor to be considered in allocating subrental space is that the tenants are normally charged for utilities on the basis of consumption. Separate meters are therefore necessary and provision for such metering should be made in the initial construction, since it will be much more costly to add wiring and controls after completion of the building. An attorney should review local taxes and regulations on utility charges to subtenants.

PRIVATE CLUBS

Another possible source of rental income is the private social club. The most practical and suitable arrangement is to lease space for club rooms or offices where the organization's staff may conduct club business and maintain membership records and books of account. Such clubs would also be likely to rent public space in the motel for meetings and functions. An arrangement of this nature would probably result in additional patronage for the dining facilities. Sometimes club members prefer to have private dining quarters, in which case the restaurant operator might serve as caterer. Ordinarily the club is expected to finance the installation of any private facility, although such costs may be included in the rental calculation.

The stability of the club is an important factor in planning facilities and services beyond the scope of guest accomodations. Disappointment has met the efforts of many owners who have sought to organize or attract a private club in order to finance more extensive facilities. Because of the non-profit, self-determined nature of such organizations, it is difficult to impose outside controls on their policies. Solicitation of their business, therefore, may be hazardous out of all proportion to the potential profits from such an alliance.

If a club venture is planned as a part of the project, care should be taken at the outset that responsibilities for club services, division of costs and expenses, operation of facilities, determination of membership privileges and adequate protection of the owner's investment are explicitly spelled out prior to the signing of leasing or operating agreements. The degree of risk is naturally greater for the operator than for the organization under consideration. Thus it is urged that an exhaustive investigation of similar ventures be undertaken. In all cases the agreement should be reviewed by a competent lawyer.

GASOLINE STATION AND TRANSPORTATION SERVICES

A gasoline station on the premises of a motel or motor hotel can offer both advantages and disadvantages. It is undoubtedly a convenience for the guest, who can have his car completely serviced while he is either enjoying the facilities or conducting his business in the area. Furthermore, a gasoline station can yield direct profits to the motel operator by attracting outside business as well as guest patronage.

Location and design of the station are especially important to the operation. The facility should not detract from the appearance and atmosphere of the motel and its recreational areas. Provision must be made for isolating the work areas from other parts of the property. It is also necessary to control carefully the disposal of waste materials, and to take special precautions in avoiding odors and noises that typically accompany this type of operation. The comfort and convenience of the guest are a first consideration in this matter.

The gasoline station is not just an additional service that will be treated as other operations on the premises. It is a separate and distinct business and will probably be managed by someone other than the owner. Naturally the manager of such a station should be qualified to supervise the many types of service expected by motorists. Stations of this type usually dispense gasoline and offer lubricating service, but some may also sell tires, batteries and accessories and make repairs.

It is frequently possible to arrange for the financing or leasing of this facility by a major oil company, which would thereby gain a retail outlet for its products. Since these companies carefully investigate all sites under consideration their appraisal should bear weight in planning for a service station operation.

One disadvantage worthy of consideration is that a gasoline station on the premises will be considered as competition by neighboring stations. Many motel and motor hotel operators rely heavily on referrals from these station operators and believe them to be an important aspect of their promotion. Often, motels and service stations cooperate closely, the former making arrangements to have guests' cars serviced by a nearby station, the latter recommending the motel to travelers. There is little likelihood that a station operator would refer business to a motel which offered him direct competition.

Related to this subject is the matter of car rentals, which has become an important aspect of modern-day travel and is also a significant source of income for many hotels and motels. Most desirable is an arrangement with an automobile renting agency so that the guest coming by plane, train or bus can have a car awaiting him upon arrival. Such an arrangement is expected by the business traveler and many hotels and motels devote space in their lobbies for car rental agencies or at least offer such service at their front desks. A number of establishments also offer private conveyances for transporting guests to and from airports and terminals and into town.

RENTAL AGREEMENTS

Shop and store space income generally breaks down into two revenue categories—concessions and subrentals. Concessions are grants to lessees for those departments usually operated directly by a motel or motor hotel. These would include the news and cigar stand, guest laundry, valet, and the restaurant operation. In such instances, the motel owner limits his service responsibilities by delegating the operation to a concessionaire who performs and is responsible for, the service rendered. Motel owners also resort to a concession arrangement in order to conserve their capital by making an agreement which will require that the concessionaire furnish and equip the necessary facilities. The concessionaire usually pays a percentage of sales or agrees to allow the motel to retain a portion of each guest charge. The latter arrangement is usually made, for instance, for guest laundry and valet, the concession for which is frequently held by an operator in the community who may service several similar establishments as well.

The newsstand and restaurant concessions are most often granted in the form of leases, with the rental fee based on a percentage of sales or profits.

Subrentals are just what the name implies—leases of space within the premises to others. Under these agreements, space is offered for use as a store or shop, with the tenant being responsible for the financing and purchase of equipment, supplies and merchandise and the hiring of all sales personnel. Such businesses will operate independently of the motel in all respects except that there may be some agreement with the motel operator covering the collection or charges incurred by motel guests. Ordinarily this space is rented for services and items that would not be included in normal motel or motor hotel operations. Such rented space may be used for offices, stores, florists' counters, ticket agencies, etc. The rental agreement usually calls for a fixed minimum annual rental, sufficient to provide a fair return on the space after covering its servicing, plus an additional percentage rental based on sales volume.

The terms of such rental agreements vary widely, depending on the desirability of the location and, to some extent, the nature of the business, some types of stores having a greater profit margin than others. The following list, based on data obtained from several real estate brokers who deal in this type of store lease, provides some indication of the range of rental percentages.

Type of Store	*Percentage Range Based on Sales Volume*
Barber Shop	8-12%
Cigar—Newsstand	5- 8
Florist	5-12
Beauty Shop	8-15
Drug Store	4- 8
Jewelry	8-10
Men's Wear	5- 8
Gift Shop	6-10
Women's Wear	5- 8
Liquor	4- 6
Photographer	6-10
Candy—Fruit Shop	6-10
Linens	6-10
Laundry—Valet Service	10-15

The length of lease, services to be furnished by the landlord, utilities to be paid by the tenant, restrictions on items sold, and operating policies should be spelled out in the lease. It is best to have legal advice on these contracts to be sure that they cover the major contingencies and contentions that may arise during the term of the lease. In many instances these details are delegated to a real estate broker who acts in behalf of the owner.

10

The Guest-Room Facilities

In Chapter Seven, the area requirements for guest rooms were indicated in a general way. Here and in Chapter Eleven, room facilities, furnishings, decoration and guest conveniences are covered in detail. Where deemed advisable, we have risked repetition for the sake of making a clear presentation. Final decisions regarding interior layout and design are the prerogative of the owner. And preparation of preliminary room layouts and of the final working drawings and construction specifications are the job of the architect. But before these preliminary or final drawings can be made the owner must provide the general specifications so that space will be planned in accordance with his desires as guided by the results of the studies described in previous chapters.

It is assumed that at this point in planning several basic decisions have been made. They would include such factors as the placement of guest rooms in relation to other major guest facilities; the choice of inside or outside access corridors; and the determination of the need for, and placement of, balconies, patios, or porches. In addition, planners will have determined the number of levels of guest rooms; the placement and space needs of elevators and stairways; the number of fire exits required by local codes; the location of parking areas; and the most logical and convenient locations for other services, control and working areas related to guest-room operations.

LOCATING THE GUEST-ROOM SECTION

The relationship of the guest room to the parking areas, maids' closets, linen room, front office, lounge and other service facilities depends to a large extent on the guest. Where his average length of stay is not expected to be more than overnight except on rare occasions, the parking area should be adjacent to the guest room. The outlook from the guest unit is not of great importance for the transient guest since he will not occupy the room during the day. If the windows of the guest unit look out on the parking area, however, the headlights of incoming automobilies may shine directly into the rooms unless particularly heavy draperies are used. Since these draperies would normally be kept closed in these circumstances it would seem an extravagance to plan large picture windows. Smaller windows that provide adequate daytime lighting but are located above the normal level of approaching automobile headlights are therefore suggested.

For the operation that anticipates a substantial percentage of terminal guests, it is often more practical to locate the parking areas away from the guest-room units, or to situate them in such a way that the outlook from the rooms does not directly confront parked vehicles. The view from the guest rooms should be a pleasant one, perhaps of the swimming pool, the lawns or even a row of screening trees and shrubs. If the location permits, the view of a distant mountain or other scenic attraction might be focused on. Spectacular scenery, however, is more often used as an attraction for the dining room or public lounge areas.

To accommodate these features, the guest-room area may be a single row of units providing access from the parking area on one side and an attractive view on the other. This is perhaps the simplest form, but may prove wasteful of land. Another plan provides a double row of guest units with interior corridors, with an outside view from both exterior walls. This type of unit is often one level above the parking areas, or where direct access to the room may be desired from outside as well as from the corridor. A third plan, also used in circumstances where it is necessary to place room units above parking areas, utilizes a double row of units with central core construction, with windows and doors in the outside walls.

The use of French doors in guest rooms for access to pool, porch or patio makes it possible to take full advantage of the view from the room and also provides the guest with a feeling of luxury and relaxation. However, many motelmen believe that the original cost of this type of sliding panel or door is not justified, particularly when it is considered that such features often do not have much impact on guests and add to maintenance and heating costs.

A common criticism of motels centers on the inconvenient location of guest-room units in relation to service facilities. Too frequently maids' closets and the linen room are an afterthought and, as a result, are located too far from the rooms to be serviced. Such poor planning can add to the payroll cost, particularly where access is by outside corridor and bad weather can make it difficult for maids and other service personnel to make their rounds. The time-saving advantages of using maids' carts between the linen room and the guest rooms can be substantial in these cases. Where guest units are spread out over a large area the use of a bicycle or a motor scooter conveyance for carrying baggage and delivering other services to the rooms should also be considered. Again, the use of schematic diagrams to study the flow of service and guest traffic is suggested.

SPACE NEEDS IN THE GUEST ROOM

The guest unit should be large enough to contain the necessary furniture without crowding, and offer sufficient open space for freedom of movement to and from the normal function areas in logical traffic patterns. These function areas fall into general categories: (a) entry, and storage of guests' clothes and baggage; (b) living and recreation; (c) sleeping; (d) bathing and dressing.

Many complaints about motor hotel room-unit design are centered on inadequate space and poorly coordinated function areas. The proportionate amount of space required for the different function areas depends on the guest to be served. The ranges outlined in the following schedule are intended as a guide.

Function	Range	Transient Guest	Terminal Guest
Entry and storage	15% to 20%	15%	20%
Living and recreation	30 to 40	30	40
Sleeping	20 to 40	40	20
Bathing and dressing	15 to 20	15	20
Total		100%	100%

Appropriate combinations can be drawn from these ratios and used in conjunction with other facts to establish an intelligent balance of function areas. All too frequently living and recreation space is reckoned only in terms of that space left over after other function areas have been provided for. This approach is most often taken when dimensions are planned without careful consideration of actual guest occupancy. If the room will house more than two people it is obvious that the living and recreation areas must be expanded proportionately. The same would naturally apply to sleeping areas, and choices of single, double, twin, studio or twin double beds.

Not all function areas need be expanded in direct proportion to the expected occupancy. The bath and dressing area that will accomodate two people will not have to be increased significantly to provide for a greater number of occupants. Nor will the entryway or storage and closet space need to be increased more than slightly.

In deciding the length and width of the guest room one should keep in mind that there are standard measurements for carpeting. If wall-to-wall carpet is planned it is advisable to design room dimensions to conform to these standard widths. Much flexibility is still possible with this arrangement since loom width can be used for either length or width of the room, provided that the pattern does not dictate otherwise. Standard loom widths are 9 feet, 12 feet and 13 feet, six inches.

Sleeping and Living Areas

In any event, at least 50 per cent of the total floor area of the guestroom unit will be devoted to sleeping and living space, which would include not only the beds but also the footage required for aisles between the beds, for the night table and bed lamps. Space for the living area normally provides for a desk and straight chair, easy chair or chairs, floor lamps, dresser or dressing table and racks for open luggage, plus the amount of lounge and card table space deemed desirable. If a separate dressing room is planned in connection with the bath, the floor area in the guest room itself can be reduced accordingly.

Additional savings in space may be effected through the use of built-in room furnishings which are particularly applicable to transient operations. As we have noted, businessmen on short trips increasingly prefer to travel light and "live out of a suitcase." The more radically designed custom-built furnishings must be considered with caution, however; it is not advisable to experiment with untested extremes.

The sleeping area may vary from 20 square feet in a single unit to more than 100 square feet where twin double beds are used. In those operations where family occupancy is anticipated, extra space should be allowed for roll-away beds or cots.

The sleeping and living functions may overlap, but they should not conflict with each other. For example, if television is provided, the set should be placed so that it can be viewed from either area. In normal circumstances it should not be necessary to move furniture in order to use either space freely. The angle of entry to either area from the outside corridor or from inside the room should also be considered. It is preferable to have the entryway lead directly into the living space so that when the door is open the view from the corridor is not of the sleeping, dressing or bath areas.

Requirements in living space are linked directly to the amount of time the guest will spend in his room and the extent to which he will entertain visitors. Suites provide additional living space, but the average guest will take only one room, and if he elects to spend considerable time in the room, living space must be provided. Some motel operators have found that this space can be made more attractive if the sleeping area is partitioned.

Entrance and Storage

The guest-room entrance includes the entrance hallway, if it is an interior corridor, or the door and space in which to open it freely if access is gained from an outside corridor. The guest-room storage area includes the clothes closet, baggage rack and dresser and the access space required by them. Storage areas should be convenient, making it possible for the guest to dispose of hand luggage and outdoor clothing immediately upon entering the room.

Clothes closet requirements have long been discussed by hotel and motel operators and no general agreement as to the best specifications has ever been reached. Neither is there general agreement as to whether closets should have doors. If doors are installed, air space for closet ventilation may be provided by a door of normal height with an open space above it. Sliding panels or accordion doors offer a space-saving advantage and are found in many newer operations.

A transient has little need for more closet space than is required to hang an overcoat, hat and business suit. However, the terminal guest may require considerably more space. (A rack for shoes and special facilities for hanging men's trousers are conveniences sometimes found in both types of accommodations.) The closet should contain a shelf or overhead rack for hats, handbags and small packages. A modern trend is to provide wall hooks for pajamas and robes in the bath area,

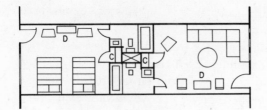

Two small units furnished in contrasting ways.

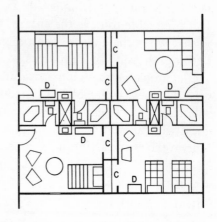

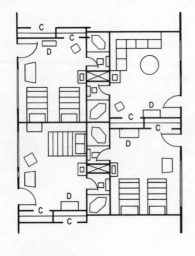

Costlier units permitting flexibility of arrangement.

CLOSET   C
BAR   B
DRESSER AND DESK   D

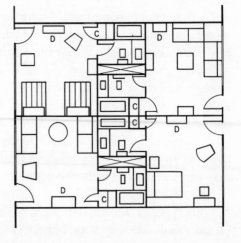

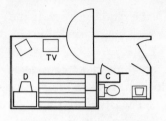

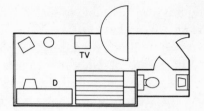

Economy is key word for this compact unit.

Comfort and compactness combined.

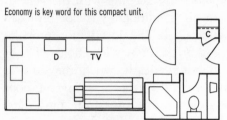

Only 20% more living space than above right, but much more than that in living area.

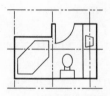

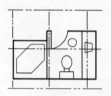

Basic bath room layouts.

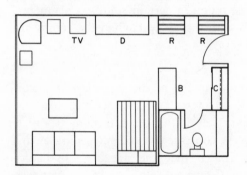

Elegant facilities for terminal guests.

LUGGAGE RACK	R
KITCHENETTE	K
TELEVISION	TV

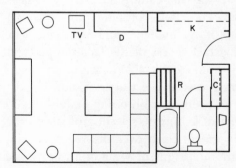

and it is also advisable to install such hooks in the clothes closet. If the dressing room has closet space, the amount of such space needed in the entryway will be reduced in like proportion.

The means of guest-room entry and exit are important considerations. A stout door supplied with an efficient lock suggests to the guest a sense of security and respect for his privacy. The style of the door and the quality of its hardware should be in keeping with the general decor of the establishment. (When air conditioning is not provided some motels offer a slatted ventilating door. This installation provides for air circulation and preserves room privacy.) A wide choice of door locks is available. One type locks automatically when the door is closed; another prevents a person with a key from opening the door from the outside when the key or lock-bolt is turned from the inside. One such device signals that the door has been locked from the inside, indicating that the guest is in the room and does not wish to be disturbed. In addition, many motels provide a draw-bolt or chain for double safety against intruders or prowlers.

Master keys are provided to the maids, valet and others who service the room and the guest, and it is essential that these keys be kept under close control. If it becomes necessary to close the room off for any reason, the management is provided with a "plug key" for this purpose. Connecting doors between rooms, found in certain suite arrangements, should be locked fom both sides with a snap-bolt when the rooms are rented separately.

Bath and Dressing Area

The private bath is no longer a luxury to the American traveler. Now the trend is toward providing more conveniences and space in this area. Because so much importance is put on bathroom facilities, good materials should be used in the construction and furnishing of this function space. Experience has shown that the use of high-quality floor, wall and ceiling materials will save substantially in maintenance costs. The choice of plumbing and wall-hung fixtures will not only figure in maintenance and replacement but will also help to determine the attractiveness of the facilities and will prove an important feature in winning guest acceptance of the overall room accommodations. If paint is used in these areas it must be particularly durable and not subject to peeling or blistering under humid conditions. Equal care should be exercised in the selection of tile so that the appearance of the bath will remain fresh over the years. Bulging or chipped tile can be one of the first signs of wear in an otherwise attractive bathroom.

A minimum of 35 square feet is necessary for the bathroom fixtures. An area in excess of 75 square feet may be required in larger units designed for multiple occupancy. The combination tub-and-shower bath is preferred by most guests. If a high percentage of single traveling men is anticipated, only a shower stall is necessary in the smaller units. However, businessmen traveling in pairs will appreciate the provision of sufficient space and fixtures in this area to allow for quicker morning preparation and departure. Thus, in a number of installations, the toilet is separated from the bath or the wash bowl, or both, and twin wash bowls placed directly in the room section have been made a feature of some modern motels.

Major points to remember in planning the bath and dressing area follow:

1. There should be adequate shelf and counter space upon which to spread toilet articles at or near the lavatory.

2. Providing proper light and a mirror for washing, shaving, make-up application is most necessary. Normally two lamps, one on each side of the mirror above the wash bowl, will suffice, but it is often advisable to supplement that illumination with additional lighting fixtures.

3. The lavatory should not be placed in a corner where cramped quarters or wrong mirror angles make use of the facilities difficult.

4. Outlets should be provided for electrical toilet accessories.

5. Adequate towel racks and hooks should be provided and placed in such a way as to be most convenient to guests.

6. A basket or covered hamper for disposing of paper and dirty linen should be placed in the room.

7. Effective safety devices and measures should be studied. These include non-skid material for tub or shower and handles placed at convenient heights and angles for entry and departure from the bath.

8. All fixtures should be so located that the amount of piping and labor required for installations within the bath and from unit to unit can be kept to a minimum.

9. All plumbing connections should be readily accessible for ease in maintenance. Some attention should also be given to suppressing noise resulting from use of the bath fixtures and plumbing—especially noises between adjacent guest units.

10. Exhaust ventilation should always be provided in the bath area, and, if the bath area is connected to the dressing area, provision should be made for confining steam and moisture to the bathroom itself.

11. It is advisable to provide the bath area with its own heating unit, which is usually placed under the lavatory where it will not take up floor space. A type of lighting fixture which also provides heat has been used in some recent installations with good results.

Additional features such as scales, two soap dishes, two rolls of toilet paper, a telephone extension, a small electric refrigerator and ice chest, extension mirrors add to guest satisfaction.

If a separate dressing area is planned it should be adjacent to or connect with the bath. Access to the bath from the guest room should be through the dressing area. In that section one usually finds a small dressing table and mirror, drawer and closet space for clothes and luggage. Often this closet space can be located so that the guest can reach it from either the dressing area or the guest room proper. Having a separate dressing area is particularly useful to the terminal guest, and such a layout has become a popular feature of many installations.

UTILITIES

The heating, ventilating and air-conditioning system should maintain comfortable temperatures without drafts and with a minimum of noise. A system of central heating and air conditioning with individual room controls appears to be most satisfactory. If the temperature is to be controlled by the guest, the control unit, or thermostat, must be placed so that the room occupant can easily reach it from either the living or sleeping area. Among the many modern fixtures currently available to the accommodations industry is a bedside panel containing all controls for utilities, telephone, television and radio units.

New uses of lighting in promoting the guest's comfort and convenience constitute one of the great advances in the accommodations industry. The guest must have sufficient light for reading and visiting in the living area and a convenient light in the sleeping area for reading in bed and making last minute preparations for sleep. Adequate light by which to enter the premises should be controlled by a switch near the entrance doorway. It may even be advisable to have all of the light and some electric outlets in the room controlled by a switch at the door, or by the turning of the door key from the outside of the room. Such an arrangement is a convenience and also helps to reduce electric bills.

Both television and radio sets are now commonly provided in motel units and the guest will often find a combination radio and television set in his room. A common mistake, however, is to provide a television set so large that it dominates a small room and makes it look crowded. Interior decorators frequently suggest that if possible the television and radio cabinets should be concealed in recessed units so that the screen and dials can be covered when not in use. This adds to the appearance of the room and makes cleaning much easier. A television set is particularly desirable in rooms occupied by guests for extended periods or in areas isolated from outside attractions or activity. However, it is frequently not needed or used by the overnight guest. Therefore, some motel operators follow the policy of having a limited number of sets available on demand instead of installing a set in every room.

11

Guest-Room Interiors

A frequent reaction of the traveler upon his first glimpse of a motel guest room is that the furniture is either too bulky and elaborate or that too many pieces have been placed in a small area, giving the impression of cramped living space. It should be remembered that as much as 35 per cent of the floor area in a typical motel unit is taken up by furniture. Fifty to sixty square feet alone will be required for a single bed and in a room with two beds, from 85 to 100 square feet or more may be necessary. If the owner attempts to place the furnishings for a twin double-bedded room in the typical 13.5-foot by 20-foot guest unit he will discover that over 50 per cent of the visible floor area is taken up by furnishings—an obviously crowded room.

In the early days of the hotel business the small single room of 150 square feet with just enough space for a bed, dresser, desk and chair was not uncommon and represented an attempt to appeal for patronage through cheaper room rates. The guest was supposed to use the lobby or public lounge areas for visiting and writing letters. With the advent of radio, television, air conditioning and increasing demands for more guest-room comfort, the modern trend is toward more living area in the guest unit and less space in the business lobby, lounges and public areas in facilities designed for the transient guest.

How far one should go in opening up living space through the use of built-in or custom-made furnishings is a matter of taste and judgment. The severity of the strictly modern may remove the feeling of comfort and relaxation that appeals to the guest. A blend of old-fashioned comfort and modern convenience is a good compromise.

A frequently neglected factor is the importance of keeping servicing and cleaning as easy as possible. If a third or more of the floor area is taken up with furniture, the maid is spending at least that portion of her time attempting to clean under and around chairs, beds, tables and lamps. Her job can be simplified in many ways. Beds can be put on rollers or built right to the floor so that it will not be necessary to clean under them. Many pieces of furniture can be hung from the walls. Upholstery, draperies and carpet can be selected on the basis of their ease of cleaning and upkeep, bearing in mind that the guest is not likely to treat these furnishings with the same degree of care he exercises at home.

Of primary importance to the appearance and maintenance of the rooms are decisions concerning the quality of materials. There are many types and grades of furniture and furnishings, certainly more than can be covered here. Some furnishings that may be attractive in appearance are not sufficiently durable for relatively carefree use over the expected life of the property. In all cases the initial investment should be weighed against the cost of frequent replacement and the added cost of maintenance that is often required for cheaper grades.

Since the lighting, color, decorating schemes and furniture arrangement are fundamental aspects of guest comfort and convenience it is advised that the selection of furniture and furnishings be made by a professional designer of interiors with direct experience in the accommodations field. A qualified designer should be able to save the owner considerable money by choosing the most suitable, attractive and durable furnishings.

FLOOR COVERINGS

The choice of floor covering depends to some extent on the section of the country in which the motel is located. In some regions, because of local soil conditions and weather, wall-to-wall carpeting is often impractical, particularly if the guest has direct access to his room from outdoors. However, there is no doubt that carpeting is most attractive to the guest. It has a very luxurious appearance, contributes to the guest's comfort and adds to soundproofing. A compromise is carpeting that leaves an open-floor border. This not only eases day-to-day cleaning problems but also makes it possible to change the entire carpet or rug more easily.

A number of types of tile floor coverings and linoleums are satisfactory for use in some types of guest units. They are, of course, generally much easier to maintain than carpeting, although frequent waxing may be necessary to keep them attractive. Such hard floor coverings are more utilitarian than luxurious and some guests may object to them in first-class accommodations. Many designers suggest using throw rugs at the sides of beds and in other strategic places when the floor is not carpeted. Another suggestion frequently made is that rugs smaller than room size be placed on a finished hardwood or tile floor. Such rugs can be taken up regularly and washed. They also can be changed easily for new color schemes.

If rugs are used, it is important to place some form of non-skid backing beneath them as a safety measure. With carpeting as well, the choice of proper padding is often as important as the choice of the carpet itself in terms of long wear and guest comfort.

When selecting floor coverings, the color schemes of the rooms should be kept in mind so that the floor coverings will blend satisfactorily with them. Whether to have a plain color on the floor, a small or large pattern, a special or stock pattern, depends entirely on the impression that is to be made on the guest, and the choice is best left to the specialist in interior decoration. As the guest crosses the threshold the floor covering often is the first thing in the room to catch his eye. Therefore, the floor covering obviously needs to have eye appeal and should conform to the general design of the interior.

Ceramic tile or a material of similar utility and durability should be used for bathroom floors. There are other sections of the guest-room area such as the dressing room space and closet floors where floor coverings other than carpet can be employed. If an exterior balcony is attached to the unit, some form of tile or concrete flooring will probably be the most satisfactory for that area, and for an outdoor patio, tile, brick or flagstone is most often installed. Larger patio areas might make use of lawn, gravel or even black-topping as a ground covering.

WALL COVERINGS

The choice of wall covering depends to some extent on the materials used for the walls themselves. In recent years cinder or cement blocks have been used to reduce construction costs. These materials and methods often simplified the problem of room wall decorations and finish, since it is possible to apply paint directly to the block. When plaster, drywall or wallboard is used, other types of wall coverings may be found suitable. A scheme which is frequently used with good results is to apply one wall of each unit to a covering different from that used for the other three. Color can be used to suggest depth or closeness, as the case may require. Color schemes can be varied from room to room to avoid an institutional look. Wall covering should be durable, easily cleaned, attractive to the eye and easy to replace.

A quantity of wall coverings and finishes meet the foregoing general specifications. Paint has become the most common, and paint manufacturers have made great strides in developing extremely durable products that are easily cleaned and maintained. It is now possible to paint a room and have it occupied the same day by a guest without his being annoyed by lingering paint odors. Paint is probably the most easily changed of the many types of wall finishes and coverings and can be touched up readily if it is stained or scratched. The chief disadvantage of paint is that the wall surface must be prepared with greater care than is necessary for other coverings.

Any type of covering has its own particular characteristics, resulting in comparative advantages and disadvantages. Possible choices are wallpaper, canvas, burlap and other cloths; plastic or plastic-coated fabrics; rubber and various types of panels fabricated of metal or other material. Many of these materials offer the advantages of durability and easy maintenance. Possibly their greatest single disadvantage lies in the task of removing them when a change in the decoration scheme is desired. Another disadvantage is the difficulty of making repairs, particularly those which involve patching over a marred section so that it will not be readily detected by the occcupant of the room. Manufacturers of these materials have made strides in overcoming these disadvantages, but at the present time paint is the most popular wall finish in motels and motor hotels, having largely supplanted wallpaper. Many wall coverings can be painted over quite simply and, provided that original installation was good, it is also possible to re-cover them with other material without difficulty.

In selecting a wall covering it is best to keep in mind the type and style of furnishings so that an intelligent and attractive blending of all elements may be achieved. The professional decorator should be consulted on this question.

DRAPERIES

The guest-room windows demand special attention, both as to their utility and furnishings. If there is a need for complete privacy from the outside, blinds or draperies should be provided. The ordinary window blind will keep out the sun and protect the privacy of guests, but because blinds lack eye appeal they have been largely supplanted by the use of draperies.

The draperies should harmonize with the general decor, and the material should be selected on the basis of both durability and appearance. There have been many new developments in drapery materials, many of which, such as those made of glass, are fire-resistant, a great advantage in itself. Where heavy draperies are demanded, linings are often used to shut out the light from the outside. The type of window to be covered will determine the choice of either "draw-drape" or those that are bound back, how draperies are to be hung and whether a valance is desirable. The appearance of the guest room and possibly

This is a typical guest-room layout at Del Webb's King's Inn, Sun City Center, Florida, containing twin double beds and living area, and looking out on an attractive lawn.

Courtesy: Del E. Webb Motor Hotel Corp.

the location of the heating unit will determine whether the drapery should come to the window ledge or to the floor. Often decorators use draperies very effectively to balance a room and to hide defects in original construction and window placement.

The use of window curtains has gone out of vogue generally, except where it may harmonize with a particular decorating scheme. Because curtains must be laundered and replaced frequently, they are now generally considered an unnecessary additional expense. The use of Venetian blinds has also been on the wane in recent years because they are dust-catchers which require a considerable amount of cleaning and replacement, and furthermore because the installation of air-conditioning has made them less necessary. In any event, the window treatment becomes an important part of the decor of the guest unit and should harmonize with the wall, ceiling and floor finish.

BEDS

In all likelihood the largest item of furniture in the guest room is the bed, and since the major purpose of a motel or motor hotel is to provide rest and relaxation for the traveler, the bed is most frequently the first piece of furniture to meet his attention. From the many types and styles of beds available on the market the motel owner should select the ones that best suit the needs of his particular operation. Unfortunately, no satisfactory formula or test can be applied as to the bed arrangement the prospective guest will prefer other than that indicated by the actual experience of others. Therefore we suggest that the owner study several existing motel and hotel operations before deciding for his own operation the relative numbers of studio or regular beds, doubles or twins.

The studio bed is particularly well adapted to the smaller room that may serve as sleeping quarters at night and as a work or living room area during the day. However, to convert the studio couch into a sleeping unit requires effort on the guest's part unless night-maid service is provided. The choice between a studio bed and a regular bed depends upon the extent to which the guest will make daytime use of the room for purposes other than sleeping.

Regular beds are always ready for their primary use, but they consume floor area and reduce living space accordingly. The typical motel room right now most often features twin beds or twin double beds, In the latter case the room can be readily adapted to family occupancy, and its added comfort will also appeal to two people traveling together. In areas where tourist or family trade is frequent, some provision should be made for portable beds and cribs. A wide variety of these portable facilities, such as the roll-away cot, is available. They present a storage problem when not in use that must be considered in planning. Whether to have the headboard of the bed affixed to the wall, a full bed stand, or a mattress mounted on an easily movable bed carriage is a further matter to be decided at this point, and the choice will affect operating service costs as well as guest acceptance.

The basic rule to follow in the bed arrangement is to remain flexible enough to make changes which are requested or seem advisable. Such a change in policy is often made necessary when the patronage of a motel turns out to be different from the type anticipated.

Innovation in bed size, shape and arrangement has often been used for purposes of advertising and sales promotion, but the real value

Typical studio room and twin-bedded room arrangements at the Executive House, Washington, D.C.

Courtesy: Executive House, Inc.

of such odd-sized furniture should be compared with higher purchase prices and the additional space required. Ordinarily, the standard sizes will serve best. Standard sizes of bed frames and mattresses are as follows:

	Bed frame	*Mattress*
Single Bed	2'11½" × 6'3½"	3' × 6'3½"
Double Bed	4' 5½" × 6'3½"	4'6" × 6'3½"
Twin Bed (each)	3' 2½" × 6'3½"	3'3" × 6'3½"

The bed should be located so that it can easily be made up by the maid. A bed placed lengthwise next to the wall or against one corner of the room adds to the time the maid must spend in the room. However, the type of location just described may sometimes be desirable if it conserves living space in a small room. The bed should be on rollers or gliders for easy mobility. The legs of the ordinary bed frame often present problems in carpet wear and floor maintenance. The bed-leg caster has long been a problem, and efforts to overcome it have resulted in changes in the bed carriage, the use of larger wheels and what is often called the "bed sled" or "glider," developments which provide a more flexible cushion, less carpet wear and less effort from the maid.

In some instances beds are installed with frames built down to the floor, saving carpeting space and eliminating the task of cleaning under the bed. There is a great disadvantage to having the bed attached permanently to the floor, however, because such construction restricts flexibility in arrangement, and it is highly desirable in commercial operations to be able to rearrange the furniture with a minimum of effort.

Since the spring, mattress and head pillows are the items that provide the sleeping surface and make the guest comfortable during what is probably the most important part of his stay, particular attention should be paid to their selection. Ordinarily the mattress and pillows should be firm and yet resilient. There are many types from which to select, and the proper choice can contribute more to the success of a motel then can a decision with respect to any other guest-room furnishings. Therefore, before making a selection, the owner of a new motel should obtain the opinion and advice of operators who have had some experience in the business. Sponge-rubber mattresses and pillows are used in many installations because of their

A deluxe, twin-bedded guest room at the Nationwide Inn, Columbus, Ohio, which offers ample space for card playing and reading.

Courtesy: Albert Pick Motels

longer wearing qualities, but they have failed to win complete acceptance from guests. The inner-spring mattress is most common today. It is advisable to have bed-boards on hand for guests who may request them.

Related to these considerations is the choice of bed linens, the wearing qualities, appearance and costs of which must be studied prior to purchase. Although the advice of an experienced housekeeper or laundryman will be helpful when making a choice of linen, it should be remembered that their opinions will be influenced by their own particular problems in handling it. Bedspreads should be selected on the basis of appearance and serviceability in that order, but with due consideration to both factors. Most often a keynote of room decor, the spread may be custom-made, displaying the motel monogram or other distinctive design to set it off. Whether to use colored linens is a matter of choice. It is a fact, however, that white linens enjoy the widest acceptance.

LIVING SPACE, LUGGAGE AND CLOTHES STORAGE

After choosing the types of beds, planners must then select other furniture that will properly complement the sleeping area and provide the necessary living space. This furniture would include the night stand and bed lamp, the luggage rack and dresser, shelf and drawer space for easy and convenient arrangement of the guest's private belongings, the desk and chairs. Such additions as an easy chair and lounge space for the extension of the living room facilities are also desirable and contribute greatly to the luxury of the room. Proper lighting and lamp arrangement are important also; and the trend has been away from the use of a ceiling light fixture and toward the use of reading, dresser and desk lamps, not only because they provide more convenient light but also because with sensible and attractive shades they add to the decor.

On the market today are wall-hung units which include luggage rack, dresser, desk and television stand. Many manufacturers and shops design custom-built furnishings in all sorts of combinations to cover the various guest-room needs and provide advantages in guest convenience and utilization of space as well as operating economies. New developments are continuous and rapid in the area of guest-room furnishings, and it is advisable to study the market closely before investing in any particular style. The trade press and the many trade shows of the motel and hotel associations are prime sources of information. Also, both the press and the associations research new products and distribute their findings.

The type of bed lamp provided does much to indicate the quality of a room's furnishings. This fixture may be a simple lamp mounted on the headboard of the bed or a more elaborate lamp standing on the night table, properly shaded for night reading. When a room has twin beds the night stand and a twin bed lamp fixture are often placed between the beds to conserve space and to reduce investment costs.

The choice of a separate writing desk as opposed to a combination desk and dresser depends on the need for economy of space and on the preference of guests. A combined unit has the obvious virtue of convenience as well as savings in space, but often at the sacrifice of luxury. In more expensive rooms the writing table is usually a separate piece of furniture. This is especially true of accommodations for terminal guests or businessmen who often work in their rooms. It also holds true in resort areas where the guest room will be a logical place for letter writing and day-time relaxation. The desk or writing shelf itself need not be wider than the normal reach of a person occupying the straight-backed chair that should accompany it. Adequate lighting should be provided to permit the person seated there to write or work. Usually the desk will have a large drawer for such guest supplies as stationery, blotters, ink, pen, guest information; forms for telegrams, laundry and valet can be placed where they will be found easily by the guest.

Two schools of thought exist regarding the best location for a telephone. Earlier installations were on the writing desk or dresser, which made them convenient for daytime use, but bedside installations are now popular. A copy of the local directory should accompany every telephone.

This is a typical guest room at the Glenwood Manor Motor House, Overland Park, Kansas, featuring a compact arrangement of furniture which increases the amount of living area. The room contains an oversized double bed and a studio couch.

Courtesy: Glenwood Manor Motor House

The extent to which the guest can be made more comfortable in the living area by adding chairs, sofas or couches, card tables and reading lamps depends on the quality of the room and the guest's willingness to pay for additional luxuries. When upholstered chairs are to be provided, the matter of wear and maintenance must be considered, and many motel operators select lounge chairs with wooden arms to minimize maintenance costs. Also, in many instances the room is protected with wall guards or panels in keeping with the decorating scheme and strategically placed to minimize wear and tear from chair backs and baggage racks.

KITCHENETTE AND DINING AREA

Owners of motels and motor hotels which are expected to have a large proportion of guests for relatively long periods often find that kitchenettes are an excellent added attraction and that they will bring in more than sufficient income to justify the investment. Motel rooms which have kitchenettes and dining space are very popular in resort areas. A demand for this facility also exists where the guest who has reached his destination may be seeking temporary accommodations while attempting to locate a permanent home. Such a demand may be temporary, of course, arising from a population movement in the area.

The equipment for a kitchenette can be purchased either in separate units or as a complete fabricated unit that includes stove, refrigerator, sink and cabinets. It is usually best to put the kitchenette equipment in a space that can be closed and locked when not in use, so that the chinaware, glassware and utensils supply can be controlled. A hard floor covering should be used in the kitchenette to prevent stains and other floor damage. A dinette or breakfast nook is often included in the kitchen area, its dimensions consistent with the accommodations provided. Newer installations frequently offer only a refrigerator for ice cubes, cold drinks and snacks.

It is important that utility lines be readily available for attaching the various pieces of equipment in the kitchenette unit. Local fire codes should be consulted to determine the requirements pertaining to kitchenette installation in residential buildings. At the time of construction provision should be made for exhaust equipment and for disposal of waste material and garbage from the kitchenette unit.

GUEST SUPPLIES

The variety and extent of supplies which can be offered to the guests are very wide but it should be remembered that each item adds to costs and must be justified by the room rate. The size and quality of soap, toilet tissue and towels should be in keeping with the impression intended to be made on the guest. Such supplies as stationery, facial tissues, wash cloths, plastic or paper bags for dirty shoes or wet bathing suits, paper cups, clothes pins, mending materials, shoe cloths, receptacles for used razor blades should be considered when room accommodations are planned and must be provided for in the original operating budget estimates. The policy of a motel with respect to these supplies will be governed to a considerable extent by the offerings of competing establishments.

Women particularly appreciate free guest supplies. An item which has much appeal is special detergent for washing stockings and other personal items. In fact, many travelers of both sexes now wear drip-dry linens which can be washed, with the help of a detergent, right in the motel bathroom. Recognition of such needs as a factor in good guest relations is growing in importance as the motel business becomes more competitive.

12

Food and Beverage Facilities

With the upsurge of promotion and investment in the motel field in recent years and the accompanying development of larger establishments, motel owners soon realized that food and beverage facilities on the premises constituted an important aspect of meeting competition for the motor traveler's business. Also helpful to the establishment of motel restaurants was the trend toward decentralization of urban areas, which moved a large share of the restaurant business to outlying areas. The catering facilities of many motels were thus able to develop local patronage to supplement their guest trade. The restaurant is now acknowledged to be an integral part of the modern motor hotel.

A recent Horwath & Horwath motor hotel study states: "The motor hotels in our study that operate their own restaurants have facilities that vary in complexity from a very simple 30-seat coffee shop to a quite diversified operation including banquet facilities and at least two restaurants seating a total of 850 persons. There appears to be no general relation between the number of restaurant seats and the number of room units that will be successful in a motor hotel. There seems to be an ever-increasing demand on the part of the motorist traveler for convenient and modern restaurant facilities."

That study and others on the subject indicate that the size and type of restaurant and bar facilities in a motel or motor hotel depend on a combination of factors, some of which are directly related to the overall motel operation and some of which are related to the demand existing in the area.

131

The type of guest expected in the day-to-day operation is one factor. It might be determined, for example, that the motel patronage will consist largely of transients, terminal guests or convention delegates. Another factor is the extent to which the facilities may benefit from the patronage of local residents and the development of local banquet and party revenue. The need for sound appraisals in the planning stage cannot be overemphasized.

THE RESTAURANT

The types of food and bar service found in motor hotels are as varied as those featured in hotels. Choices depend on the size of the operation, the type of patronage expected and the location of the establishment.

Regardless of what facilities may seem to be most suitable at the outset, it is a serious mistake to proceed with planning them until a study has been made to determine probable tastes and preferences of the guests and patrons. Such a study, if properly conducted, can be expected to indicate the kind of food service most likely to meet specific demands; the number of seats which would be economically feasible; the expected rates of seat turnover by days of the week and months of the year; and the anticipated check averages at the various meal periods. All of this information in turn will serve as an important guide in estimating the total food and beverage income.

Every food operation is, in effect, a manufacturing business in which the full circle of procurement, preparation and sale of the product takes place on the premises. As in every manufacturing plant, the smooth flow of merchandise through the various processes is of utmost importance to an efficient operation.

A chart illustrating the natural flow of traffic in the food and beverage department is shown on an accompanying page. A similar chart, prepared with a specific project in mind, should be helpful to those responsible for allocating the working and serving areas and deciding the layout of equipment. Preparation of this type of flow chart should be the first step in planning catering facilities. It will serve as a guide to the architect and others in arriving at the most efficient arrangements and will minimize or avert many departmental problems and serve also as a check list of the functions to be covered in actual operation.

The various types of food and beverage facilities are described in the following paragraphs:

Figure A

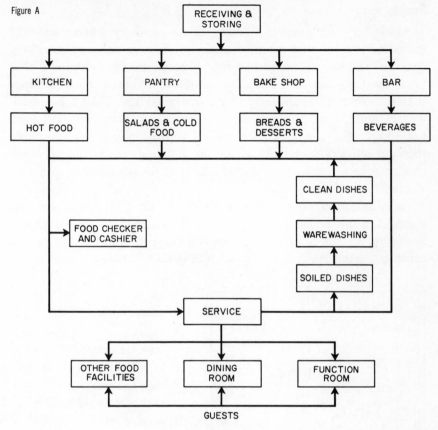

FLOW CHART
FOOD AND BEVERAGE OPERATIONS

Continental Breakfasts

This is an informal service usually restricted to sweet rolls or doughnuts, fruit juice and coffee and is served in the office or lobby area of the motel without charge. Ordinarily, this is offered on a self-service basis and is provided as a convenience where there is either no food service available or where the dining facility does not open until later in the day. Some motels serve Continental breakfasts in the guest rooms.

A number of motels have installed an automatic coffee maker in each room; envelopes of instant coffee and cups are provided so that guests can brew their own coffee at whatever time they choose. The value of this self-service is a controversial issue among motel operators, but many guests who feel the need for a cup of coffee before venturing out at an early hour do appreciate the convenience.

Snack Bars

Snack bars are usually installed as an auxiliary service adjacent to swimming pools or other recreational areas or for service at odd hours of the day. They add to the informal resort atmosphere that has proved popular in many motels and motor hotels. Such facilities usually operate independently of the main kitchen. They serve sandwiches, griddle and fountain items and soft drinks for the most part, but often offer liquor service where allowed. Generally speaking, they are self-service operations insofar as the guest is concerned, although waiter and waitress attendance is made available in many instances.

An illustration of a combination snack bar and service bar designed for the poolside of a large midtown motor hotel is shown in Figure B. This compact arrangement, occupying 250 square feet, is capable of handling complete snack and beverage service.

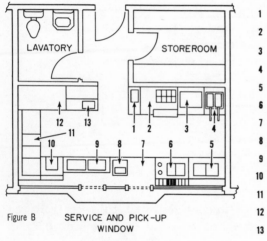

1	SINK
2	SANDWICH UNIT
3	GRIDDLE ⎱ EXHAUST HOOD
4	DEEP FAT FRYER ⎰ OVER
5	ICE CREAM FREEZER
6	SODA FOUNTAIN UNIT
7	SERVICE COUNTER
8	CASH REGISTER
9	BOTTLE COOLER
10	COCKTAIL UNIT
11	SINKS WITH DRAINBOARDS
12	BACK BAR WITH CABINET BASE
13	ICE MAKING MACHINE

Figure B   SERVICE AND PICK-UP
                        WINDOW

Counter-Service Coffee Shops

Coffee shops providing only counter service should be considered for projects where the demand for food service is expected to be limited, faster service is deemed desirable and the dining area is small. The length of the counter would depend entirely on the probable peak demand but should seldom exceed 40 linear feet, or a capacity of 20 persons. If more than that number of seats appears to be necessary, it would probably be advisable to consider a combination counter-and-table-service arrangement.

Ordinarily, a counter-only coffee shop provides a menu limited to short orders, sandwiches, salads and such items as can be prepared with counter-top equipment. The grill cook normally doubles as a server, depending on the number of seats and the service demands. No separate preparation kitchen could conceivably be justified for this type and size of operation, nor should meat cutting or fresh vegetable preparation be considered. Pre-cut and pre-portioned meats, frozen vegetables and other convenience foods should be utitized in order to conserve space and minimize the payroll. Usually the server also acts as cashier, although in the larger and busier operations a cashier's station is provided near the entrance of the shop.

An illustration of a counter-service coffee shop is shown in Figure C. This is a 12-stool operation in a 30-unit motel situated on a highway several miles from a middle-sized town. Because no restaurant existed in the immediate vicinity of the motel it was felt desirable to provide this facility for the guests. By adhering to a limited-service schedule and benefiting from the patronage of local residents as well as transients, it was able to show satisfactory operating profits.

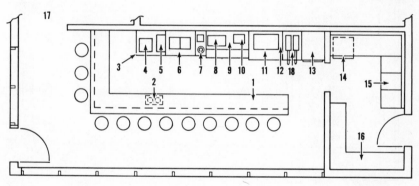

Figure C

1	SERVICE COUNTER	10	TOASTER
2	COFFEE WARMER	11	GRIDDLE
3	CABINET BASE	12	EXHAUST HOOD MOUNTED BELOW DISPLAY CASE
4	CASH REGISTER		
5	COFFEE MAKER	13	REFRIGERATOR
6	ICE CREAM CABINET	14	PORTABLE UNDERCOUNTER DISHWASHER
7	SINK AND DIPPER WELL	15	SINKS WITH DRAINBOARD
8	SANDWICH UNIT WITH SHELVING BASE	16	SHELVING
		17	FOYER AREA
9	DESSERT DISPLAY CASE (WALL MOUNTED)	18	DEEP FAT FRYER

Counter-and-Table-Service Coffee Shops

Coffee shops which provide both counter and table service are more numerous than any other type. This is because such operations have great flexibility, permitting them to be of many sizes and to offer a variety of services. They range from the very simple to the elaborate, depending on the location, size and character of the motel or motor hotel in which they are situated. Clearly, the greater the seating capacity, the more the operation must depend on outside patronage for its support.

Most combination counter-and-table-service restaurants require a preparation kitchen. A reach-through service window, which makes

Figure D

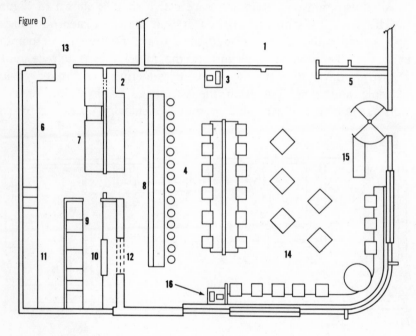

1 MOTEL LOBBY	9 RANGE AREA
2 SOILED DISH PASS-THRU	10 COOKS' TABLE
3 WAITRESS SERVICE STAND	11 PREPARATION
4 COUNTER SERVICE AREA	12 ORDER PICKUP WINDOW
5 COAT RACK	13 SERVICE CORRIDOR
6 REFRIGERATION AND PREPARATION AREAS	14 TABLE SERVICE AREA
7 DISHWASHING	15 CASHIER
8 COFFEE SHOP COUNTER	16 WAITRESS SERVICE STAND

it unnecessary for waitresses to enter the kitchen, is frequently employed. Such an arrangement minimizes the area required for preparation and usually lends itself to fast service. In this type of facility the server may also act as cashier, although usually there is a combination cashier's station, tobacco and candy counter. Figure D illustrates a typical call-window type of operation, while a more conventional service arrangement is shown in Figure E.

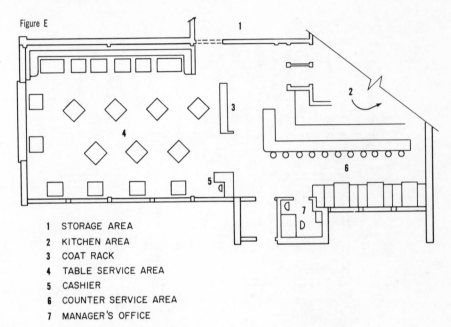

Figure E

1   STORAGE AREA
2   KITCHEN AREA
3   COAT RACK
4   TABLE SERVICE AREA
5   CASHIER
6   COUNTER SERVICE AREA
7   MANAGER'S OFFICE

Dining Rooms

Dining rooms, as distinguished from table-service coffee shops, are usually more formal and dignified in decor and service appointments. In general, such dining rooms are found only in motels and motor hotels having upwards of 80 units. It is sometimes the case, however, that one with fewer units can anticipate a volume of business from community sources that will support a dining room. On the basis of Horwath & Horwath studies it has been concluded that an average annual food revenue of from $1,200 to $1,500 per seat is the minimum required to justify large restaurant facilities. It would be expected that in such dining rooms the menu would be more selective and the prices higher than in the less distinctive table-service coffee shops.

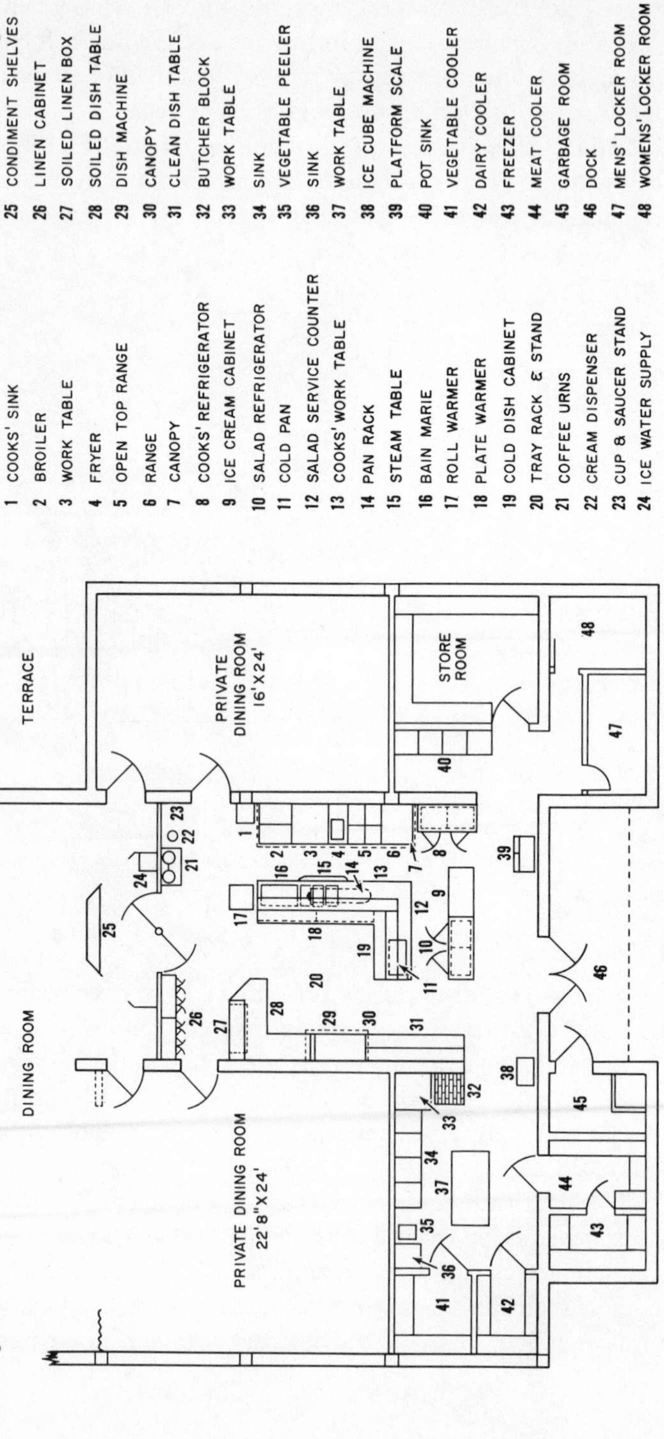

1 COOKS' SINK
2 BROILER
3 WORK TABLE
4 FRYER
5 OPEN TOP RANGE
6 RANGE
7 CANOPY
8 COOKS' REFRIGERATOR
9 ICE CREAM CABINET
10 SALAD REFRIGERATOR
11 COLD PAN
12 SALAD SERVICE COUNTER
13 COOKS' WORK TABLE
14 PAN RACK
15 STEAM TABLE
16 BAIN MARIE
17 ROLL WARMER
18 PLATE WARMER
19 COLD DISH CABINET
20 TRAY RACK & STAND
21 COFFEE URNS
22 CREAM DISPENSER
23 CUP & SAUCER STAND
24 ICE WATER SUPPLY
25 CONDIMENT SHELVES
26 LINEN CABINET
27 SOILED LINEN BOX
28 SOILED DISH TABLE
29 DISH MACHINE
30 CANOPY
31 CLEAN DISH TABLE
32 BUTCHER BLOCK
33 WORK TABLE
34 SINK
35 VEGETABLE PEELER
36 SINK
37 WORK TABLE
38 ICE CUBE MACHINE
39 PLATFORM SCALE
40 POT SINK
41 VEGETABLE COOLER
42 DAIRY COOLER
43 FREEZER
44 MEAT COOLER
45 GARBAGE ROOM
46 DOCK
47 MENS' LOCKER ROOM
48 WOMENS' LOCKER ROOM
TERRACE
PRIVATE DINING ROOM 16'X24'
STORE ROOM
DINING ROOM
PRIVATE DINING ROOM 22'8"X24'

Figure F

Waitress service stations should be located at strategic points in the dining room, one service stand being required for approximately every 50 seats. The pick-up station for food is located in the kitchen, and a food checker is usually provided. The checker may also act as cashier; or, as is often considered desirable, a cashier's station may be located in the dining room area.

Figure F illustrates a kitchen and service arrangement designed for a conventional dining room, supplemented by two smaller private dining room or function room areas.

Specialty Rooms

Specialty room take many forms, such as open-hearth operations featuring steaks and other broiled items; nationality rooms specializing in foods of European, Oriental or other foreign origins; restaurants which specialize in one or more foods such as chicken, seafood, pancakes and waffles. In this classification one finds steak rooms, rib rooms, chicken and seafood restaurants, luaus, as well as other types. The most common facility today is the open-hearth visual cooking arrangement which specializes in broiled foods. These restaurants have proved to be quite successful generally, in part because they have been able to substitute unique atmosphere for entertainment, which has become increasingly costly. A typical open-hearth dining room and kitchen layout is illustrated in Figure G.

Cocktail Lounges

Cocktail lounges in motor hotels range from the ordinary to the exotic, their size and style dictated largely by the number of units and other characteristics of the project.

It is generally agreed that the ideal location for the cocktail lounge is adjacent to the dining room so that the food and beverage services may complement one another. Frequently the separation of the dining and lounge areas is effectively accomplished without sacrificing space by means of plantings or an ornamental divider.

Whereas dining patrons may prefer well-lighted rooms, bar and cocktail lounge customers definitely desire more subdued lighting and a lesser degree of exposure to public view. It is therefore preferable to locate the bar and lounge away from outside windows that front on a thoroughfare or other public place. Such considerations would not apply if the lounge and bar were situated on an upper floor where an interesting outside view might be had without the loss of privacy. Indeed, wide windows on upper-floor facilities may prove an added inducement to patronage.

Figure G

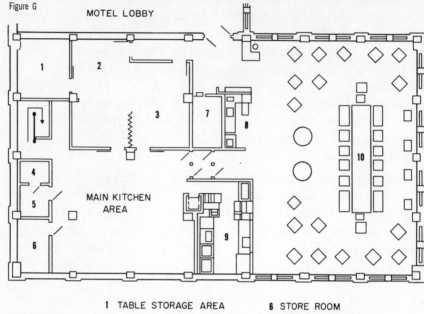

1 TABLE STORAGE AREA	6 STORE ROOM
2 FUNCTION ROOM NO.1	7 CHECK ROOM
3 FUNCTION ROOM NO.2	8 WAITRESS STATION
4 FREEZER	9 VISUAL COOKING AREA
5 COOLER	10 PLANTER DIVIDER

Figure H illustrates a moderate-sized cocktail lounge and open-hearth dining room combination.

Service Bars

In the majority of motor hotels there is no need for a service bar, since the requirements for beverage service to the dining rooms, guest rooms and pool-side can usually be accommodated from one or more of the conventional bars, or, as in the case of function service, from a portable bar. However, circumstances of physical layout occasionally dictate the desirability of such a facility; two instances are where beverage service is required in an area remote from the regular bar or where the volume of dining room and room service beverage sales is too great to be served from the regular bar.

Normally, service bars require comparatively little space, the requirements being limited to a conventional work station, a sink, a bottle cooler and a reasonable amount of shelving for stock. Usually, an area measuring 7 feet by 8 feet for each bartender will be found sufficient.

Figure H

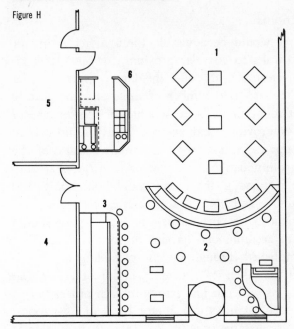

1   DINING AREA

2   COCKTAIL LOUNGE

3   COCKTAIL BAR

4   LOBBY

5   KITCHEN

6   VISUAL COOKING AREA

Figure I

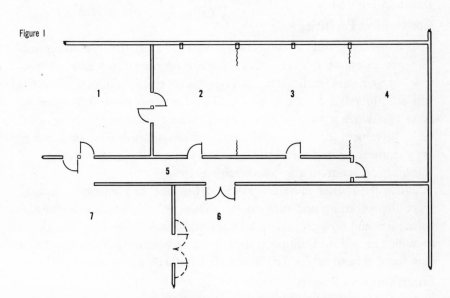

1 KITCHEN AREA	4 FUNCTION AREA #3 49 SEATS
2 FUNCTION AREA #1 42 SEATS	5 CORRIDOR
3 FUNCTION AREA #2 56 SEATS	6 LOBBY
	7 DINING ROOM

Banquet and Party Rooms

Generally speaking, it would be advisable for a motel or motor hotel of more than 50 units to consider providing private party facilities. The greater the number of units, the larger these facilities should be. The ratio between the number of units and the seating capacity of the banquet rooms must be reasonable, of course. One of the principal reasons for providing banquet and party facilities is to encourage business groups to occupy the guest rooms because of the convenience of such accommodations. On that basis, a 600-seat ballroom could hardly be justified if the motel could house only 300 persons, unless a definite demand from local sources existed.

The arrangement of the ballroom and private party rooms should be sufficiently flexible to accommodate groups of various sizes. Such flexibility can be accomplished through the use of sliding or airwall partitions. Care should be taken to provide soundproofing so that meetings in adjacent rooms will not interfere with each other.

An arrangement of such facilities in a motor hotel of 150 rooms situated in the central business area of a city of 100,000 population is shown in Figure I.

Convention Facilities

The banquet and meeting rooms discussed in the preceding section are essential to convention accommodations. In order to provide proper and satisfactory service, however, additional facilities and accommodations are required. The first and most important of these is a kitchen with a good layout, proper equipment and a location convenient to the service areas. Next in order of importance are the means for quietly and efficiently removing soiled dishes and transporting them to the warewashing area.

Other needs that must be provided for are: (a) adequate storage space for recording and projection equipment; (b) an elevator of sufficient size and capacity to house bulky and heavy equipment and doors of sufficient width to admit it; (c) portable platforms for a stage or a dais for the head table; (d) portable bars; (e) check-room facilities.

Entertainment Rooms

Entertainment rooms providing music, dancing and floor shows are found in only the most elaborate motor hotels. These rooms, being in the "supper club" class, should be distinctive in decor and atmosphere and provide cuisine and service with a Continental flair.

Because rooms of this type are expensive to build and very costly to operate, careful consideration should be given to the desirability and sales potential before they are definitely made a part of the plans. As stated in a previous chapter, this type of room represents a close approach to "show business," and that factor sets it apart from the ordinary restaurant operation, which usually confines itself to providing meal service in a pleasing atmosphere.

An interesting example of a circular terraced entertainment room is illustrated in Figure J.

Figure J

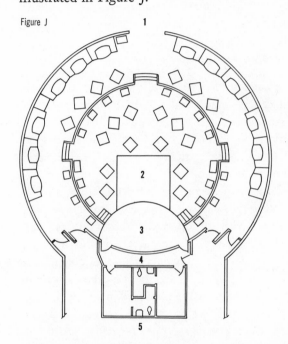

1 FOYER AREA

2 DANCE FLOOR

3 STAGE

4 DRESSING ROOMS

5 KITCHEN AREA

PRINCIPLES OF KITCHEN AND DINING ROOM LAYOUT

The selection of kitchen equipment of the type and capacities best suited to the particular needs of an operation and the designing of a layout that will function efficiently are extremely important factors in successful restaurant operation.

The objectives of modern kitchen planning include:

1. Proper preparation of food.
2. Fast and efficient service.
3. Minimum payroll.
4. High standards of sanitation.
5. Adequate merchandise control.

The basic facts that must be determined before arriving at any decisions regarding equipment requirements or arrangement are:

1. Type of service contemplated.
2. Composition of the menu.
3. Number of seats.
4. Potential patronage.
5. Peak load periods.
6. Hours of operation.
7. Whether baking will be done on the premises.
8. Extent of linen service.
9. Location of receiving dock.
10. Locker and washroom requirements.

Once these matters have been settled, an intelligent approach to the problem of kitchen layout can be made and the final planning of the areas can be undertaken. At this point it is prudent to engage someone experienced in food operation to collaborate with the architect in space allocation essential to the restaurant operation. Such experience is necessary in planning the equipment layout of kitchen, storerooms and service areas so that proper facilties can be provided for receiving, storing, issuing, preparing and serving food and beverages. Unless the services of one thoroughly familiar with the operating details in "the back of the house" are obtained it is likely that important points affecting service, merchandise control and traffic flow may be overlooked. Too often the architect's original allocation of space for the preparation and storage areas is inadequate or improperly placed. When the kitchen engineer and the architect work together from the start of the project even the framing of the buildings can sometimes be revised to fit the columns, pipe shafts, stairways, elevators and other obstructions to the flow of traffic into a plan that will best serve the operation.

The proper function of the kitchen engineer is to specify only such equipment as will be required to do the prescribed job and to arrange it to provide an orderly flow of merchandise from the receiving and storage areas through the various steps of preparation and service. Provision for adequate working areas, wide aisles, convenient refrigeration and water supply, the avoidance of cross-traffic and compliance with local sanitation codes are equally essential to planning.

Every project has individual problems of space allocation and for that reason any discussion on the subject must be generalized. However, there are several basic considerations which apply in nearly all cases.

The area required for the dining room is directly related to the number of seats and the type of service desired.

The recommended area per seat in the various types of dining rooms is as follows:

	Number of square feet
Formal dining room	15-17
Coffee Shop	
Table service	12-14
Counter service	18-20
Cafeteria	16-17
Banquet	9-10

Table size is usually related to the type of service contemplated, as indicated in the following guide:

Type of Service	Number of Seats	Tables Oblong	Round or Square	Full Width	Booths Table Width	Table Length
Luxurious	2	30" x 36"	—		2'	2'
	4	48"-54" x 36"	36"-42"	4'10"5'6"	1'8"-2'	3'6"
Intermediate	2	28" x 28"-30"	—		2'	2'2"-2'6"
	4	48" x 28"-30"	32"-34"	5'2"-5'6"	2'-2'2"	3'9"-4'
Economical	2	24" x 24"-26"	—		2'	2'6"
	4	24"-26" x 42"-48"	30"	5'8"-5'10"	2'4"-2'6"	4'-4'2"

Counters range in width from 16 inches to 24 inches, and 2 linear feet are allowed per stool.

Aisle widths should offer minimum dimensions of 36 inches for general circulation and 24 inches for service.

A mistake frequently made in restaurants is to provide an excess number of tables for four and too few tables for two, with the result that the percentage of table occupancy suffers because of the use of large tables for one or two persons. As a general rule, 60 per cent of the seating capacity of motel dining rooms should be in "deuces" and 40 per cent in "fours." That proportion provides flexibility of table arrangement, as two "deuces" can be either placed together for a party of four or used individually.

Although there can be no standardization of kitchen layout because of the many variations in sizes and types of service and differences in physical structures, general average ratios regarding space requirements may prove helpful in the initial planning stage. It is true that a smaller kitchen may result in lower payroll costs, but an inadequate kitchen area may also prove quite costly when later revisions are restricted because of structural barriers.

For a conventional dining room operation the approximate percentage relationships of the various function areas to the total kitchen and back-of-the-house area are as follows:

Receiving	5%
Dry storage	15
Refrigerated storage	8
Pre-preparation	4
Cooking equipment	8
Salad and cold food	8
Baking	10
Pot and warewashing	8
Work and service areas	17
Trash storage	5
Employees' facilities	12
Total	100%

Additional pointers that apply in nearly all kitchen planning are:

1. Provide a working surface adjacent to the deep fat fryers.
2. Provide a water supply over ranges.
3. Provide a convenient sink and reach-in refrigerator for the cooks.
4. Provide proper ventilation and lighting.
5. Place all fixed equipment on a cove curbing, unless local regulations prevent this.
6. Utilize portable equipment as much as possible for:
    (a) Vegetable bins, flour bins, etc.
    (b) Dollies for garbage cans, dish and glass racks.
    (c) Self-leveling equipment for dishes.
    (d) Work tables.
7. Provide pre-rinse and rinse injector equipment on dish machines.
8. Utilize waste disposal units where possible.

9. Provide for self-service in cafeteria lines where possible. (Self-service coffee urns and milk dispensers should be considered.)
10. Provide sufficient areas for dry, refrigerated and frozen-food storage.
11. Where possible, provide reach-through refrigerators and food warmers between the preparation and serving areas.

RECEIVING AND STORAGE AREAS

Probably the most frequently underspaced areas are those allocated for the receiving and storage of merchandise. The problem can usually be traced to the desire of the owner and architect to concentrate on guest accommodations and revenue-producing space in the front of the house. While it is desirable to devote maximum space to such purposes, it is just as important that necessary operating facilities not be sacrificed in the bargain.

The receiving area should be of sufficient size to allow proper verification of the weight or count of the items delivered. There should be room for adequate and convenient scales, desk space, etc. Provision should be made adjacent or convenient to the receiving door for the handling of waste matter, empty cases and bottles, soiled linen and other pick-up items.

The storage areas should be as convenient to the receiving door as possible, particularly the food storeroom, which is the most active area in this part of the operation. Steps or ramps between the storeroom, the receiving area and the kitchen should be avoided whenever possible. In other words, the extent of the transportation of merchandise should be minimized, because each trip adds to operating costs and multiplies the chance for loss through careless handling and pilferage. Access to the storage areas should be controlled at all times and the areas should be locked when not in use.

The number and size of the storage areas required is dependent upon the size of the motel, the volume of its food and bar business and its location in respect to available markets. Where deliveries are infrequent, the storage facilities, particularly refrigerators and freezers, must be sufficient to accommodate greater quantities. With the steadily increasing availability of frozen and other forms of convenience foods, it is important to give special consideration to the adequacy of freezer space.

The storage of liquor, wines, beer and soft drinks demands certain special requirements. Some wines must be refrigerated and others should be stored horizontally. Bins for the storage of varieties and brands of whiskies should be set up in a well-ventilated, theft-proof area.

If draught beer is to be served, special provision must be made for refrigerating the kegs. Bottled beer and soft drinks can be stocked in a well-ventilated and safe area, and small quantities can be kept under refrigeration in the bar. Space should also be allocated for sorting and storing empty bottles and cases to be picked up by the supplier.

WAREWASHING

Great strides have been made in recent years in the warewashing department. The conventional rack-type machines have been vastly improved by the addition of pre-rinse units, automatic detergent controls, wetting and drying agent injectors and more efficient washing action. Additionally, the development of the flight-type dishwasher has meant that more and better work can be accomplished with less help where the volume of business justifies that type of equipment. With flight-type machines the clean-dish table is eliminated and clean dishes are placed in portable trucks or self-leveling equipment as soon as they are taken from the machine. Glasses, cups and soup bowls are placed in appropriate racks before washing and the filled racks are set on the belt pins and sent through the machine. As they emerge the racks are placed in self-leveling equipment or stacked on dollies or mobile carts for transportation to the service stations. Not only does this minimize handling, but it also substantially reduces breakage.

The location of the warewashing department deserves careful thought. Both convenience in bussing and the possible noise factor must be considered. In small operations, where the bussing of china, glassware and silver is directly to the dishroom, the soiled-dish table is usually located in the kitchen area and to the right of the doors leading from the service area. In larger operations, however, the warewashing department can be more remote, often on the floor below or above, with both vertical and horizontal dish conveyors transporting the wares between the dining and warewashing areas.

Substantial savings in bussing payroll can often be achieved in soda fountain and other counter operations by providing an under-counter conveyor which transports the soiled wares directly onto the soiled dish table. Also, in coffee shops where a kitchen call window is used, a conveyor belt might be installed under the window so that waitresses can buss soiled dishes at the same point their orders are given and picked up.

MODERN PLANNING

Appearance, utility and durability are combined to provide the modern kitchen with many facilities and conveniences that were unheard of a few years ago, making it a show place instead of a facility to be hidden, creating customer interest and acceptance. Convection-type and electronic ovens, infra-red broilers, fully refrigerated food trucks and other mobile equipment of all types and kinds make it possible to do a better job faster and often with fewer employees than was possible in the conventional kitchen of years past.

Planning of the restaurant facilities is based upon two main considerations: (a) the needs of the typical guest; and (b) the need to obtain the ultimate in efficient operation. Since the food and beverage operation is a comparatively low-profit service, it is essential that the facilities answer a real need and are properly planned so that neither space nor labor is wasted.

In order to take full advantage of the latest developments, the owner, architect and kitchen planner must weigh carefully all aspects of this operation. It is worthwhile to lay out a scale model of the kitchen so that spacing and traffic can be judged accurately.

13

Recreation and Entertainment Areas

Previous chapters have touched upon the need for guest recreation and entertainment. The extent and variety of these services depends on many factors, but basic considerations are the needs of the guest and the space available.

If a substantial share of the motel's guests are expected to stay for extended periods it is frequently necessary to offer them some of the less strenuous forms of outdoor sports and recreational facilities. The number of businessmen who travel with their families and combine business and pleasure is on the increase. This trend makes it advisable to consider the allocation of space for family recreation during the day. The most popular of these facilities is the swimming pool. Next is the playground area, which may include a slide, swings, sandbox and other play equipment.

Many motels and motor hotels have found it worthwhile to offer shuffleboard, badminton, tennis, golf, bowling and even horseback riding. All such activities require not only ground area but also considerable capital investment and therefore must be justified on the basis of their direct income-producing potential or their role in attracting additional patronage.

THE SWIMMING POOL

The most recent figures available indicate that at least one out of every three motels or motor hotels has a swimming pool or is planning to add one. Since the swimming pool has probably the widest appeal to

150

guests, including those who actually go swimming and those who prefer to use the area only for lounging and sunning, the balance of this chapter will be devoted to that recreational facility.

Direct and Indirect Benefits

Although it is seldom possible to obtain sufficient direct revenue from a swimming pool to cover the cost of maintenance and operation, there are a number of less tangible side benefits that can justify it. Many people who do not use the pool like to watch the swimmers, and the pool usually becomes a center of attraction. It may also serve as a drawing card for the motel's restaurant and cocktail lounge, especially if their windows face the pool area. The restaurant can be extended into a patio section at the pool, with full outdoor service provided in good weather. Sometimes a snack bar or luau for beverage service is located on the pool's deck area.

Pool and patio area of the Golden Triangle Motor Hotel, Norfolk, is in full view of the main section of the structure. The cabana section is an attractive feature of these facilities.

Courtesy: Golden Triangle Motor Hotel

The extent to which the pool may be used by others than house guests should also be studied. Considerable local demand for such a facility should encourage the operator to seek ways in which admission fees or dues from a club membership arrangement might be used to defray the pool's cost and expenses and perhaps, at the same time, increase local patronage of the dining room and bar. Use of the pool by "outsiders" would entail the necessity of constructing bath and dressing rooms and the normal facilities associated with a bath club, such as locker rooms and administrative and control areas.

The manner in which such a club is promoted is highly important to the motel owner. If outside membership is to prove practical, the operating control of all facilities should remain in the motel owner's hands. Otherwise, local patronage may hamper free use of the pool by house guests.

Although local patronage of the pool has on occasion contributed substantially to a motel's profits, more often the response has not been as great as expected, resulting in facilities that have proved to be far more extensive and costly than necessary. Ordinarily the motel operator considers the swimming pool only a side attraction and does not attempt to enlarge upon it.

Many interesting aspects of pool use have come to light in various studies. One motel operator reported that guests of his establishment who were visiting industrial plants in the area frequently brought back friends from the plant to use the pool facilities. Such practice generally resulted in additional dinner business and certainly helped to spread word-of-mouth advertising and gain local acceptance and support for the motel. Swimming pools are sometimes located so that they act as an advertising medium in themselves, attracting people from the highway. Such a location may prove a drawback, however, if it exposes guests in the area to the noise, dust and odors of nearby highway traffic and robs the pool of privacy.

If the pool can be heated and the area shielded from sharp winds, the swimming season can be extended. Also, if properly designed, the pool can be converted to an ice-skating rink in the winter in certain climates. If sufficient demand exists for year-round or extended-season operation, the pool may be sheltered or covered by a variety of new materials and devices. Some motor hotels offer an additional indoor pool, but investment in space and capital for two pools is high in relation to probable return and there has been no extensive trend in this direction.

Professional Guidance

Factors influencing the choice of location, type, size and shape of the pool and the method of operation must be studied before construction begins. Selection of the materials and most suitable auxiliary equipment for the job requires professional guidance. The architect should be consulted on location, layout and design. He should plan the most feasible way to integrate the pool with the overall scheme of facilities and landscaping. A professional engineer experienced in pool construction and operation should also be consulted and should supervise the actual installation.

Location of Swimming Pool

Location of the pool depends substantially on the type of construction that is best adapted to the area and on the funds allotted to this part of the project. Generally speaking, it should be in a spot that receives direct sunlight for a maximum number of hours and is screened

The pool and outdoor dining terrace at the Nationwide Inn, Columbus, Ohio.
Courtesy: Albert Pick Motels

from prevailing winds without being so near trees and shrubs that an accumulation of fallen leaves and branches will present a problem. The pool area should be easily accessible from the guest rooms, particularly if no poolside shower or dressing rooms are provided. It should be brightly illuminated at night but should be kept free of insects that are often attracted by lights. Many pool areas are illuminated by open gas flames or torches, which are attractive in themselves and also act as a means of pest control.

Surrounding the pool with a terrace or deck area that is at least as large as the space occupied by the pool itself will enhance the spaciousness of the facility. The deck or terrace might even be twice that size if the pool is located in the center of it. To make the most of its appeal it should be placed where it can be seen from the various public areas, especially the dining rooms.

Auxiliary equipment will demand space on the site. Filters, pumps and heating equipment are normally located below ground and can sometimes be installed in the basement areas of the motel building. If the pool is a considerable distance from the guest rooms it will be necessary to install toilet facilities for both men and women, a provision frequently required by local ordinance.

Determining Size and Type

The size of the pool area will control the extent of its use by motel guests and local patrons. Pool authorities say that from 20 to 30 square feet of pool and terrace or deck area will be required by each person actively using the pool. Fewer than half of the persons who use the pool are expected to be in the water at one time, the remainder occupying poolside space. A crowded or cramped pool area destroys the element of luxury and greatly reduces its utility and attractiveness. Most often it is more important that the terrace area rather than the pool itself be spacious.

Small pools were installed in early tourist establishments to enable their proprietors to advertise that a pool was available. The rapid development of pool facilities in hotels and motels since then has indicated that where a motel operator does not have sufficient space to exploit the advantage of a swimming pool as an attraction to the guest, he had better devote his space to other attractions.

Motel operators should acquaint themselves with all local laws concerning swimming pools. Regulations normally specify water depth and slope requirements. Pools that are too short or that slope sharply are dangerous and may be prohibited by law. Diving areas must be planned to offer proper depth under and near the diving boards. Diving boards can be a dangerous addition to pool facilities and in most cases, particularly where the pool is primarily for guest use, they are not offered. Depth of water should be marked at intervals along the sides of the pool. A rope supported by floats to indicate the limits of deep and shallow areas is another common safeguard.

A set of pool regulations should be provided and strictly maintained. It is suggested that children be prohibited from using the pool unless a parent or attendant is present or there is reasonable assurance that they are capable swimmers. Some swimming areas offer a separate wading pool for children. Regulations should also control the hours during which the pool may be used. Related to rules for use of the pool are regulations which stipulate which areas of the motel are "off limits" to persons wearing swim clothes.

The type of pool most suitable for a particular motel will depend on the location, the shape desired and, to some extent, local soil conditions.

In many instances the swimming pool is given an unsual shape to enhance the atmosphere of the pool area and provide a conversation piece. Some pools are available only in rectangular shapes which may neither fit the space allotted for the pool area nor harmonize with the landscaping or the design of the motel building. Some pools are installed above ground, but sunken pools are more common. Many multi-story motel buildings have a pool on the roof or at one of the set-backs, in which case installation plans for the pool area must be coordinated directly with the building operating plan; and the architect must be certain that the structure will be strong enough to support the additional weight.

Pools intended for the public must be constructed more solidly than those intended for private use. For example, pools that are constructed by installing a plastic liner over cement, earth or other material are generally not recommended for public use because of the danger of tearing the liner. Pools endorsed for heavy use are those which are: (a) prefabricated of either metal or plastic; (b) partly fabricated of concrete, concrete blocks and steel, for example; or (c) fabricated on the site with materials such as poured concrete, dry-pack concrete or pneumatically applied concrete or plastic. Most pools are tile-lined or coated with a water-resistant composition paint.

The choice of materials and other aspects of pool construction should take into account plot characteristics and regional climatic influences. Certain of these materials need the support of solid ground rather than loose fill. Others of these materials are adversely affected by special stresses or strains as well as by sharp changes in temperature and weather conditions and therefore may prove unsatisfactory in certain parts of the country. The difference in weight between an empty and a filled pool can often cause difficulties, as can water pressure accumulating beneath the pool during thaws, causing the pool to bulge and develop cracks or other defects. Many pool owners keep them filled in winter and leave logs in the water to absorb ice expansion.

Another factor to be considered in the choice of a pool is the amount of maintenance that will be required. Some pools, particularly those made of steel, will have to be painted at least once a year if a good appearance and satisfactory sanitary conditions are to be maintained. Where the inside of the pool has a tile surface, annual painting is not necessary, but the tile joints will have to be kept tight. Generally speaking, the prefabricated or fabricated-on-the-site plastic pools require no additional interior finish, but such products are relatively new and their durability has not been completely established.

The materials available for use in constructing the terrace or deck area must also be considered in terms of maintenance requirements. The surface of such areas must be kept smooth and free of slippery spots. They must have no jutting or ragged edges, be easy to keep in a sanitary and attractive condition and be capable of standing up under abuse from the constant moving of deck furniture and pool equipment. If the pool area is accessible to the public during off-seasons, the pool should be provided with a cover or a fence that can be kept locked. Covers are available that will stretch across the entire pool surface and prevent any accumulation of debris in the water, at the same time permitting rain to penetrate so that covers need not be removed frequently. If the pool is too large to be covered, it will have to be surrounded by a fence to pevent unwary persons or animals from falling in.

All pools require such equipment as pumps and filters. The minimum capacity of this equipment is normally determined by local regulations which specify the number of times the water must be changed. As with the equipment required for heating and ventilating the motel, the capacity of the pool equipment should be slightly greater than the maximum demand so that it will not be necessary to use auxiliary and emergency equipment. All pool equipment should be located where it can be reached easily for maintenance and can be connected to utility lines without undue difficulty. If such equipment is improperly selected or installed, the pool may be condemned by local authorities; later correction of the defect could involve substantial additional investment.

Because much of the piping, the sanitary and safety items must be installed prior to the completion of the pool, it is imperative that the planning of construction be left to professionals and that plans be completed early enough to allow proper integration of the pool area with the master plan of the motel.

Auxiliary Facilities

If they are required, toilet facilities and showers, dressing rooms and lockers for men and women in the pool area should be constructed at the same time as the pool. Frequently such conveniences are provided in private or semi-private facilities, commonly called "cabanas," which afford a shaded area, chairs, lounges and tables for rest and relaxation. These facilities are sometimes sufficiently furnished and equipped to serve as auxiliary guest-room units and are a fair source of added income. The construction of more permanent dressing areas or cabanas should be considered in a community where they can be rented by the season to local residents as well as being offered to guests of the motel. Such cabanas are usually placed around the pool area with an open deck space facing the pool. Cabanas can be temporary structures, consisting of tents of colored fabric or of canopies which provide sufficient privacy for dressing and lounging. In such instances bathroom facilities are centrally located. An arrangement of this nature is adequate if the pool is used only to a minor extent by persons other than room guests.

When considering whether the cost of cabanas or dressing areas for other than regular house guests is worthwhile, it is advisable to think of alternative means of meeting the needs of pool guests. Some motel operators have set up a schedule of day rates for guest rooms located near the swimming pool. These rooms can double as bath houses when

Because of the layout of the pool and terrace area of the Pen and Quill Hotel, Manhattan Beach, California, guests have an unobstructed and pleasant view of pool activity right from their rooms.

Courtesy: Pen and Quill Hotel

the demand warrants. This plan requires design and furnishings that will facilitate such dual use. The floor coverings and furniture in these units must be of a type not easily damaged or soiled by moisture and dirt. Guest-unit furniture can be designed for easy storage and can be replaced with pool furniture when the rooms are used by bathers. Up-holstered pieces can also be covered with water-resistant plastic material. The bed presents a problem in such rooms and perhaps the studio-type bed serves best. It is advisable to consider using guest rooms for the convenience of bathers only in an area where such use may be occasional or where the motel site is too small for the construction of cabanas or dressing rooms.

Pool accessories, furniture for the patio or terrace and life-saving equipment form an essential element of auxiliary equipment and deserve careful study. Lounge chairs, umbrellas or canopies, metal tables and chairs for snack and bar service and card-playing, sunning pads, water floats and water-game equipment are among the many items in this category.

Pool Area Income

An analysis of the possibilities of income from the rental of cabanas, fees for the use of the pool, lockers and dressing rooms, and sale of food and beverages in the pool area should be made and the resulting estimates studied before determining the extent of the facilities. In each instance the additional investment necessary for providing permanent auxiliary facilities, the cost of services connected with them and the cost of required maintenance should also be calculated. If the estimates

The pool section of the Highway Inn, Dallas, is accessible to both parking areas and guest rooms.

Courtesy: Alsonnett Hotels

of income exceed the estimates of expenses by a favorable margin, there will be good reason to believe that pool facilities are economically feasible. Even if the net revenue is not sufficient to pay the cost of maintaining and supervising the pool operation, the investment may be justifiable because of the pool's advertising and promotional value to the motel. (Of course, the usefulness of other recreational areas may also be augmented with auxiliary conveniences, such as catering service, dressing and locker rooms, etc., although to a lesser degree.)

Operating Costs

The cost of operating a swimming pool breaks down into three general categories:

1. Direct expenses, which would include the payroll of lifeguards, attendants and cleaning personnel; cleaning supplies; towels and other linens; laundry; sanitary supplies; water and filtering process supplies, etc.

2. Maintenance, including painting, pool cleaning and upkeep of equipment. The extent of such cost depends largely on the type of construction used for the pool and the size of the terrace or deck area.

, 3. Supervision and control, which will depend on local regulations and the extent to which persons other than house guests use the pool. (Some motel operators have employed closed-circuit television as a means of supervising and policing the pool area.)

An estimate of operating costs should be prepared in advance, based on the type of pool and style of operation. There is no established guide for measuring pool operating costs since some types of expense bear little relationship to either pool size or location. The cost may fluctuate from as little as $2.00 per square foot of pool area to as much as $10 or $15 per square foot. The simple recreational-type, patronized almost exclusively by motel guests and located in a climate where the swimming season is relatively short, will probably not cost more than $2.00 per square foot annually to maintain. However, any extension of the swimming season and fluctuations in the cost of local utilities will affect this figure. Costs are also influenced by use of the area surrounding the pool and the policies followed for pool operation.

Advice pertaining to pool installations and operation is available from the National Swimming Pool Institute in Howard, Illinois. Further information may be obtained from other trade organizations and associations in the recreational, hotel and motel fields.

14

Cost Estimates and Capital Requirements

After the market study is made and the site is determined, two highly important steps remain prior to undertaking the construction and furnishing of the facilities. The first is to make a preliminary estimate of the amount of investment involved, which entails a study of the cost of land, buildings, the furnishings to be provided and the amount of working capital necessary to carry on the actual operation. The second is the projection of income and expenses in a preliminary budget estimate to determine the possibilities and probabilities of a return on operations sufficient to warrant the investment involved. Both of these preliminary projections and estimates will have a direct bearing on the feasibility of the project in the eyes of the investors, and lending agencies that will be expected to furnish the funds for construction, furnishings and operation.

The lending agency is interested primarily in probabilities rather than possibilities, but both should be projected in order to portray the full picture. If the preliminary cost and profit estimates are not encouraging, they will indicate whether it is more advisable to abandon the project before large sums are spent or to change its conception in order to make it a sound investment. At this stage many owners of property who had hoped to develop a motel project have found that it is better to take a small loss at the start by investing a few dollars in such preliminary calculations than to lose their entire original investment in an unsound venture.

The projections should be made by persons familiar with costs and net income possibilities. It is advised that the architect consult with an accountant experienced in motel and hotel operations. When these preliminary projections have been prepared and the investors have aligned sufficient funds to complete the project, it is time for the architect to prepare more detailed final working drawings and specifications for use in obtaining contractors' bids.

PRELIMINARY CONSTRUCTION COST ESTIMATES

As a rule, the investor is aware of the exact cost of land at the time the project is first conceived. Thus he is able to use a known quantity for figuring the first capital investment. Since the total investment in the project will not be definitely known until final construction has been completed and the doors are open for business, the balance of the cost estimates must be made beforehand, based as nearly as possible on realistic computations and logical reasoning. The preliminary rough estimates can be accomplished in a number of ways, among which are:

1. The application of "rules of thumb" established in the industry and based on studies of motel or motor hotel construction. They often take the form of costs per room or guest unit. The range is wide, depending on the size and style of the units involved, their furnishings and the amount of public space, catering and recreational facilities, etc. In the early days when only guest units were built and construction costs were much lower it was not unusual to estimate from $3,500 to $5,000 per unit, compared with the present range of from $8,000 to $15,000 per unit. The cost per unit now sometimes exceeds $15,000 in elaborate establishments.

2. An analysis of the costs of similar projects built in the same area.

3. A projection of costs based on the planned square footage or cubic footage of the proposed facilities multiplied by costs per foot of similar construction in the vicinity.

Since it is vitally important that the estimates indicate the maximum probable investment, it is best that all three methods be used in order to provide a reasonable cross-check. The estimates must be realistic; actual costs very frequently exceed the estimates when preliminary figures are not compiled with due care.

A study of the balance sheets of a number of motels and motor hotel projects indicates the following average investment breakdown:

Land and site improvement (including landscaping, parking area, swimming pool, etc.):	10%-20%
Buildings:	65%-70%
Furniture and equipment:	15%-20%

The foregoing figures are averages intended to be used only as a check on the estimates of costs involved in a specific project. The basic fault in applying these ratios to the cost per room unit is that the restaurant and other auxiliary facilities which may be contemplated are, of course, a part of this total cost. Since these facilities are not necessarily directly related to the number of guest rooms in the project, however, one might easily get a distorted picture from an estimate based on the cost per guest unit.

In the final analysis it is best to consider inclusion of any or all of these auxiliary facilities only to the extent of their contribution to the success of the operation. Therefore it is better procedure to again check the original estimates made on the basis of methods previously suggested by computing the cost of each major facility separately. The facilities must then justify ther inclusion in the overall plan on the basis of direct profit contribution or their less tangible benefits.

Exterior view of Del E. Webb's Towne House, San Francisco, illustrating a high-rise structure requiring a hotel approach to cost estimates.
Courtesy: Del E. Webb Motor Hotel Corp.

We repeat the warning that the use of general industry "rules of thumb" on a per-guest-unit cost of construction is only a starting point and is frequently unreliable because of the tendency on the part of some promoters to use the figure that fits a predetermined total investment. As previously stated, a recent analysis of motor hotel construction costs reveals an extremely wide range, depending on location and type. Also, in using the cost of a similar establishment as a guide, adjustments must often be made to cover the differences between the facilities of the existing operation and those contemplated for the proposed motel. By far the best and most reliable method to use is the one involving the cost based on the square or cubic footage of the entire project, using the experience of local construction people to determine costs. This method also lends itself to a detailed breakdown, which is preferred to cost estimates made on the basis of lumping the various improvements to the property into general categories.

As an example, the following breakdown may be used:

1. Land. The cost of the property is usually known or can be appraised. A factor should be added for landscaping and preparing the site for the facilities to be placed on it.

2. Parking, entrance and driveways. The local grading and paving costs per square foot should be multiplied by the number of square feet in the area planned for this use.

3. Building construction. The rough preliminary layout drawings of the improvements to be constructed on the plot are used as a guide for these cost estimates.

    a. Guest units, administration and control areas. The square or cubic footage requirements should be multiplied by local rates for similar construction, adjusted for elevators and other mechanical equipment which may be peculiar to the project and therefore not included in these rates.

    b. The restaurant. The square footage required to accommodate the number of patrons projected should be multiplied by local rates for similar construction.

    c. Recreation and auxiliary facilities. Firms experienced in the construction of swimming pools or other, similar, facilities should be consulted, and the one providing the best facility for the money should be selected. For stores, shops and other public areas the square footage requirements multiplied by the local construction rates should produce a reliable estimate.

When the computation of construction and site improvement costs has been completed, the total should be increased by an estimate of the fees of the architect, decorator and other consultants involved in the planning, the cost of financing and carrying the property during construction, and a reasonable reserve to provide for contingencies. It is usually the case that construction costs exceed the original estimates. This is due mainly to the "extras" that are the result of changes often found necessary or advisable during the course of construction. There are always omissions or changes that come to light only as the project materializes.

Recent experience indicates that construction costs are rising steadily and may well increase between the time of the original projection and the letting of contracts. Therefore it is suggested that a reserve of 10 per cent to 20 per cent be added to the estimates for conservative projection of costs at this point. The resulting figure should then be converted to a per-unit basis for comparison with figures available from general studies and the analysis of construction costs of similar projects.

COST OF FURNISHINGS

At a recent show a minimum set-up for room furnishings was exhibited at a cost of $750, and such estimates range from that low figure to $2,500 per room and more. The use of general "rules of thumb" in computing the cost of furnishing the motel is subject to the same problems outlined in the previous section on construction costs. Cost figures available for the industry or for similar projects do not indicate any general pattern for determining the ratio of the cost of equipping the administrative and control areas, restaurant, recreational and attendant facilities, or of obtaining the furnishings necessary for the guest units. In fact, it should be obvious that these costs vary substantially among the several different projects that might be studied as guides. Therefore the estimate on furnishings should be made by considering first the guest-room units alone, next adding the estimates for the public areas, administration and working spaces.

A sound method for determining the probable cost of furnishing the guest-room section of the motel is to set up a model room and discuss it with the person who will be engaged in completing this part of the project. Professional interior decorators frequently have available lists of prices for all types of furnishings and are in a good position to make a reliable estimate of the probable cost of furnishing a typical room. Many furnishings houses have contract departments that will furnish such information for preliminary estimates and are in a position to follow through to the installation of the various items.

Since it would not be feasible to set up samples of each type of room to be offered in the final project, it is best to base the estimate at this stage on one or two typical units, considering the result to be the average cost. This figure is multiplied by the number of guest units contemplated, and an additional margin for contingencies is added. Then the cost of furnishing the corridors, lobby and administrative areas is computed and added to the estimated cost of furnishing the guest units. Much of the information necessary for this calculation can readily be obtained from the purveyors who deal in these items. Further insights may be gained from a visit to one of the hotel or motel shows, contact with one of the trade associations, or a perusal of the trade press.

The estimated cost of furnishing and equipping the restaurant, including service, preparation and storage areas, should be based on an analysis conducted by professionals with experience in this department, preferably a reliable kitchen consultant and an interior decorator who will work as a team with the architect. General specifications as to quality and performance must first be set; then the price range of the furnishings and equipment best suited to the project can be determined. Since the cost of equipping a restaurant can range from a few hundred dollars per seat for a simple coffee shop to several thousand dollars per seat for the specialty restaurant, decisions must be reached in the very beginning with respect to the type of establishment and extent of the service desired. Once again, when the estimates are finally prepared they can be compared with industry averages in order to test their reliability.

In making estimates for furnishings and equipment, one should not forget to include the cost of office furniture and machines, furniture for the pool area, laundry equipment, equipment for other working areas such as the linen room and engine room, and furnishings for the help's locker rooms and dressing rooms. Often these items are submerged in the original calculation, a fact which can widen the spread between the original calculation and the final determination of capital investment.

OPERATING EQUIPMENT

Such necessities as linens, china, glassware, silver, utensils and uniforms are usually grouped in a classification called "operating equipment." These items must be replaced constantly as opposed to furnishings and other types of equipment normally charged to operations on a depreciation basis. Control of these short-life items is usually by means of frequent inventories, if there is control at all, and they are listed on the financial statements at their inventory values. If they are handled from the start on an inventory basis, the same way as other supplies, the operator will obtain a more accurate idea of his replacement costs on operating equipment items than is possible by having only replacement cost figures. Such replacement expenditures may vary considerably from one period to another because replacement purchases are infrequent and often distort the picture of the operating results. In a smaller operation it is often impractical to keep detailed records of these costs. As a result, the original equipment is often lumped in the records with the total furniture and equipment, leaving no alternative but to charge the cost of replacements to expense as they occur.

Since the estimates on furniture and equipment considered in the previous section do not include the cost of the operating equipment items, it must be added to those estimates so that the total original capital investment required for the project can be established.

"Linens" includes not only sheets, pillow cases, towels, napkins and table cloths, but also bath mats, shower curtains, mattress pads, table pads, bed spreads and blankets. Classified as "china and glassware" in addition to tableware are such rooms department equipment as ashtrays for guest rooms and glasses for the bathrooms. "Silver" is both tableware and flatware. "Utensils" includes any tool or piece of equipment that must be picked up in order to be used, although usually only the utensils in the kitchen, bar and cocktail areas are so classified, while such items as brooms, pails, mops, etc., are considered "supplies." Also in this category are soaps, wash cloths, dust rags. The "uniforms" category covers clothing purchased for use of employees, examples being shirts and trousers for maintenance workers and uniforms for kitchen employees, bellmen, maids, waiters and waitresses.

Estimates of the requirements for operating equipment can be based on a per-unit figure, or better, a standard unit of measurement times the logical requirements. For example, the requirement for rooms linen should be the number of room units times the linen requirement for one unit. The linen necessary for guest occupancy should be multiplied by four to give the total linen requirement for operation, allowing provision for changes and laundering as well as for the set in the guest room itself. A similar procedure should be followed in determining the requirement for table settings of china, glassware, linen and silver in the restaurant operation, figuring the anticipated maximum turnover in patrons per seat per day, with adequate provision for warewashing and changes. In each instance it is well to have reserve stock on hand for emergency use. Consultation with kitchen experts will provide the necessary checklist for estimating utensil requirements.

A count of the number of employees who will wear uniforms should be multiplied by at least two so that one set can be worn while the other is being cleaned or laundered. Since in many instances uniforms must be fitted to the person who is to wear them, this double requirement is often disregarded, although there should be some reserve for emergencies.

WORKING CAPITAL REQUIREMENTS

To the funds required for the investment in land, furnishings and equipment it is necessary to add the money required for house funds to finance inventories of supplies and accounts receivable and to meet current bills. Such money is commonly called "working capital" and, although in the ordinary process of operation the project will also incur obligations for supplies and expenses which do not demand immediate cash payment, there should be some provision made to insure that the project will start operations with a good credit standing.

Working capital can be classified as follows:

1. Cash on hand. This consists of change funds for the front-office staff and cashiers who will handle the cash transactions with guests and patrons resulting from sales or payments of account. The amount of money required usually ranges from one-half to three-quarters of one per cent of the estimated revenue from all sources. It is necessary that the employees at the front desk have sufficient money to make change and to cash checks for guests who have proper credit standing. Such service is a convenience often expected by the guest.

2. Cash on deposit. The amount required for this purpose is a variable that depends primarily on the extent of the owner's desire to maintain a liquid and good credit position with respect to current obligations to be paid by check. It is advisable to have sufficient funds on deposit to at least meet current payrolls, utility charges, etc. In the beginning it is also advisable to have enough money to meet emergency expenditures that might occur and to pay expenses until sufficient cash income has been generated to carry on the operation in a normal manner.

3. Accounts receivable. In these days of the credit card it is more necessary than ever to finance the guests' charges. Hotels were formerly considered to be a cash operation, with the guest paying at the end of each week of his stay, or, in the case of shorter stays, upon departure. Many guests and most patrons paid cash for their meals and services in other departments too, whereas these charges are now added to their bill, even including tips, which the motel may find convenient to pay the employee in cash. Today the guest frequently presents a credit card upon checking out, and the bill is collected through the credit card agency or from the guest or his company after he has returned home.

The local resident who patronizes the restaurant has also become credit-minded and frequently charges his meals, receiving a monthly bill against what is called a "city-ledger" account. At any rate, the transaction results in an account receivable to be collected at a later date, and this results in bookkeeping detail and also in the necessity of financing those transactions until they are paid. The current figures on receivables indicate that they average from 3 per cent to 4 per cent of estimated annual revenue from all sources; in other words, total income from motel operations for a 10- to 15-day period.

The foregoing data applies only to regular guests and patrons. If considerable function business is conducted and credit cards are used extensively, the number of days' business represented (frequently called the "spread") may be even higher, depending on the billing policy of the motel. Most motels render their bills immediately upon departure of the guest or at the time that a function is held, but some follow the policy of sending all city-ledger bills out once a month, which obviously means that the accumulation of unbilled accounts will be correspondingly higher.

4. Inventories

    (a) If food inventories turn over approximately 3.33 times per month, the value of the inventory at any one time would average one per cent of annual food sales. An inventory turnover of four times per month is considered quite good. If the establishment cannot obtain most of its food items in the local market it will be necessary to maintain a higher-than-normal inventory to allow for the extra time it will take for shipment of merchandise.

    (b) Beverage inventories can be maintained at 5 per cent to 6 per cent of estimated annual beverage sales, which results in a turnover approximately once every two months. This figure varies, depending on such factors as the ratio of beer and soft drink sales to overall sales and the amount of wine stock carried. A monthly turnover in the beverage inventory is excellent in the ordinary bar and cocktail lounge with a predominant sale of liquor and a well-stocked bar.

    (c) The proper level of supplies inventories is difficult to determine as both items and necessary quantities vary considerably between establishments, depending on local circumstances, contract and delivery requirements. Ordinarily we would estimate one per cent of annual revenue as the capital required for supplies inventories and prepaid expenses. Prepaid expenses also vary in different areas, but for the most part consist of prepaid insurance premiums, license fees and utility deposits. They may also include prepaid property taxes, interest, etc.

All of the items listed, therefore, are commonly called "current assets" and they are offset by "current liabilities" in arriving at the working capital. Although it is possible to operate with a one-to-one ratio—that is, one dollar of current assests to one dollar of current liabilities—it would be prudent to have sufficient cash on deposit to raise the ratio above that level. A current ratio of $1.50 to $1.00 is considered excellent.

The offsetting current liabilities are estimated as follows:

1. Trade creditors' accounts payable. Since most trade creditors' accounts are on a monthly basis, this item can be estimated at one-twelfth the annual cost of sales and services to be supplied by purveyors.

2. Accrued expenses.

  (a) Payroll and payroll taxes can be estimated at one week's gross payroll.

  (b) Other accrued expenses usually consist of utility bills, local taxes, social security and unemployment taxes, etc., and can be estimated at one per cent of total revenue from all sources as a starting point.

  (c) The mortgage, equipment notes and other note obligations will all require current payments of interest and principal which should be included in the current liability section of the financial statement. The normal policy is to include in this category the interest to the date of the statement and the principal payment due within one year from that date.

At the beginning of operations, however, the trade creditors' accounts will not have been fully developed, and when the preliminary estimates of investment capital are prepared the loan commitments may not be known. Therefore the preliminary estimates of working capital must be made up with careful consideration of how such liabilities will affect the financial picture when they become a reality.

PREOPENING EXPENSES

Funds will be necessary to pay the current payroll and other costs incurred prior to the actual opening of the business. A full month's payroll and ample funds for promotion and advertising should be considered as an integral aspect of the capital requirement, a factor that is often overlooked in preliminary calculations. This can be a major item, depending on the ability of the owner to build his operating staff and on his luck in timing the completion of the project to coincide with peak demand season.

It takes time to build a staff, acquaint employees with their duties, clean up after the contractors have finished and put the house in order to receive its first guest. Key personnel will have to be available on the premises at least a month or two before the house is open to the public, and it would not be wise to have the working staff arrive just a day before the guests. Supplies must be received and stored, equipment must be tested, and those responsible should be made familiar with its use. Everyone must be acquainted with his surroundings, his duties and responsibilities, and be indoctrinated in service policies. Price structures should be established and control procedures must be rehearsed. Utilities must be in good working order days before the opening. The advertising and promotion program should have been started long before operations begin. Sometimes operating efficiency is more quickly attained by conducting a series of trial runs before actual opening. As the project nears completion, however, owners and operators understandingly grow anxious to see the revenue start coming in.

SUMMARY

The total investment required for a motel project can thus be summarized as follows:

1. The cost of the land.

2. The cost of preparing the land for the improvement contemplated, incuding parking areas, entrance and driveways.

3. The cost of construction, including all related fees and the cost of financing, insurance, etc., during the construction period.

4. The cost of furnishings and equipment.

5. The cost of the swimming pool and other recreational areas.

6. The cost of operating equipment such as linens, china, glassware, silverware, utensils and uniforms.

7. The necessary working capital to provide cash for house funds; financing of receivables; inventories of food, beverages and supplies; and for prepaid expenses such as insurance, utility deposits, taxes and licenses, plus a sufficient bank balance to meet current expenses.

8. Sufficient funds to cover preopening expenses such as payroll, advertising and promotion.

15

Getting the Right Advice

The need for the prospective investor to seek out expert advice may appear to be overstated. However, as enticing as this field may look, much that is critical to a successful operation can neither be readily observed nor absorbed by the newcomer without professional help. Furthermore, competition becomes keener by the day, increasing with it the advantage of established operators over beginners in the field and making essential a closely guided appraisal of one's chances for success.

The order in which the advice of different specialists is sought can vary, depending on the topography of the site, the potential of the overnight accommodations in the area and the type of operation planned. The major consideration is to take each step in proper sequence so that time and funds devoted to the project will be in proportion to the known facts relating to the project's economic feasability. In general, the following order is acceptable and in most cases will prove to be the most practicable.

The market analyst should be called upon first to determine the need for the facilities, to advise on the proper development of the site and on the extent to which the facilities planned are adequate. He should also prepare a preliminary estimate or budget of the revenue and expenses based on the specific improvements contemplated. Furthermore, it is advisable at this point to consult a good lawyer and perhaps a banker or other person experienced in finance for assistance in determining the proper financial setup, adequacy of capital, clearance of titles, conformity with local restrictions and related legal and financial matters. If the prospects for the project look encouraging at this point, the architect should be contacted, first to determine exactly what type of facilities can be erected on the site and, second, to prepare preliminary sketches suggesting ways of placing the building or buildings most advantageously from the standpoint of appearance and operating efficiency.

As the architect develops his thinking, he may, together with the owner, seek the consulting services of a surveyor, engineer, interior decorator, kitchen equipment engineer, swimming pool expert, etc. These professionals will want to enter the picture before the construction has proceeded too far, thus avoiding restrictions on their work which might add to construction costs and eventual operating expenses. Their specialized experience can be quite valuable at this time, provided that they are not committed to preconceived ideas; and here we would be inclined to defer to the judgment of the architect, since he is the one who can best determine whether the suggestions of each specialist are in keeping with his conception of the entire project.

When the preliminary layout of the buildings, parking areas and recreational facilities has been satisfactorily developed, it will be necessary to check the need for any revision of income and expense provisions made when plans were less specific. Definite decisions can then be made concerning the legal, tax, financing and accounting problems connected with the project and the ultimate form of the business structure of the operation itself. Those in charge of the project will now have to decide the way in which capital is to be provided to cover all costs of the project up to the point where it will be supported by income from operations.

Questions having to do with the sources and extent of available equity money, the sources, extent and terms of any loans or mortgages and the most desirable methods of financing the equipment must be answered before bids can be taken on construction and furnishings. Although quite often the contractors will extend some credit and even participate in the financing, it is good business to have sufficient equity capital at the start so that the project will not be placed in jeopardy because of lack of funds before it is completed. The lending agency, be it a mortgage broker, insurance company, savings and loan association or some other type of financial institution, will ordinarily demand information on the feasibility of the project to help determine the soundness of the loan. The lenders will be interested primarily in learning whether the operation is likely to generate sufficient cash income from the start to repay the loan as required, as well as the relationship of the amount of the loan to the amount of the entire investment.

When the financing of the project has been fully arranged, final plans can be developed and bids taken from various qualified contractors. Once construction is under way it is time to give top priority to obtaining advice on the actual operation of the establishment. If the owner is to operate the motel himself, he must begin to get his crew together, particularly the key people. If a manager is to be hired, he should be on the premises in plenty of time to familiarize himself with the property. It would be well for him to be in close contact with the architect, builder, and others involved in developing the property during the early stages of construction so that his experiences can be utilized. He might, at the same time, be employed in such preopening activities as advertising, promotion, and employee training.

Quite often the selection of the manager is made before the financing has been arranged. Financial institutions believe it extremely important that the type of management be decided early in the planning stages. They may refuse to make the loan unless they have adequate assurance that the management is experienced and professionally proven.

It may be elected to lease either the entire premises or a part of them, such as the catering department, in which case the terms of the lease will help to determine the extent of the landlord's investment, while the rental terms will determine his share of the income generated by the project. Because the tenant becomes, in effect, a partner in the business he should be qualified and able to justify the economic feasibility of the venture through his ability to operate profitably. Any investment made by the tenant will become security for the lease, and the extent of that investment, his responsibilities and obligations, will be spelled out in the lease. His credit standing and history as an operator will be investigated by the lending agencies as well as by the owners.

Many chain organizations in the hotel and motel field have an established pattern of operation. There are also franchise organizations which assist in determining a project's economic feasibility and offer to help or take an active part in the financing, design, construction, furnishing and operation of a motel. Both groups also stress their value as referral organizations in developing sales. A few organizations offer their services as professional operators on a management contract basis. Each of the various types offers both advantages and limitations from the standpoint of participation and experience in operation. The motel owner must base his decision on whether or not to team up with them on his particular circumstances.

MARKET ANALYSIS

Before calling on the professional analyst to determine the extent and type of need in a given area for motel or motor hotel facilities, it is best to make one's own appraisal of the location. The time involved in such a study will vary, of course, depending on the type of operation contemplated. For example, determining the most suitable type of overnight accommodations for a resort area may require an extremely extensive study of the visitors' backgrounds. Before undertaking such a study the prospective investor might make a personal visit to the area and its surrounding approaches to determine whether sufficient activity exists to warrant a more detailed examination.

Construction of a motel on a through highway should not be considered until the traffic patterns of tourist and business travel within a radius of at least 150 miles of the site have been reviewed. Adding to the present facilities in an urban or suburban location should not be considered until the prospective investor has visited the locality and studied the effectiveness of existing accommodations in serving community needs.

Those persons who are acquainted with a particular area, its economy and prospects should be interviewed, particularly if they have some influence in the community, either political or financial. Discussions with local bankers, municipal authorities, chamber of commerce executives and state and local highway department personnel should be very helpful in ascertaining the need for additional motel or motor hotel facilities.

It is entirely possible that the knowledge gained from such interviews will discourage the prospective investor from further consideration of the development, especially in an area where the public evidences a negative attitude. However, experience has shown that most municipal authorities and local business leaders, being boosters of their communities, desire to encourage the construction of new motor hotel facilities, whether or not there is an actual need for them. It is therefore imperative that after the prospective owner's appraisal has been completed a professional market analyst be called in to evaluate the reliability of the data on which the initial conclusions are based. If the prospective investor is already the owner of the land under consideration, his judgment may be warped by his own desire to develop the site, and thus he needs the corroboration such a professional study can give him, even more than the individual who does not have a strong reason for building on that particular site.

The market analyst selected should be an impartial professional with years of experience. He should not be in a position to gain materially from the conclusions of his studies. The selection of a consultant should not be based on the amount of his fee, but rather on the amount of direct experience he has had in the field of guest accommodations and the access he may have to helpful facts and statistics upon which to base his conclusions and suggestions. He will be asked to study the area, determine the need for guest facilities there and suggest the way in which the site under consideration can best be developed to answer that need. He should also be qualified to make realistic projections of income and expenses at reasonable levels of business for the type of facilities which would seem best suited to the local market and the site. The economic feasibility of the project should be determined on the basis of his projections.

Most reputable firms qualified to handle this type of assignment will agree to perform it in two steps: (1) a discussion of the findings of the actual market study with the client; (2) a presentation of suggestions for sitedevelopmentand projections of earnings for the types of facilities suggested. Naturally, if the market study results are negative —and they often are—there would appear to be no economic justification for going ahead with part two of the study. On the other hand, if the market study indicates a need for a type of facility not originally considered by the developer, a revision of the original plans should be discussed with him before continuing the study. If the market study is encouraging, the continuation of the assignment into its second phase by the expert who has gathered and prepared the background material would, of course, be advisable.

ARCHITECTS AND ENGINEERS

The selection of an architect with previous experience in the field of motels and motor hotels frequently has many side benefits. Not only does he have the experience that will enable him to design facilities that are most practical, but he also usually knows of engineering consultants and other experts in related fields. The American Institute of Architects will recommend qualified architects to a person considering the construction of a particular type of building. The individual or firm chosen should have the consulting services of a local architect in order to insure full compliance with local codes and ordinances in the final plans and specifications. Since the relationship between architect and developer is often a personal one, the best results are obtained when their personalities are compatible. The final selection for this assignment can be made only on the basis of personal judgment, and the fee should not be the primary consideration, being far outweighed by the values of experience, ability and personality.

Almost all areas and communities have local zoning and building regulations which must be met. As soon he has been selected, the architect should be provided with as many specifications as the developer can prepare and should be asked to submit preliminary drawings and sketches of the proposed facilities. The owner's specifications should include some idea of the size and type of operation to be constructed and the amount he believes he can afford to spend on the project. A copy of the market analyst's report should be given to the architect, and all of the consultants and professionals engaged to participate in the project should be encouraged to cooperate with him, for from the moment he is brought into the picture, the architect becomes the key man on the job.

LEGAL, ACCOUNTING AND TAX ADVICE

Professional advice should be sought with respect to gaining title to the property, complying with laws pertaining to its development, selecting the most advantageous financing structure and initiating a system of accounting and control once the operation opens for business. Early in the planning stages the investor should engage the services of an attorney familiar with local and state regulations relating to the operation of motor hotels and to business organizations in general and an accountant or accounting firm with broad experience in the accommodations field and in tax matters.

Their counsel will bear on decisions such as: whether the facilities will be owner-operated or leased; what licenses must be obtained; ways of handling other regulatory matters and tax aspects of the proposed project to best advantage; how to organize the operating budget; and the most effective way to recruit and train operating personnel.

OTHER CONSULTANTS

That consultant who advises on problems of finance might be the owner himself, a promoter, lawyer, accountant or banker. It is most important that he be capable of putting the financial structure together in the proper way, to ensure as nearly as possible that there will be sufficient capital to enable the project to reach the point of self-support on a sound basis.

The other consultants who would normally be used are advisors in interior decoration and furnishings, swimming pool and recreational areas, food facility engineers and those in any other area where special experience may be needed. Certainly someone familiar with actual operations should also be employed early in the program if the investor is not an experienced operator or does not intend to manage the property himself.

SUMMARY

The questions on which professional advice is usually sought are presented in the following checklist:

1. Market Analysis
   a. What are the indications of economic growth in the area?
   b. What is the probable future course of development of the community?
   c. How keen would the competition be from existing and contemplated housing and feeding accommodations in the area, and what is the present status of each of those operations?
   d. Is the property readily accessible to private and public transportation?
   e. Is the proposed development of the site economically feasible?
   f. What are the needs of the guest and the community?
   g. Where will the business come from?

2. Architectural and Engineering
   a. Can the proposed facilities be adapted to the limitations of the site?
   b. Are utilities such as sewage disposal, water, fuel, electricity and gas service readily available?
   c. Do zoning and building restrictions permit the type of development proposed?
   d. Are the costs of developing the site and its improvements justified by the potential income of the proposed motel?

3. Legal, Tax and Accounting
   a. Can clear title to the land be obtained?
   b. Is it advisable to purchase or to lease the property?
   c. How should the venture be financed? Can a sale- and lease-

back arrangement be used to advantage? What terms should be sought on a loan?

d. What form of financial organization would be best?

e. What is the most effective system of internal control and book-keeping?

f. What forms for reporting information on operations should be prepared daily, weekly and monthly?

g. What are the income tax problems involved and how are they best handled?

h. What are the local property taxes, the requirements for licenses, inspections, etc.?

4. Operational

a. Should the property be leased to an operating group? If so, in whole or in part?

b. Is the location suitable for promotion of group business, social events, conventions and business meetings?

c. What are the local employment problems?

d. What will be the status of the owner, operator and management of the project in the community?

e. What are the local housing problems in connection with executive personnel; which employees of the motel will be expected to live on the premises?

f. What, if any, are problems of transportation for both employees and guests?

The foregoing list is by no means exhaustive. Additional questions will undoubtedly occur as the project progresses. Many of the subjects mentioned in this section are dealt with in greater detail in other chapters. Our only purpose here has been to indicate the areas in which professional advice is available and to stress that it is generally good policy to seek it and heed it.

16

Business Structures and Financing

We have presented a general picture of the evolution of the motel and motor hotel business, tracing its beginnings from the early tourist court and motel. These facilities were usually financed and operated by individuals as sole proprietorships and records were kept on a simple cash basis. Particularly in those businesses operated only as sidelines, records were often buried in a presentation of the individual's overall financial picture. Even though the field grew steadily in importance, demanding full-time involvement for many operators, the sole proprietorship form of financial structure remained dominant. However, as projects became larger and more elaborate it was obvious that a greater amount of capital than many individuals could afford to risk in a single venture was becoming a prime requisite. As a result it became necessary to finance these larger ventures through a more involved structure.

Sole proprietorships, partnerships and corporations are the most common forms of financial organization, although others exist, such as cooperatives, joint ventures, syndicates and trusts. The extent to which these three forms exist and influence the motel field is indicated in the figures compiled by Dr. Howard A. Morgan of the University of Arizona, who directed a study made under a research grant from the Small Business Administration. A report on this study's preliminary findings was made at the "Motorama" trade convention, held by the National Restaurant Association and the American Motor Hotel Association in May, 1962. The following figures on the relative popularity and size of the different types of financial structure, based primarily on published Bureau of Census findings, were taken from Dr. Morgan's study with his permission.

LEGAL FORMS OF ORGANIZATION

	Year 1948 Number	Per Cent	Year 1954 Number	Per Cent	Year 1958 Number	Per Cent
Establishments						
Sole proprietorships	19,314	74.7%	23,177	78.9%	32,330	78.4%
Partnerships	6,082	23.5	5,015	17.1	6,599	16.0
Corporations	463	1.8	1,177	4.0	2,319	5.6
Total	25,859	100.0%	29,369	100.0%	41,248	100.0%

Sales Receipts	Amount	Per Cent	Amount	Per Cent	Amount	Per Cent
Sole proprietorships	$124,380,000	63.8%	$277,651,000	61.1%	$454,333,000	53.6%
Partnerships	55,700,000	28.6	111,128,000	24.4	190,489,000	22.5
Corporations	14,721,000	7.6	66,097,000	14.5	202,205,000	23.9
Total	$194,801,000	100.0%	$454,876,000	100.0%	$847,027,000	100.0%

Payroll	Year 1948 Amount	Per Cent	Year 1954 Amount	Per Cent	Year 1958 Amount	Per Cent
Sole proprietorships	$13,072,000	58.3%	$30,809,000	48.4%	$51,538,000	38.7%
Partnerships	5,620,000	25.0	15,547,000	24.4	32,299,000	24.3
Corporations	3,754,000	16.7	17,354,000	27.2	49,218,000	37.0
Total	$22,446,000	100.0%	$63,710,000	100.0%	$133,055,000	100.0%

Number of Employees	Number	Per Cent	Number	Per Cent	Number	Per Cent
Sole proprietorships	10,562	62.6%	18,444	51.6%	34,988	46.4%
Partnerships	4,412	26.1	9,397	26.3	17,980	23.8
Corporations	1,903	11.3	7,918	22.1	22,445	29.8
Total	16,877	100.0%	35,759	100.0%	75,413	100.0%

Averages Per Establishment	*Sales Receipts*	*Payroll*	*Ratio to Sales*	*Number of Employees*
Sole proprietorships				
1948	$ 6,440	$ 677	10.52%	.55
1954	11,980	1,329	11.09	.80
1958	14,053	1,594	11.34	1.08
Partnerships				
1948	$ 9,158	$ 924	10.09%	.73
1954	22,190	3,100	13.97	1.87
1958	28,866	4,895	16.96	2.72
Corporations				
1948	$31,795	$8,108	25.50%	4.11
1954	56,158	14,745	26.26	6.73
1958	87,195	21,224	24.34	9.68

The foregoing statistics indicate significant changes in the motel business over the past decade. While the continuing growth and numerical dominance of the smaller motel are evident, the figures also reflects a substantial increase in the number of larger and more elaborate establishments, with an accompanying growth in influence. As a result, there was a steady increase in the total volume of business of motels using the corporate form of financial organization.

The payroll figures indicate that the ratios of costs to sales and the number of employees per establishment were comparatively low in the sole proprietorship group, largely because the proprietors themselves did much of the work in those motels and, for the most part, did not draw salaries or wages. In partnerships, there was some management payroll but it was not a true cost of the services rendered because the partners, too, tended to keep their own salaries at a minimum. In the corporate form the number of employees and cost ratios are more truly representative of services rendered and therefore may be used for purposes of comparison in measuring efficiency of operation and setting up budgets or estimates of income possibilities.

The sole proprietor—and to some extent the partner—often reflects in his net profit not only the return on his capital investment, but also compensation for his operating efforts. This point is sometimes overlooked by the inexperienced motel purchaser who is then in danger of paying a price based on a profit figure that is inflated by the failure of the motel owner to draw fair compensation for his services.

SOLE PROPRIETORSHIPS

In this form of financial structure all of the required equity capital is provided by one person, who therefore receives the total profit after providing for the expenses of operation and the costs of any borrowings needed for the motel project. The owner of a sole proprietorship is primarily an independent operator, although it is likely that he will belong to a referral organization in the motel field. He may even hold a franchise, although most of the franchise chain establishments are comparatively large and are likely to be partnerships or corporations. The facilities may range in size from the small man-and-wife operation to the most elaborate type of motor hotel, the distinguishing factor being that of sole ownership.

By joining a referral, endorsing or franchise group for the purpose of gaining some of the competitive advantages of a chain operation, the owner of a sole proprietorship restricts his freedom to the extent that he agrees to meet the group's specifications as to operating policies and facilities in order to qualify for membership. He remains independent, however, since there is no division of actual ownership with others under the arrangement just described. Often it is argued that the local economy is better served and civic responsibility is more evident when the property is owned by a local independent operator. He has a more direct personal interest in management, whereas the policies of the chain operation may be influenced by the fact that ownership and management control are directed from outside the community, which circumstance could adversely affect both community and guest relations. It is in this group of independent operators that the direct contact of the host and guest is most evident, and since motels are a personal service business this is an advantage on which the owner of a sole proprietorship can capitalize.

PARTNERSHIPS

In this form of financial structure more than one person provides the equity capital and participates in the operating results. Quite often the partnership is a team consisting of two or more persons who are to conduct the operations and others who provide the necessary capital but are not active in management. An individual may do no more than provide capital for an operation, becoming what is known as a "silent partner," in that his name and connection with the project may not become publicly known. He is, in effect, the financial backer of the project, with a participation in the profits as his incentive for investment.

Some states recognize a limited partner's status, but the general conception is that all partners are personally responsible for the liabilities and acts of the partnership. The contributions to equity capital and the division of earnings are determined by the partnership agreement. Although a partnership may be formed by oral agreement or by implication, it is advisable that the agreement be in writing and prepared by good legal counsel in order that there be no subsequent misunderstanding between partners as to each one's authority, responsibility and rights of participation in the affairs and profits of the partnership. Thus the agreement will outline the manner in which each partner will make his contribution to capital and the amount of capital he must maintain, the manner in which his profit participation is to be determined, the circumstances under which he may cash withdrawals and the extent to which he is responsible for the obligations of the partnership and its operations.

If one partner is to have charge of management, the contract should outline his compensation and perquisites as well as the extent of his authority and responsibility for determining policies, incurring debts, hiring staff, etc. The agreement should also outline the method of settling differences between partners, the circumstances and manner in which the contract may be terminated, the extent to which the claims of heirs and assigns may be considered and the basis on which assessments may be made to cover possible losses. Often the capital contribution of one of the partners may be the land or other property involved, in which case its value to the partnerhip must be assessed.

There are many forms of partnership, and it is not possible to mention the variety of contingencies that would cover them. The best advice is to arrange for legal counsel familiar with the parties involved and the intent of the partnership to draw up the agreement in a form that will best protect all concerned.

In a partnership the usual accounting is to show each partner's capital contribution as his equity account, to which his share of earnings is added. If the original capital is deemed sufficient to warrant that any earnings may be subject to withdrawal, the practical way to treat the accounts during operation is to credit each partner's earnings to a drawing account and to charge his withdrawals against that balance. The typical partnership arrangement is that the participation in earnings should be in proportion to the capital invested by each partner and that withdrawals should be made in like proportion. However, these agreements are flexible and they often specify that the distribution of profits shall be on a basis not at all related to the capital contribution of the partners. For example, it could be arranged that any profits would first be used to pay the silent partner a specified return on his capital contribution, with any excess being distributed equally to the partners.

It is usually true that the larger the numbers of partners in a venture, the greater is the necessity of carefully working out the legal aspects in order to insure a smooth continuity of operation. Projects that are syndicated by the purchase of "units" or "participating certificates," are really forms of partnership. In those instances the affairs of the partnership are usually placed in the hands of a management committee approved by the participants, with members of that committee looking after the affairs of the group. Often, arrangements are made by the committee to hire a manager for the actual operation of the motel or to lease the facilities to a person or organization with experience in motel management.

Several of the organizations granting franchises enter into a partnership arrangement with the operators of individual motel properties holding their franchises. Tax considerations often are an important factor in bringing about such an arrangement, but there are other, additional advantages.

The partnership form of financial structure is used mainly by the independent motel or by the motel belonging to a referral or franchise group. Generally, the establishment owned by a partnership is larger than the sole proprietorship motel but smaller than that owned by a corporation. The obvious advantages of partner ownership are that it does not demand one individual's total resources for equity capital and that it may allow for more extensive facilities. A few partnerships have grown into chain operations, but more generally they are limited to independently operated establishments.

CORPORATIONS

The corporate arrangement is used when investors desire to limit their financial responsibilities and liabilities to the amount of their investment and the organizers of the project find it easier to acquire the necessary equity capital for the project by putting their participants in an investment position with respect to the amounts involved. The advantages of the corporate form in terms of flexibility, stability and limitation of liability are quite evident in the larger operations, particularly the chain or group businesses.

A corporation is an artificial entity created under the laws of the state to act as an individual; as such, it must meet the requirements of the state in which it is incorporated with respect to the extent of its responsibility and area of operation. The application for a corporation charter usually states the number and kind of shares to be authorized, the type of business to be conducted, the life of the corporation and the number of shares subscribed. The articles of incorporation and bylaws must be outlined in detail and be in conformity with state law.

These laws differ from state to state in many respects, with some of the differences involving requirements of stock ownership for officers and directors, the number of stockholders and directors that a company must have, voting rights and methods of voting, the frequency of stockholder meetings, the keeping of minute books and other corporate records, and the types of reports which must be made. Therefore it is vital that these organization and operating procedures be advised and directed by a competent lawyer.

The equity capital of a corporation is represented by shares of stock issued for value to those who invest in the company. Once its shares have been issued, the corporation becomes an entity which operates through its directors, who are elected by the stockholders. There are many variations in the kinds of stock, the ordinary common stock being considered the prime evidence of equity ownership. But in many cases certain preferences are given to investors as to their participation in the earnings and capital distribution by issuing a separate class of stock to cover these benefits. However, we will not attempt to elaborate on these points and will confine the discussion to the corporate form itself.

The major advantages of a corporate setup are:

1. The limitation of the liability of the shareholder to the amount payable for the shares purchased.

2. The fact that capital is represented by transferable shares, usually in sufficiently small denominations to make their sale or distribution quite flexible.

3. The corporation is a distinct legal entity for all business purposes.

4. The corporation provides stability and permanence of organization.

5. The management is in the hands of an elected board of directors acting through its officers and agents.

6. The fact that the first five advantages listed make it an easier and more practical way to obtain equity capital.

The major disadvantages are:

1. The limitations of activity to what is outlined in the charter and permissible under the corporate laws of the state.

2. The taxation of earnings before distribution of profits to the owners, and the need to pay franchise and capital stock taxes.

3. The need to file many reports both to the state and to shareholders. Being a creature of law, the corporation must conduct its business in compliance with the law and all of its proceedings must be a matter of written record.

4. The need to make certain corporate affairs a matter of public record in order to comply with state and federal requirements.

The extent of liability for federal and state income taxes has become a major consideration in determining the best form of financial organization for a given situation in the field of motels and motor hotels, just as it has in all business endeavors. For that reason it would be well to have the advice of a tax expert before making a final decision to use the corporate form. The present rates of taxation on income tend to overshadow the other advantages of the corporate form to the point where the tax effect of the transaction is sometimes considered before thought is given as to whether the motel involved is a good risk.

If the individual stockholders are in a high tax bracket, they may find it advantageous to build up their equity by letting the profits accumulate in the corporation and holding their shares over a period of more than six months in the hope of eventually selling them at a profit, which would be a long-term capital gain taxable at a lower rate than straight income. If the stockholders are not in the high tax brackets and are interested in receiving a cash distribution of corporate profits, this can be accomplished only by means of a dividend. Thus the earnings of a corporation have already been taxed and the dividends again are taxed as income when received by the individual investors. Starting in 1958, however, Sections 1371-77 of the Federal Tax Law gave stockholders in a domestic corporation having one class of stock and ten or fewer individual shareholders the option, upon their election, of eliminating the liability for the corporation income tax and being taxed instead as individuals on their respective share of the earnings. This was done to assist small business operations by putting their shareholders in a position to enjoy some of the advantages of the corporate form without subjecting them to the "double taxation" just described. Because motels and motor hotels are largely in the "small business" category that tax relief provision might be expected to have wide application in their field. However, it has been used only sparingly. What has prevented it from gaining greater popularity is the requirement that all stockholders must agree to add their share of the corporate income to their own taxable earnings.

In a closely held corporation it is possible that certain distributions to the stockholders directly involved in the operation may be justified when paid as officers' salaries. Also, some justification may exist for regarding a portion of the funds furnished by interested parties in connection with the original financing as loans or secondary mortgages, the interest on which would be deductible for tax purposes. The payments of principal on such loans are tax-free and are made possible by having some of the earnings retained in the business. Both the officers' salaries and interest paid on loans from stockholders are closely checked for proper justification by the income tax authorities and sometimes, if abuses are found, these items are considered to be dividends not deductible for the corporation, yet taxable to the recipient.

It is readily apparent that as motels have developed into large, costly projects, the corporate form of financial structure has become the most suitable. In the majority of cases its use makes it easier to raise substantial amounts of equity capital and to obtain professional management. The advantages of securing financial backing through the sale of stock seem to outweigh by far the disadvantages related earlier in this section. The increase in the use of the corporate form indicates that the motel business has firmly established its position in the travel market.

SUPPLEMENTAL CAPITAL

The form of legal and financial organization best suited to the project depends on how and by whom the initial equity money is contributed. The next consideration in financing is how supplemental funds are to be obtained, for ordinarily the equity holder does not have sufficient funds to finance the entire project himself and must borrow in order to complete it. His own investment may even be too small to give him a sufficient equity to interest anyone in making a loan on the project. In that case he must either find one or more partners or incorporate and sell stock.

Because of the risk involved, a purchaser of an equity interest in a motel or motor hotel would probably expect a return of 10 per cent to 15 per cent on his money, plus some assurance of the safety of principal until it is fully repaid. In the event that the project is attractive and interesting to people in the community as a civic improvement, the factor of return on the investment would not be as important a consideration as would otherwise be the case. For the most part, however, equity funds are obtained from private sources. If the project is a corporation and the stock is to be sold publicly in a given state, it must be qualified under that state's "blue sky" laws. For national distribution it must also qualify under the Federal Securities and Exchange Commission laws and regulations.

"Going public" has become increasingly popular in the past few years, with the general public showing as great an interest in the stock market as it did in real estate bond issues in the 1920's. Since that earlier era, however, the S.E.C. and state authorities have initiated procedures of disclosures on security issues to be offered publicly. These procedures are intended to ensure that the investor has available to him sufficient facts about the stock to buy with his eyes open. Complying with the various state and federal regulations is a complicated process requiring the filing of a great deal of information in order to obtain clearance of a stock issue. Naturally, the work involved should be handled by lawyers and accountants familiar with the procedures.

Companies which have had their securities cleared for public sale must issue statements to be filed at regular intervals with the commission in accordance with their regulations, certified to by public accountants and attested to by the officers of the company. There are exemptions outlined by both local and federal laws and regulations based on the size and extent of distribution of security issues. A lawyer will be familiar with those regulations and should be consulted to insure that the securities issued by smaller and more closely held projects comply with them.

Many of the chain motel and motor hotel groups have sold stock to the public. For a long time the stock of hotel chains such as Hilton, Sheraton, Hotel Corporation of America, and Knott has been traded on the New York and the American Stock Exchanges. Shares of Howard Johnson's recently were admitted to trading on the New York Stock Exchange. The prices of Holiday Inn stock and several other motel chains are quoted daily in the "over-the-counter" listings.

Regardless of the extent to which the equity capital is distributed, it is just good business to prepare a financial projection of the capital requirements of the project, the manner in which the capital is expected to be obtained and the investment which would seem warranted by the potential income from the operation of the property. We assume at this point, of course, that the feasibility study has been made and that its indications are encouraging. This first involves adding up the costs necessary to bring the project to completion, ready to open for business. Next comes the projection of the amount that might be supplied by long-term debt. It may also be necessary to plan for a commitment on interim funds required until the long-term loan becomes operative. A decision must be reached as to whether financing will be aided by leasing the project or sections of it, and consideration must be given to the possibilities of reducing the requirement of equity capital by obtaining secondary financing, including equipment contracts or leases. The balance of the required capital must come from equity funds. One of the hazards to the success of any business is that of being under-financed, a situation which often occurs when the original financial projections are made haphazardly or are ignored by the original promoter and equity investors.

To many investors one of the attractions of an investment in improved real estate, such as a motel or motor hotel, is the possible income tax advantage or "shelter" that is inherent in depreciation allowances under current income tax law. The use of accelerated depreciation to reduce the income tax burden during the early years of operation often makes it possible to pay off long-term obligations at a fast rate and to increase the equity holdings proportionately. In fact, securities have been sold on the premise that the funds would be invested in the purchase of properties on which a high depreciation could be taken, enabling the company to make regular payments to its security holders as a "tax-free" return of capital. In such instances it is expected that the depreciation charges will enable the company to show an operating loss even though sufficient cash has been generated to make possible regular distributions to security holders. This is an extreme condition, quoted to illustrate the importance attached to "cash flow," not as a recommendation for such securities.

The equity owner is interested in cash flow, and the projection of operations should include a statement prepared on that basis. However, it is preceded by the regular projection of earnings, for the cash flow statement must start with an estimate of available income.

Being theoretical and based on the plan and expected potential of the motel facilities, the projection of income is intended only to give some idea of the possibilities of earnings, usually determined by using industry averages of income and costs. The accuracy of the estimates is dependent on the experience of the individual who prepares them. It must be understood that such estimates or projections are not a guarantee of what actual future operations will produce.

Later chapters on accounting provide examples of operating statements based on averages from recent annual studies. Here the computation of cash flow is explained by example:

We have assumed the existence of plans for a 150-room motor hotel requiring a total capital investment of $1,500,000. The estimated gross operating income—the estimated annual earning available for financing, depreciation and income taxes—is $200,000. Note that the capital investment is 7.5 times this earnings figure, the rough basis often used as a starting point in the purchase or evaluation of a hotel or motel property.

The owners of the project usually want to obtain as large a first mortgage as possible in order to ease the problems of producing equity money or obtaining secondary financing. Lending agencies have just the opposite view, for they are interested primarily in the security of their commitment. Therefore, most of the primary, or first-mortgage, loans furnish only 50 per cent to 60 per cent of the total capital requirement. Sometimes a larger loan is made if prospects for the success of the project appear to be unusually good. Another yardstick often used by lending institutions in determining the amount of a loan is that the available earnings before interest, depreciation and income taxes should amount to twice the annual loan requirement for payment of interest and principal.

To the lending party, money is a commodity and its price is determined by the rate of interest, the commissions or discount and other concessions to be paid and made by the borrower. The rate of interest is also influenced by conditions in the current money market, including variations in the supply of funds available for lending. Interest rates on first mortgage money vary considerably, depending on the risks involved. At present, 5 per cent money is scarce, the present rate now ranging from 6 per cent to 7 per cent.

Another factor is the term of the loan, which is the length of time the debt is expected to be outstanding. Most first mortgage loans now must be repaid in from 15 to 20 years, with interest and principal payable monthly on the basis of a set schedule. This amount is often called "the constant," in that as the principal and interest are paid off in installments the amount of interest diminishes, and the payment of principal is thereby made correspondingly larger. This accelerates the repayment of principal and results in the cash requirement for interest and principal payment remaining constant throughout the term of the loan. For our example we have assumed a 20-year loan at 6.5 per cent and show the cash flow on the basis of both a 50 per cent and a 60 per cent loan.

In our example the first calculation is that of estimated net profit after subtracting the amounts of the first year's mortgage interest and federal income tax provision at current corporation rates from the gross operating profit. We have also assumed that the capital investment is made up as follows:

Land	$ 150,000	Swimming pool	$ 25,000
Building	1,000,000	Organization and	
Furnishings	275,000	preopening costs	50,000
Total	$1,500,000		

Straight-line depreciation is calculated at 3 per cent for the building and 10 per cent for the furnishings and swimming pool.

Calculations are as follows:

	Based on $750,000 loan	Ratios to $750,000 equity	Based on $900,000 loan	Ratios to $600,000 equity
Gross operating profit	$200,000	26.67%	$200,000	33.33%
Deduct:				
Depreciation	60,000	8.00	60,000	10.00
First-year interest	48,193	6.43	57,832	9.64
Total deductions	$108,193	14.43%	$117,832	19.64%
Taxable income	91,807	12.24	82,168	13.69
Federal tax provision	42,240	5.63	37,227	6.20
Net profit	$ 49,567	6.61%	$ 44,941	7.49%

The next step is the cash-flow calculation, summarized as follows:

Cash Flow	Based on $750,000 loan	Ratios to $750,000 Equity	Based on $900,000 loan	Ratios to $600,000 Equity
Gross operating profit	$200,000	26.67%	$200,000	33.33%
Deduct:				
Annual loan payment (principal and interest)	67,102	8.95	80,522	13.42
Estimate of annual replacements of furnishings	20,000	2.67	20,000	3.33
First year's income tax	42,240	5.63	37,227	6.20
Total deductions	$129,342	17.25%	$137,749	22.95%
Cash flow to equity investors	$ 70,658	9.42%	$ 62,251	10.38%

The loan requirement of principal and interest, based on constant monthly payments, is met about three times for the 50 per cent loan and two and one-half times for the 60 per cent loan, indicating that the higher loan might be obtainable on this basis of measurement.

Since the depreciation charge does not require a cash outlay it is added back to the net profit in calculating the cash flow. However, in its place there will be expenditures necessary for replacements of furniture, fixtures and equipment during the life of the project; and experience indicates that they average from 50 per cent to 100 per cent of the depreciation charge. In this example, we used two-thirds of the furnishings and swimming pool depreciation to cover that estimated cash outlay.

It is apparent that if the accelerated depreciation method is used for income tax purposes, an additional deduction of $60,000 would be allowable in the first year, reducing the income tax by $31,200 in the first instance and $30,577 in the second, which if added to the cash flow would leave $101,856 (13.58 per cent) to equity investors with a 50 per cent loan and $92,828 (15.47 per cent) to those with a 60 per cent loan, thus advancing the equity leverage in the first years of the project considerably and indicating why these depreciation methods are a factor in making real estate improvement projects attractive to many investors. The hitch is, of course, that the depreciation must be earned in order to take full advantage of this factor, and in the early years of a motel project it takes time to generate the earning power anticipated in the preliminary projections. In earlier days motels showed profits immediately upon opening, but as competition has grown, the cost of advertising and promotion, the preopening costs and the expenses incurred in settling down to a smooth operation have more often than not resulted in a period of a year or more before the net earnings are realized and stabilized.

Most equity investors regard a portion of the principal payment on the loan as an element of increase in their equity values, since the loans are usually over a 15- to 20-year term and the property itself is expected to have a much longer useful life. As the loan is paid off it may also be possible to refinance at a much lower basis of payment, and at the time the loans are paid off the equity investors can realize the entire value of the property. Thus they are interested in the cash flow from two points of view, first as an indication of the possibilities of a cash return on their investment and second as an indication of the rate of increase in equity value through debt reduction.

BORROWED CAPITAL FUNDS

Theoretically, a mortgage is a transfer of the property title to a new owner with the condition that the original owner, or mortgagor, may reacquire title by paying the loan for which the mortgage is security in accordance with the terms of the obligation. In practice, the mortgage is regarded as a pledge of property as security for the loan, and the person lending the money, called the mortgagee, has the right to acquire the property under foreclosure proceedings in the event of default on the terms of the loan. Thus, the ownership of the property remains with the borrower for all practical purposes so long as he complies with the terms of his obligation and meets the stipulated payments of principal and interest on the loan.

In the event that the amount of the loan is too large to be financed by one person or group and necessitates the sale of this obligation to many persons, the mortgage instrument becomes a "deed of trust" and the bonds that are issued under this deed are the security evidence or receipt for the amount loaned by each person, indicating that portion of the mortgage that is owned by the holder of the bond. The mortgage or deed of trust and bonds issued under its terms are involved legal documents; to insure their proper execution, both mortgagor and mortgagee should turn to legal counsel.

The first mortgage form of borrowing is typical of motel and motor hotel projects. This type of mortgage gives the mortgagee a lien on the property covered in the mortgage and on the income resulting from its operation to the extent of the sums involved, prior to all other obligations except those exempted by state or federal law, such as taxes and wages. Thus it takes precedence over the claims of trade creditors and other current obligations of operation, as well as any secondary financing or claims of the equity holders. It holds the primary or first claim on the net earnings generated by the operation of the motel, further secured by a first claim on the title to the property in the event of default.

The sources of first mortgage money are many and varied, including individuals, insurance companies, building and loan associations, certain fraternal and religious organizations, pension and employees' welfare trusts, etc. Banking institutions confine themselves primarily to short-term loans, but are instrumental in providing interim funds for construction periods secured by mortgage commitments and in the financing of loans for rehabilitation and improvement of properties where the sums are not large and the bank officials' knowledge of the property and its management warrants their confidence. The Small Business Administration of the federal government is also in a position to make loans in cooperation with the local banker for purposes of rehabilitation and improvement of existing properties.

The local banker is in an excellent position to help plan the financing and should be consulted at an early stage of the development of a new project or in the event that cash is needed for rehabilitation, expansion or improvement of an existing property. However, persons attempting to place a first mortgage are most usually concerned with financing a new property and will either deal directly with the lender or act through a mortgage broker. Many lending institutions prefer to have their commitments handled through a broker because of his familiarity with their loan requirements and limitations and the fact that it may be more practicable for the broker to assemble the necessary data to support the feasibility of the loan.

In making a loan the mortgagee will want to know that title to the property is free and clear and that the project is a sound venture capable of generating sufficient earnings to cover the loan requirements and to warrant sufficient return to the equity owners to minimize the chances of financial difficulty and the possible costs of foreclosure. The lender will also be interested in seeing a projection of the range of earnings based on various levels of occupancy and sales volume, preferably compiled by an unbiased and financially disinterested person, such as a public accountant familiar with motel and motor hotel operations. He will need to have all background material covering the feasibility of the project and will want to examine the background of the owners and proposed management. In the same manner he must be satisfied as to the ability and experience of the architect and, through contractor's commitments, the reliability of cost estimates for the project. In many loan contracts, the money for construction is advanced upon the presentation of the architect's certificates for payment to the contractors and the presentation of invoices for equipment and furnishings. Also important to the mortgagee is assurance that all zoning requirements, licenses and other legal necessities are covered.

If the motel is to be constructed on leased land, it will very probably be necessary for the landowner to subordinate his lease rights, since otherwise the mortgagee's position as first lien holder on the property would be weakened, and lending institutions hesitate to make loans unless the fee or land title is clearly a part of their security. Most often the furniture, furnishings and equipment are also included in the mortgage agreement through a chattel mortgage on such property acquired or to be acquired. However, there are instances where the financing is intended to cover only construction and the security is confined primarily to the real estate, with chattel-mortgage rights being subject to the prior lien of the furnishings house based on their chattel or installment equipment contract, which usually passes title to the motel upon full payment.

Financing through a first mortgage implies that the major risks of the enterprise are borne by the equity holders, with less risk taken by the holders of secondary financing such as second mortgages, chattel mortgages and equipment contracts. The risk factor will be weighed by the mortgagee in determining the interest rate and other considerations which may be involved in making the loan. Thus, although a 60 per cent loan may be justified, the loan cost factors might be lessened with a 50 per cent loan. The term, or life, of the loan is also influential. A 15-year pay-off usually means a smaller interest factor than a 20-year loan.

Making a loan involves certain costs to the lender which are usually covered by a discount factor if the loan is made direct; or if those costs are borne by the mortgage broker, by the payment of a broker's commission. These discounts and commissions vary considerably, depending on the desirability of the loan and the current money market. They may range from one per cent to as high as 7 per cent or 8 per cent, averaging between 2 per cent and 3 per cent.

Sometimes an additional inducement is necessary in securing a loan, such as enabling the lender to participate in the equity earnings through the issue of stock; or, with individuals, arranging a partnership participation as a bonus or added fee for granting the loan.

Compared with the terms for a first mortgage, secondary financing is usually obtained at higher rate of interest and is repaid over a shorter length of time, usually not longer than five years. Here, because of the added risk involved and the demands of the primary financing, the lender wants a fast pay-off of principal, and the interest and discount factors might range from 8 per cent to as high as 18 per cent. This is where most projects run into trouble, because of the fixed burden on earnings and the possibility that the original projection of finances was too optimistic and resulted in the project's being under-financed.

It is often deemed feasible to finance furniture, furnishings and equipment on an installment contract basis or through a rental arrangement. Such methods have been used frequently in the installation of air conditioning, television and radio sets, and large signs. The lender or renter, as the case may be, retains title to the equipment and often provides for servicing and repairs. If the equipment is leased, the rental becomes a deductible expense for tax purposes, a factor often advanced as an argument in favor of this arrangement, although the major advantage to the motel is that no capital outlay is necessary. It seems logical that if a piece of equipment is worthwhile to the operation, its purchase will prove cheaper in the long run than a lease, since the lessee must also cover his costs and profit in financing and servicing the item. The question of whether to lease or buy is best answered by the circumstances present in a company's finances.

The method of repaying the principal sum of a mortgage is prescribed in the terms of the loan. The lender may either rule that no prepayments may be made or that limits be set on the time and amounts of such advance payments, often stipulating a penalty of one or 2 per cent on the amounts so paid. Conversely, the loan arrangement may require that additional principal payments be made based on a percentage or arbitrary amount of the net earnings after meeting the original fixed loan requirement. In this case it is especially important that sufficient provision be made for covering replacement and improvement expenditures which may be required by the property, a contingency that is often overlooked in such arrangements.

LEASES

The answer to the question of whether the owner will operate the motel or lease it depends on several factors. The owner may have the property and the equity funds for such a project but may be otherwise unqualified. Or he may consider the investment attractive but be unwilling to devote the necessary time to it, preferring to remain in an investment position. He may be unable to finance the entire project and will therefore seek a tenant to assume the major risk of operation and also contribute a part of the equity capital as a guarantee of the rental income. Naturally, in a lease situation the landlord desires to obtain sufficient income to cover his capital requirements and give him a fair return on his investment. Additionally, the enterprise must offer sufficient earnings potential to give the tenant a similar return plus satisfactory compensation for his management, his operating skills and his acceptance of the basic risks inherent in the business.

The lease is fundamentally a partnership agreement between landlord and tenant. This means that the lawyers for both parties should draw it up in order that their respective rights and responsibilities will be properly protected. Since the terms of a lease are decided by negotiation, there is some advantage in having the second party present the initial draft, thus giving the first party the advantage of review and correction.

It is essential that the lease fully and accurately describe the property involved and specify the length of time for which the tenant is to be in possession, the amount of rental and basis of its payment, the extent of the rights to the income produced by the property and responsibility for the costs of operation and upkeep, the types of protection necessary to proper conduct of the business and care of the property, the insurance coverage to be carried, the rights or restrictions of assignment, the collateral security for the rental and the rights of heirs and assigns of the original parties to the agreement.

The typical motel lease covers only the land and building, with the tenant owning the furnishings, fixtures and equipment which become security for the lease. On occasion, however, the landlord may also own the furnishings, in which circumstances the rental is determined accordingly and the lease specifies the manner in which they are to be maintained or replaced by the tenant. When the landlord owns the furnishings, security for the lease may be the payment of the last year's rental in advance or the provision of a security deposit, the handling of which also varies widely depending upon the terms of the lease. For instance, the deposit might either be placed in escrow or used by the landlord to ease his financing problems. For income tax purposes it might be in securities returnable to the tenant with the interest or in dividends payable to him during the life of the lease.

There are some cases where the land involved can only be obtained by lease and cannot be bought, being held as an investment by the owner. The rental paid is usually based on a fair return on the appraised value of the land, usually ranging from 6 per cent to 7 per cent annually. The land lease usually covers a long period, typically from 50 to 99 years, with provision for rental adjustments from time to time to cover inflation and other contingencies that may influence land values during the term of the lease. Furthermore, the lease will probably stipulate what use will be made of the land and the extent of the improvements to be placed on it.

Since the useful life of a modern motel or motor hotel property is from 25 to 40 years or more, depending on the obsolescence factors inherent in the industry, the ordinary lease period on a motel may extend from 10 to 25 years, with the probability of options exercisable under certain conditions for extension of the term by the tenant. If the tenant owns the furnishings and has made considerable leasehold improvements, he may prefer a shorter term, with options for extension, in order to take advantage of the larger depreciation and amortization deductions for income tax purposes which might then be possible.

In the way of reviewing a point explained previously, the rental is usually based on a fixed rate of return on the owner's capital investment or is based on a division of the operating income of the property, either as a percentage of sales or a division of profits, with a minimum guaranteed rental to cover the fixed financial requirements of the landlord. The lease will also specify which party is to pay property taxes, insurance and upkeep. Such costs are usually assigned to the tenant, making the rental a net income to the landlord. However, there are also instances in which the landlord agrees to pay the property costs or a portion of them. More often such an agreement is limited to providing that any increases in property taxes will be divided between landlord and tenant, as might also be the cost of any major repairs, particularly repairs to what is termed the "outside of the building," such as roof, walls, roadways and sidewalks.

The owner may feel that the need for special experience and knowledge in restaurant operation makes it advisable to lease the restaurant part of the premises to an established operator, in which case the restaurant tenant may be expected to participate in the financing of the project to the extent of paying for the interior decoration, furniture, furnishings and equipment needed for that department. The rental basis is usually a percentage of sales with a minimum guaranteed rental. The rates, if the premises are furnished by the tenant, range from 3 per cent to 5 per cent of food sales and from 7 per cent to 10 per cent of beverage sales, although there are cases where it has been found necessary to reduce these rates in order to attract a desirable operator. If the premises are furnished by the landlord, the percentages would be proportionately higher—from 5 per cent to 8 per cent on food sales and from 10 per cent to 15 per cent on beverage sales.

Whether the tenant leases all or a portion of the motel operation, he will want to take some part in the determination of the type of facilities to be constructed. For this reason he should be brought into the picture before the final plans have been prepared. If the owner is not experienced in this area the tenant may be better qualified to pass judgment on the plans and to supervise their execution.

The integrity and proven ability of the management are key factors in obtaining financial backing. It is therefore possible that leasing the operation to a recognized and reputable chain operator will result in favorable mortgage terms for the owner. Furthermore, such a tenant may have sufficient connections in the field to aid in placing the loan. The same advantages are open to the operator who associates his establishment with a national franchise operation.

In the 1930's and later, several professional management organizations specialized in the operation of hotel properties on a fee basis. Recently we have noted similar contracts negotiated in the motor hotel field. Compensation for this management service is usually in the form of a fixed fee which covers administrative costs, combined with a division of income between management and owner based on either a percentage of gross income or profit. The contract usually specifies the fixed charges and the other costs which must be met before profit. The advantage of such an arrangement is that the owner obtains professional management and supervision of his property.

More often we have seen a management contract in the form of a lease, wherein the lessee provides only the working capital necessary to the operation. This form appears to be a more practicable arrangement for obtaining management services because the tenant is held more accountable for the business results. His compensation is based primarily on the profits produced, the rental agreement specifically spelling out the division of income between owner and tenant. Most rental agreements further require that the tenant assume financial responsibility for the success of the operation to the extent of his own financial resources.

17

Chain Operation, Referral Organizations and Trade Associations

Chain operation, a natural step in the development of the motel business, has received its greatest impetus in the past ten years. Many motel owners have sought to build on the success of their first ventures by the development of additional facilities in other likely locations. The early dream of having under one organizational banner motel accommodations strategically located from coast to coast has become a reality in the rapid spread of chain, franchise and cooperative ventures in the motor hotel field. This same motive has encouraged many existing hotel chains to extend their operations into the motor hotel field and capitalize on their experience and established reputations in serving the traveling public.

The traveler has been quick to react to the "brand name" approach, which became an important factor in motel sales promotion with the entry of the chain and franchise groups into this field. The approach has been accentuated by readily recognizable facilities marked by standardized architectural patterns, color and decor, as well as by the names, symbols and slogans stressed prominently on uniform entrance signs, road signs, guide books, and emphasized in national advertising programs.

The growth of the chains has caused the independent operator to turn to cooperative and referral groups, organized to give his facilities a favorable standing with the traveling public. In addition, these associations have activated advance registration and guaranteed reservation plans, national advertising and sales promotion campaigns to augment the cooperative sales efforts of their membership. They all have minimum standards for facilities and service which the establishment must meet in order to qualify for membership. These standards are enforced by a system of inspections intended to give the public assurance of finding in each member operation the quality that the association's name and symbol are intended to signify.

Having realized the relationship between quality standards and public acceptance, these associations are quite rigid in their requirements and strict in their inspections. They also offer educational programs for members and their staffs and publish bulletins for their members on new developments in the field. Both the franchise groups and cooperative organizations encourage their associates to participate in making policy decisions. Sectional and national meetings of the owners and operators of member motels are held regularly.

Because the influence of chains, franchise groups and referral organizations has increased so dramatically in recent years, it is advisable for the individual interested in the motel and motor hotel field to acquaint himself further with this aspect of the business. We believe this end is best served here by the presentation of pertinent information on several of the major companies and associations now in operation. What follows is not all-inclusive; the field is still growing and has by no means reached a final stage of development. Additional information on referral, franchise and chain operations can be gained by contacting the hotel and motel trade associations and by reading the trade press.

CHAIN OWNERSHIP AND OPERATION

Because chain operation is still comparatively new as an important force in the motel field, the listings of chains available in published directories are relatively incomplete. Today's list may not be truly representative next year and surely will not be representative five years hence. We have prepared a list of motor hotel groups or chain operators which include some of the names best known to the traveling public. There are many more, particularly smaller chains, which should also be included in any complete listing. The hotel companies that have entered the motor hotel field in the past ten years are marked with (H). This designation will serve to indicate the extent to which hotelmen have been influential in the growth of the motor hotel field. Several motel chains existed prior to 1950; the oldest listed are the Alamo Plaza groups, which originated about 1939.

The majority of chain operators own their properties, although some run them on a lease basis. The franchise groups are regarded as chain operations because of the close affiliation of the units.

NAME	HOME OFFICE
(H) Affiliated Vance Motel Hotels	Seattle, Wash.
Airway Hotels, Inc.	Buffalo, N.Y.
Alamo Plaza Hotel Courts	Dallas, Tex.
Alamo Plaza Hotel Courts	Waco, Tex.
(H) Alsonett Hotels	Tulsa, Okla.
Americana Motor Hotels, Inc.	Denver, Colo.
Aristocrat Inns of America	Chicago, Ill.
(H) Associated Hotels	Chicago, Ill.
(H) Boss Hotels Company	Des Moines, Iowa
(H) Caravan Inns (Western Hotels, Inc.)	Seattle, Wash.
Congress Inns	Santa Monica, Cal.
(H) Dinkler Hotel Management Corp.	Atlanta, Ga.
(H) Doric Hotels	Seattle, Wash.
Downtowner Corp.	Memphis, Tenn.
Executive Inn Motor Hotels Corp.	Cincinnati, Ohio
(H) Executive House, Inc.	Chicago, Ill.
(H) The Futterman Corp.	New York City
(H) Hilton Hotels Corp. (Hilton Inns)	Chicago, Ill.
Holiday Inns of America, Inc.	Memphis, Tenn.
(H) Hotel Corp. of America (Charter House)	Boston, Mass.
Hyatt-Chalet Motels, Inc. (Hyatt House)	Los Angeles, Cal.
Howard Johnson's Motor Lodges	New York City
Imperial '400' Motels, Inc.	Englewood Cliffs, N.J.
(H) Jack Tar Hotels	Galveston, Tex.
(H) The Kahler Corp.	Rochester, Minn.
(H) Knott Hotels Corp.	New York City
(H) Manger Hotels	New York City
Marriott Motor Hotels	Washington, D.C.
(H) Pick Hotels Corp.	Chicago, Ill.
Ramada Inns	Phoenix, Ariz.
(H) Schimmel Hotels Corp.	Lincoln, Neb.
(H) Sheraton Corp. of America	Boston, Mass.
Tisch Motels-Hotels, Inc.	Miami Beach, Fla.

	Tourinns, Inc.	New York City
	TraveLodge Corporation	San Diego, Cal.
(H)	Treadway Inns	Boston, Mass.
(H)	Van Orman Hotels	Fort Wayne, Ind.
	Del E. Webb Motor Hotel Corp.	Phoenix, Ariz.
	Western Hills Hotels	Fort Worth, Tex.

VOLUNTARY COOPERATIVE ASSOCIATIONS

Through affiliation with a respected referral organization an independent owner and operator unites his efforts and resources with other independents. Through this type of organization the independent operator gains primarily the sales promotion benefits and advantages of chain operation without sacrificing the individual control of his establishment, at the same time gaining other collateral benefits that come from direct contact and association with others in the business. The sunburst emblem of Quality Courts, the lariat of Best Western, the four-leaf clover of Superior Motels, the Capitol dome of Congress Inns and the brass door knocker of Master Hosts are symbols well known to the modern-day traveler.

Referral associations, which are organized on a non-profit basis, are owned and controlled by the members, who elect their own directors and vote on policies. The first cooperating groups were formed in the days when the individual motel operator had the field to himself and realized that such organization was necessary to overcome the harmful publicity that roadside housing received in some areas during the 1930's. Their purpose was to help the individual operator to police himself and to guarantee the maintenance of proper standards as well as to undertake cooperative advertising and sales promotion campaigns fashioned to project their image as a respected and established part of the accommodations business. As the competition from chains grew, the independents found it more vital than ever to band together with others to maintain his place in the travel picture and to survive successfully the growing pains of the industry.

Each group, organized as a non-profit corporation, is patterned by its own members and thus reflects the character which best fits the section of the travel market to which they cater. Naurally, independent operators in a given area desire to have exclusive referral rights insofar as possible. Therefore not only does the independent motel operator have to find a group which has requirements and standards suitable to his type of operation, but he must also find one which is not already represented in his territory by one or more of his competitors.

The following selection of major cooperating groups is representative but not all-inclusive.

Quality Courts United, Inc.*

Quality Courts United was organized in 1939 and held its first annual convention in Daytona Beach, Florida, the location of its present headquarters, in June 1942. By 1962 this association consisted of 605 members and a total of 30,112 guest room units, an average of about 50 units per motel. Each membership is held by the individual authorized to commit the motel he represents financially, not by the motel itself. To keep the association one of independent owners and operators, its bylaws limit it to members having not more than three properties.

There are 17 persons on the headquarters staff and two field men. The board of directors consists of 11 persons elected by the membership; the directors in turn elect their officers. The eleven directors together with ten other members designated by the board make up the inspection team, which adheres to a set program of annual inspections of the member establishments plus additional inspections including those of applicants for membership and member motels which have changed hands. The term of the president is limited to two years and that of each director to not more than six years. The board meets six times a year, and regional membership meetings are held, presided over by one of the board members. Attendance by members is required.

To qualify for membership the applicant must meet the minimum standards outlined in the bylaws. In order for a motel owner to maintain membership, his motel must pass an inspection of facilities, service standards and character. There are ten facility requirements: wall-to-wall carpets, full air conditioning, television, modern tiled bathrooms, free ice, room telephones, restaurant facilities, paved driveways, swimming pool or similar recreational facility and acceptance of American Express credit cards. Specified standards are outlined for such items as the heating system, mattress and box springs, door locks, the type and complement of bath linens and bath mats, and size of soap.

In addition, the member must agree to distribute directories or travel guides, two in each room and one to the arriving guest; to use the illuminated display sign; to maintain adequate registration records,

*Quality Courts United, Inc. has recently announced the formation of Quality Courts Motels, Inc., an organization that will evolve into a franchise chain. Its president is John Lacock, president of Quality Courts United.

guarantee room rates and cooperate in the free reservations program, using the phone-ahead or TWX system. (When the American Express rate on collections was changed to 4 per cent the headquarters office stopped serving as a clearing house on these charges and they are now handled directly by the member motel.)

The public relations and sales promotion program entails a million-dollar expenditure. Approximately 6 million guide books are now distributed annually. The association reported 1530 road signs in use in 1962, with about 1350 additional signs paid for by individual members and carrying the Quality Courts emblem. The association road signs are located at heavy traffic spots not necessarily near member motels. National advertising in magazines, trade press, and metropolitan newspapers is also an important part of this program.

The dues and advertising assessments change from year to year depending on the budget which is adopted at the annual meeting. The 1962 rates were as follows:

	Annual Dues		*Advertising Assessments*	
Number of Rooms	*Per Room*	*Maximum Total*	*Per Room Per Day*	*Maximum Daily Total*
1 to 12	—	$ 425.00	2.5¢	$ .30
13 to 75	$20.00	1,685.00	2.5	1.875
76 to 100	15.00	2,060.00	1.875	2.34275
100 to 150	10.00	2,560.00	1.25	2.96775
Over 150	5.00	—	.625	

The entrance sign is leased by the member facility and remains the property of Quality Courts United. Current sign rentals are determined by the optional pay-out term adopted by the member and are based on the cost of the sign. The member also has the option of having a marquee, but the general format of the sign is specified by the association. Sizes range from 27 to 32 feet in height and are 18 feet in width, thus dominating the entrance and giving the member facility a prominent and definite tie-in with the association.

Western Motels, Inc.

The Best Western organization, with headquarters in Long Beach, California, was organized along lines similar to Quality Courts in the 1940's and affords somewhat similar benefits and services to its members in the western part of the United States. Its members make the rules and regulations and elect their officers. The area in which it operates is divided into 52 districts, each with its own district governor, who must inspect all member motels in his district twice a year and furnish a written report on his findings. There is a paid headquarters and field staff which handles the administrative work and supplements the inspection program. In addition, each member is required to visit and submit a written report on three member motels per year, thus assisting in the inspection program and at the same time benefiting from personal contact and acquaintance with other members.

Qualification for membership is based on minimum standards required for first-class motel facilities and operation. Restaurant facilities are not a requirement. Regional conferences are held each year and the annual convention is held in October, the attendance ranging between 800 and 900 persons.

The 1962 membership was reported to be 665, with a total of 32,228 rooms, averaging 48 rooms per motel. The largest motel in the group had 750 rooms. The major item in advertising and sales promotion is the travel guide; approximately 5 million are distributed each year. Advertisements in area mediums, AAA directories and other publications are also included in the program. A monthly bulletin is published to keep members up to date on activities in the motel field.

The free advance reservation system and referral program are augmented by TWX or telephone contact. The association also uses the American Express credit card set-up, and has a life and health insurance program for owners and employees. It operates a cooperative buying plan by which quantity prices and discounts are obtained for furnishings and supplies. This plan was reported in 1962 to be running well over a million dollars per year in purchases to cover the pooled needs of its members. The illuminated "Best Western" sign and emblem are prominently displayed at the entrance or office location of each member.

The dues of this association also vary from year to year. Based on the annual budget of 1962, for example, a 15-unit motel would be charged $272, one of 100 units, $870, and one of 200 units, $920.

Best Western Motels and Quality Courts cooperate on referrals and distribute each other's travel guides. Members of either group will accept reservations for the other.

Superior Motels, Inc.

This association of motels and motor hotels was founded and incorporated in Hollywood, Florida in 1950, with 33 charter members as a cooperative group linked under one common identification with a registered trademark emblem. It is merged with Eastern Motels of New England in 1957 and set up a plan of controlled expansion into the West. It is now operating from coast to coast in the United States. In 1962 the membership was reported to exceed 500 motels ranging from 12 to 200 units and totaling about 16,000 rooms.

In 1959 its headquarters office was moved from North Carolina to Hollywood, Florida and placed under the supervision of a full-time executive vice-president. It is owned by the membership and operated through a 15-man board elected at its annual meeting.

Prescribed qualifications for membership are enforced by rigid systematic inspection. The property must be located in a desirable environment; the building must be of good design, soundly built and well maintained; the grounds must be well kept and the drives clearly defined. The bedrooms must contain adequate living space, be soundproofed and have good ventilation and heat. There must be adequate parking space for each guest, and room and telephone service must be available at all times.

The guest-room furnishings must include wall-to-wall carpeting, two easy chairs and one desk, luggage storage and clothes-hanging facilities, adequate lighting, mirrors, and wastebaskets, ash trays and related items. Free ice must be convenient to the guest rooms. Tiled baths are required, as well as linen supply, soap and a sanitary bath mat. The office or lobby must be proportionate to the size of operation, easily available to, and identifiable by, guests. There must be a properly attired host on hand to meet and serve guests. Accurate registration of all guests and vehicles is required, and no member may publicly display price or rate signs. Rates are quoted in the directory listings distributed by the association.

In addition to these conditions there are also rules on housekeeping and maintaining the conduct of the business on a high moral plane. The need for a reasonable flexibility, depending on local conditions, is recognized with respect to such items as swimming pools, room telephones, children's playground, air conditioning, paved driveways, room television, and restaurant facilities.

Members must prominently display the official "Superior" emblem on the property and on road signs. They must also distribute the association directories, two in each room and one to each arrival, participate in the advance reservation system, cooperate with the programs of the membership and be open to inspection without notice by the association's representative at all reasonable times.

"Superior" currently prints and distributes approximately three million directories a year and has recently adopted a program under which 500 uniform road signs will be erected annually. Five thousand road sings now display the trademark emblem, including member's signs. There is also a national advertising program in selected magazines and metropolitan newspapers.

A free prepaid reservation system is operated by all member motels as a guest service, all supplies to implement it being furnishied by the association. The cost of telephone calls is absorbed by the motel receiving the reservation. The association has also established a central purchasing plan and a distribution organization through which motel supplies, furnishings and equipment are available to members at volume price.

The association holds regional educational meetings in addition to its annual convention and distributes information to the members to keep them abreast of developments in the motel field.

The association has recently established a $50,000 scholarship program under which annual scholarships will be granted to young people from the industry enrolled or planning to enroll in any college or university with a recognized school of business administration and adequate courses in motel and hotel management.

Membership dues are determined at the annual convention based on the budget adopted by the association. The 1961-1962 dues schedule was as follows:

	Annual Dues	
Number of Room Units	*Per Unit*	*Maximum Total*
First 12 units	——	$225.00
13 to 50 units	$8.00	529.00
51 to 100 units	6.00	829.00
Over 100 units	4.00	

In addition each member is required to deposit $150 on the "Superior" illuminated emblem, payable $50 with the application for membership and $25 per year for the next four years.

Master Hosts Hotel Association

The Master Hosts Hotel Association was organized in 1953 by three Texas motor hotel operators and held its first national meeting in Fort Worth, where its headquarters are located, in April, 1954, with 36 members attending. In 1962 the association reported a membership of 210 motor hotels comprising 29,000 rooms, an average of 145 rooms per establishment. Nearly all members are men with hotel experience who have built or converted their properties to meet the pattern of combined motor and resort facilities.

The association is a democratic organization divided into four districts (eastern, western, east central, and west central), with the bulk of its membership in the southern and western areas of the United States. Each district elects five board members, one of whom becomes the district vice-president. The board then elects a president, who becomes chairman of the board after his presidential year, and a secretary-treasurer, these 23 men making up the governing body.

The headquarters office is operated by a general manager, whose staff is augmented by four full-time inspectors.

To qualify for membership an operation must conform to the standards set up in the bylaws of the association, which include the following ten guarantees to the guest:

1. Capable management—hospitable, experienced, ethical.
2. Complete hotel service—dining facilities operated by the hotel; room service, guest laundry and valet, porters or bellmen, a folio system for all accounts.
3. Ample free parking for both rooms guests and restaurant patrons.
4. Adequate swimming pool or comparable recreational facilities.
5. All rooms with private baths.
6. All rooms with telephone and 24-hour switchboard service.
7. Year-round air conditioning.
8. Free "Master Hosts" reservation service.
9. Superior quality.
10. American Automobile Association approval.

Members agree to five guarantees of cooperation: (a) To provide Bell System National Typewriter Exchange Service (TWX) where possible; (b) to furnish each room with a "Master Host Directory" and Teletype reservation form; (c) to have an approved lobby or front-office rack for brochures of Master Hosts member hotels; (d) to display an outside illuminated emblem sign and to use the "Master Host" emblem and promotional tools; and (e) to adhere to all policies of the association as provided in the bylaws.

The applicant is first cleared by an inspection team, which makes two inspections of the motor hotel. The membership is notified and given 10 days to comment on the application. The inspection reports and members' comments then go to the board of directors for action. If the property is under construction the plans and cost estimates are reviewed by a blueprint committee which reports to the board.

Considerable emphasis is placed on the advantages of active co-operation of the members in the promotion of room sales, not only for regular referrals, but also for conventions and other types of group business. The association contemplates opening regional offices to promote group sales and has already conducted a direct campaign by contacting business firms with teletype equipment for that purpose. An advance, instant reservation service, available free to guests through teletype, is a major factor in the cooperative plan.

The 1962 budget called for the printing of 1.5 million directories to be distributed by the association and its members, the cost of such directories being a part of the regular operating budget. Rates are publicized in the directories, but the posting of rates at the entrance of the motor hotel is prohibited by policy. The special advertising campaign includes space in national magazines, the trade magazines of travel agencies, hotels and motels and over three hundred highway bulletins paid for by the association. This promotion is in addition to the 1700 member road signs bearing the "Master Hosts" emblem.

The guest is also asked to participate in the program of the association by filling in forms which seek his compliments and complaints about service and facilities. The guest is asked to mail these forms direct to the home office and they are followed up by letter, both from the home office and manager of the property involved. These forms supplement the regular annal inspection and re-certification program.

The association also conducts contests for the members and their employees, using such items as referrals and advance reservations, compliments, and ideas on operation and sales promotion as bases for competition. It furnishes members with manuals on operation for employee education and on conducting staff meetings. The Master Hosts emblem is available for use on uniforms, name plates and tie bars.

Two regional meetings are held annually in each of the four districts. These meetings and the annual convention are attended by key personnel and outsiders in the business, as well as by regular members. In addition to business meetings and social functions, educational talks are included on the agenda.

The 1962 annual dues were $750 for year-round operators in the continental United States. Members outside the continental United States were charged $360, and seasonal operators paid $75 for each month of operation. In addition, the 1962 national advertising assessment, which totaled $300,000, was based on four cents a room for the first 100 rooms, three cents a room for the second 100 rooms and two cents a room for all rooms over 200.

The entrance sign, an embossed plexiglass illumination of the association's emblem 6 feet by 8 feet in size, costs each member $450. The cost of embellishments for existing signs runs from $40 to $87, and that of the "coast-to-coast" embellishment, from $28 to $38.

Congress Motor Hotels

Congress Motor Hotels was organized on May 1, 1955, as a national business-promotion association for motor hotels. It is operated by and for its members and has its own offices and directors. The headquarters office is located in Los Angeles, California.

There are two groups of motor hotels included in the membership of this association. One group consists of operators who wish to retain the established names of their motor hotels and therefore participate only in the referral and national advertising and promotion programs of the organization as a member of the association. The other group consists of operators who use the name "Congress Inn," the franchise program launched March 1, 1959 for motor hotels meeting required standards of facilities, service and character; and who, in addition to participating in the referral and business promotion programs, receive other services in connection with planning, financing and operation. These operators are granted exclusive rights to represent the organization in their particular areas for 10 years.

As of June 30, 1962, there were 300 participating licensees and 34 Congress Inns. The participating franchise fee at that time was $500, plus a royalty fee of $1.00 per rental unit per month up to a maximum of 60 rooms. The Congress Inn franchise fee was $5,000 in addition to a royalty fee of $2.40 per rental unit per month, the life of the license being 10 years, with renewal options. All franchise holders automatically become members of Congress Motor Hotels, which receives its dues income from the franchise fees paid to Congress International, Inc. The current rate is $12 per year per licensed room unit. The association may vote additional direct assessments on the members. The association is, in effect, a cooperative referral and business-promotion group whose membership is determined and controlled by the franchise organization, Congress International.

The right to use the name "Congress" and to display the registered trademarks is granted by Congress International, Inc., which has its main office in Miami Beach, Florida. Three types of official emblems are in use, all carrying the Capitol dome on a shield bearing one of three designations. One bears the designation, "Member, Congress Motor Hotels," and is used together with the member's own name as the identifying emblem of motor hotels holding a participation agreement issued by Congress International. The second designation is "Congress Inn," which identifies those establishments holding license agreements with Congress International. The third designation, "Congress, Coast to Coast," is used by all members to make the public familiar with the trademark of this network of motor hotels.

This organization divides the United States into ten regions, with two additional regions in Canada and one in Mexico. Each region has a director elected for a three-year term. The directors elect the officers. A full-time executive officer operates the association program and directs the headquarters office and staff. Each region holds its own meeting and, in addition, the entire membership attends the annual national convention. The members are required to attend at least one meeting a year. The directors serve as a budget committee for the association and approve all expenditures.

The membership is pledged to uphold the standards of the association and to comply with its bylaws. The Congress code requires that each establishment offer generally attractive premises; sanitary bathrooms; neat and well-kept rooms, lobby, office and grounds; modern bedding, up-to-date furnishings and appointments, adequate lighting, ample hot water and linens; courtesy and orderliness in service to guests; adherence to published rates and cooperation with the Congress program.

All members are required to offer guests advance reservation service to other Congress members using the "Reserva-Check" and "Reserva-Charge" systems. The receiving members pay the cost of calls, and the service is free to guests. All members are required to honor American Express, Carte Blanche, and Diner's Club credit cards.

The association publishes a travel guide directory of member hotels. Members are required to place these in each guest room and make them available at the registration desk. The cooperative "Ad-Plan" is based on a "due-bill" arrangement whereby each member receives advertising from the participating publication at the same dollar value that is represented by the accommodations granted to "due-bill" guests. Each member is required to incorporate the Congress emblem in his highway sign and printed advertising and on guest stationery, match covers, glass wraps, etc. Approved "Reserve Ahead" signs and stickers must be posted in the lobby and guest rooms.

Each member is expected to call on at least five others each year in his referral area and to report these calls in writing to the home office. The association also prepares a desk book containing a complete description of each member establishment which each member must keep current for use as ready reference on referrals.

The franchise operation of the Congress Inns specifies facilities and services beyond those required of the participating members of the association. These more extensive requirements include restaurant facilities, 24-hour telephone service and swimming pools. The Congress Management Company operates those company-owned motor hotels not placed under lease, sets up management and control procedures for licensees seeking such assistance and provides professional management for motel investors who are not experienced operators. Included in the franchise package are the services of a legal staff, financial and architectural counsel, room planning and layout service, personnel indoctrination, outlines of operation and accounting procedures, a volume purchasing plan and a group life and medical insurance plan.

American Automobile Association

The endorsement most highly prized by motels and motor hotels is probably that of the American Automobile Association. Headquarters for this association's travel service are at 1712 G Street, N.W., Washington 6, D.C. This federation of automobile clubs was founded in 1902 and has 750 clubs and branch offices, with a total membership just short of 7.5 million.

Listings are based on rigid inspection continuously carried on by more than 40 field representatives, who certify that the standard requirements for recommendation and listing are complied with. There is no fee required for listing. If an establishment qualifies it may be authorized to rent and display the American Automobile Association emblem, the 1962 rates being as follows:

Number of Rooms	Annual Rental
Under 12	$140.00
13 to 25	155.00
26 to 100	175.00
Over 100	200.00

The establishments may display the association's emblem by "official appointment" and must sign an agreement to comply with the requirements for endorsement and listing. The 1962 tabulation of listings for the United States follows:

	Number Listed	Entitled to Display Emblem
Hotels and resorts	2,301	1,641
Motels	10,789	9,933
Restaurants	2,448	1,123

The association issues about 6.4 million tour books, 15 million state and regional maps, and 80 million strip maps. Annually, the various offices will prepare 12 million tours or trips for members.

The requirements for recommendation of motels and motor hotels by this association are summarized briefly:

THE ESTABLISHMENT

1. Those having fewer than 10 rental units are ineligible.
2. Every unit must have a private bath.
3. Buildings of over 2 stories must have two adequate exits on each floor and have adequate fire protection.
4. Rooms must have a safe and adequate heating system.
5. Rooms must be soundproofed.
6. Buildings over 3 stories must have an elevator.
7. Motels must have an adequate and easily identifiable office.
8. Establishments located in undesirable environs are ineligible.

EXTERIOR

Establishments creating an unfavorable impression from the highway due to poor design, neglect or obsolescence will not be approved. The grounds, if any, should be nicely landscaped. Driveways should be two-lane, preferably paved. Covered doorways and walkways are desirable. Entrance, parking area and walks should have adequate all-night illumination.

INTERIOR

1. Good maintenance and cleanliness are essential.
2. Supplementary locking device for room doors must be provided to ensure guest privacy and safety.

3. There must be adequate, free floor living space in guest rooms.
4. Each unit must have good ventilation.

GUEST-ROOM EQUIPMENT

The guest room must contain good furnishings and have attractive decor, including:

1. Comfortable beds, linens, blankets, spreads, pillows, mattress pads, all in good condition.
2. A desk and dresser or combination unit. Luggage and clothes-hanging facilities.
3. Good light for reading at the bed, desk and easy chair.
4. Shades, draperies or blinds on windows.
5. At least one easy chair and one wastebasket.
6. A good, clean, well-lighted mirror.
7. Stationery.
8. A light switch convenient to the door.

BATHROOM EQUIPMENT

Basic fixtures are essential, of course, and there must be:

1. A door separating the bath from the rest of the unit.
2. At least one bath and one face towel for each occupant.
3. A good, well-lighted mirror.
4. A window or other adequate ventilation.
5. Good shelf space.
6. Heat when needed.
7. Razor-blade disposal facilities.
8. A hook on bathroom door.
9. Wastebasket, facial tissues, wash cloths, bathmat, safeguard for persons using tubs.
10. Ceramic tile baths are preferable.

MANAGEMENT

1. Operation must be of high moral character.
2. Management must be hospitable.
3. Establishment must declare its rates for publication. (It is preferable that rates be posted in each guest room.)
4. Daily linen changes should be provided when a daily rate is charged.
5. A responsible person should be in attendance at all times.
6. Check-out time should not be earlier than noon.
7. Personnel should be neat and well-groomed.

The AAA also reserves the right refuse recommendation to any establishment for any reason it deems sufficient, even though the establishment may meet all the outlined qualifications. Optional facilities, where available, will also bear inspection as to operating condition and appearance.

Motels and motor hotels usually display the AAA emblem at the entrance to their establishments and also use it on their private listings, stationery and sales-promotion literature.

TRADE ASSOCIATIONS

The trade associations of the accommodations industry provide major opportunities for motel and motor hotel operators to get acquainted with each other, educate themselves in the ways of the business, keep up with its development and protect their interests through combined efforts. Attending association meetings, receiving their bulletins, learning about their research projects and actively participating in their programs benefit the motel operator in many ways that would be difficult, if not impossible, to match by any other means.

Although the referral and recommending groups mentioned earlier in this chapter perform some of the functions of education in the business that are also a part of the trade associations' program, they do not supplant the major functions which make trade association membership an important consideration, and most such organizations recommend that their members also belong to a trade group. Many independents and chain operators find that the services and functions of the trade association suffice for their needs as to group action, information and research, and realize the importance of gathering together to discuss mutual problems and to give themselves and their establishments the status and protection that come through joint effort.

In most instances the state associations are directly affiliated with the national groups; joining the state association automatically makes one a member of the national group. There are also regional, city and special groups, such as those in the resort field, that supplement the functions of the state and national associations and devote their programs to special problems and interests.

Several of these organizations hold trade shows and exhibitions where equipment and products used in the business can be seen and direct contacts with suppliers can be made. These shows are usually combined with educational programs, discussion groups and social functions. Several regional groups also sponsor short courses or other training programs for the benefit of members and their staffs.

The other major functions of the associations are to represent the industry in legislative affairs, to develop a public relations program and to promote the general welfare of the business. The two major national associations are currently meeting with the National Restaurant Association to determine the areas where they might benefit by combining forces on a common ground, thus making each association more effective in its efforts on behalf of its membership.

American Hotel and Motel Association

This association's headquarters are located at 221 West 57th Street, New York 19, New York. It was organized in 1910 as a successor organization to the American Hotelkeepers' Protective Association and the Hotelmen's Mutual Benefit Association, which dates back to 1879. It is a federation of state associations, including all 50 states, the District of Columbia and Commonwealth of Puerto Rico, the provinces of Canada; Mexico, the Bahamas, Bermuda, Jamaica, the Virgin Islands and Venezuela.

Although the state association is the official member, voting rights are based on one vote for each 50 active members of its group, and the 1962 membership was comprised of over 5,500 hotels representing a total of 650,000 rooms. Since the member establishments are, in effect, determined by their membership in the state and regional associations, the extent to which motels and motor hotels are represented cannot be readily established. However, they now definitely make up a sizable part of the membership total. At the 1962 annual convention the association's name was changed to include the word "Motel." Over half the state associations have made similar changes, including "Motel" or "Inn" in their titles. These changes are indicative of the increased membership of motel and motor hotel establishments in this federated group.

The dues structure is modest, starting at $25 for hotels of 40 rooms and under and continuing on a sliding scale based on the number of rooms in the establishment, ranging from 75 cents per room for the next ten rooms to $1.25 for all rooms over 500, with seasonal resorts paying 62.5 cents per room for all rooms over 40.

The association also has an allied membership consisting of firms servicing hotels, the 1962 count listing 371 members who pay $200 per year. These members are included in a special directory issued to all member hotels. Although they participate in the annual convention program, they have no vote in the association's business meetings.

In 1927 the Hotel Red Book Directory Corporation was organized with rights to publish the annual official directory of hotels, called the "Hotel Red Book," which is widely distributed to travel agencies, commercial organizations and travel transportation facilities, and has been long recognized as an official reference and guide to hotels. In 1961 the listings were restricted to members of the association and arrangements were also made in 1962 to prepare special pocket-sized area guidebooks for the state and regional associations desiring them for distribution. The corporation is operated for profit; the annual income, after taxes, is paid into the association.

The association is controlled by a board of directors, one from each member state or territory. They are elected by their respective local bodies for a two-year term. The officers are elected at the annual meeting by the member associations, based on voting rights previously outlined. The board meets at the annual convention and once at midyear. An executive committee of 17 members, which includes the six officers and eleven elected members of the board, is elected by geographically outlined districts. The directors also elect a special annual budget committee from their membership. The annual budget amounts to approximately $650,000.

The administrative affairs of the association are in the hands of a full-time executive vice-president appointed by the directors. The activities and services are controlled by the 17 standing committees appointed annually by the president of the association.

The association has now been divided into five regions, each serviced by a direct field representative. The association also maintaains an office in Washington, D. C., whose full-time manager and staff work directly with the chairman of the governmental affairs committee. The New York office staff also has full-time directors for the departments of education, employee relations, and public relations, as well as a search or service department. These people prepare special studies and bulletins in their respective fields to assist members with their problems and keep them abreast of current developments. There is also a staff of advisors in the areas of law, accounting, insurance, architecture, kitchen planning, and laundry operation.

The association has endorsed and distributes a booklet outlining a uniform system of accounts for hotels. It also has had prepared a simplified system for smaller hotels and motels. It has published and distributed from time to time other booklets devoted to subjects pertinent to the industry. Upon the sale of the Universal Travel Card to the American Express Company, proceeds were assigned to the American Hotel Foundation, organized primarily to distribute these and other funds assigned to it for scholarships and other educational and scientific purposes.

The members of the association also organized and financed the American Hotel Institute several years ago, which now operates through Michigan State University in providing home study and group study courses relating to hotel operation. Enrollment in these courses reached a total of 2300 in 1962. Group study cost is set at $15 per course and home study at $25, these costs very often being paid by the member establishment employing the student.

American Motor Hotel Association

This association was founded in 1943 following several prior attempts at organization dating back to about 1937. The original purpose of organization was to establish a code under the National Recovery Act; the present organization was brought about by the problems connected with federal rent control. It started as an affiliated membership organization of state groups and in 1951 the bylaws were changed to make state associations affiliate members, but with motels as direct members, dues being assessed on a per-unit basis. In 1952 the offices of the association were moved to Kansas City, and a full-time executive secretary was installed. It has now expanded to five staff members and its present address is V.F.W. Building, Broadway at 34th, Kansas City 11, Missouri. In 1959 the governmental affairs program of this association was expanded by adding a staff position and secretary to cover Washington, D.C.

Current membership is reported to be more than 7500 motels and motor hotels, with 43 affiliated state associations. It also has an associate membership made up of persons serving motor hotels, as well as sustaining members, those members contributing $50 or more to the association. The annual dues are $15 per member. The state association must agree to collect the national dues along with its state dues and to remit them to the national association as they are collected. Direct members are solicited from states which do not have an affiliated association membership. Their 1962 schedule of dues is $25 up to 20 room units, $35 from 21 to 40 units, $40 from 41 to 60 units and $50 for over 60 units. Members also pay a rental fee of $10 for the right to display the association's standard identification sign, which sign remains the property of the association.

Only affiliated members are entitled to vote at the meetings. Each member association is allowed one vote for each 50 members in its group up to a maximum of 5 votes, and has one delegate to the annual convention for each vote. The association's affairs are primarily in the hands of the board of directors, who approve the annual budget and employ the executive vice-president. The officers consist of a president, three regional vice-presidents (east, central and west), and a secretary-treasurer elected by the delegates to the annual meeting. The officers together with the immediate past president constitute an executive committee, acting on behalf of the board and subject to its approval.

The bylaws state the objectives of the association to be: (a) to foster the interests of its members and those in any way related to the motor hotel industry by common business interests; (b) to encourage high business standards and fair treatment of the traveling public in providing for their comfort, protection and convenience; (c) to establish and maintain uniformity and equality in the customs of the motor hotel trade; (d) to acquire, preserve and disseminate valuable information and to encourage closer relationship among those engaged in this industry; (e) to stimulate friendship and fellowship among those engaged in the motor hotel industry; and (f) to do anything necessary, suitable and proper for the accomplishment of any purposes herein set forth or which might be recognized as proper and lawful objectives of a trade association, all of which shall be consistent with the public interest as well as in the interest of this industry and trade.

The association publishes a monthly magazine for its members, an annual directory of motels and informational bulletins of the "how-to-do-it" type. It sponsors an annual trade show. (The 1962 show was held in conjunction with the National Restaurant Association show in Chicago.) It sponsors a member reservation system, called "Televation," is active in governmental affairs, represents the industry with all allied interests such as U. S. Travel Services, handles public relations for the industry on a national basis and assists state affiliated organizations in membership development and program evolution. It also sponsors and distributes a uniform system of accounts manual and a program in the field of workmen's compensation insurance.

18

Franchise Groups

Franchise organizations offer to the motor hotel field the advantages of their national reputation, the successful merchandising of a tested pattern of establishment and services and the advantages of direct affiliation. Although franchise arrangements differ according to individual circumstances, there are two main types, one deriving its income through a licensing agreement calling for an initial franchise fee and royalty payments based on room income, the other obtaining a division of profits through a joint-venture or partnership agreement with the individual operators of the establishments involved.

These organizations assist in the selection and development of the site, have basic plans and requirements for construction and furnishings as well as for operation, accounting and control. Uniformity of design for easy recognition and identification is stressed and each has its own entrance sign, emblem and slogan, providing the advantages of a brand name or trademark in advertising, sales promotion, referral and advance registration programs.

The five examples used in this chapter do not comprise the entire field but were selected as typical of the two major types of franchise operation.

HOLIDAY INNS OF AMERICA, INC.

The first Holiday Inn was opened in Memphis, Tennessee in 1952 and was soon followed by three additional establishments. Originally a partnership, the company was incorporated under the laws of the State of Tennessee in 1954. The first inns were company-owned. The franchise or license policy was resorted to soon thereafter for more rapid expansion. This naturally involved a lower direct investment, the licensee in most instances finding and acquiring the land, clearing any local zoning problems and handling the financing, construction and direct operation under the licensing agreement.

Common shares of the company were first offered for public sale in 1957, the control remaining in the hands of the original owners. Including stock dividends and stock splits there were 2,072,862 shares outstanding at the end of November, 1961. The company has recently formulated a program to acquire the properties of certain of its licensees through an exchange of stock. Although the income from license fees and services is a material element contributing to company profits, management believes a better profit can be gained from direct operation of the properties. A new Class A common stock, restricted in voting rights to one-tenth of a vote per share, was authorized to implement this program. The licensee receives a package deal of one share of regular and three shares of Class A common stock on a tax-free exchange basis for its stock, the values involved being based on the earnings potential of the property involved.

Most of the licensee establishments are closely held corporations; Holiday Inn stock is readily salable on the over-the-counter market and has definite collateral value. Therefore this arrangement has appeal to those owners who want to be relieved of operating responsibility and prefer to be in an investment position, subsequent sales of this stock also being at capital gains rates.

As of midyear 1962, there were 61 company-owned properties, 24 of which were acquired in stock trades; 208 franchise operations, 63 franchise sites and four company-owned inns reported to be under construction. These properties represent a total of 36,743 rooms in the United States and Canada. The largest operation reported at that date was the 18-story structure in New York City; the average size was 110 rooms. There are units in 35 states and Canada, the majority located in southern and mid-western states.

In the fiscal year ending June 30, 1961 the company derived 40 per cent of its gross revenue from rooms, 25 per cent from food and beverage sales, 20 per cent from its supply company sales, 9 per cent from fees and services and 6 per cent from other sources.

The original company policy was to lease out the restaurant operation. This was changed in 1958, the catering operations now being placed under direct company operation and control as their leases run out. The restaurant facilities are patterned to fit the establishment and its patronage potential. They include snack shops with counters, tables or booths; coffee shop operations with tile floors, paper napkins and table doilies; or carpeted dining rooms with a complete linen complement, proper atmosphere and decor. Standards of operation are strictly controlled.

The initial franchise fee is $10,000. The licensee then pays a royalty of 15 cents per room per night, or 2.5 per cent of gross rentals, whichever is larger. The licensees receive direct advice and assistance on feasibility analysis, basic plans and financing. All units are of similar design, with standard room sizes and appointments specified by the company. All are air conditioned, offer swimming pools and other recreational facilities, restaurants and meeting rooms.

The licensee also gets the benefit of national advertising, the current assessment for which is 8 cents per room per night, and leases the $14,000 entrance sign, which is standard to all properties. A system of free advance reservations and referrals, augmented by the distribution of travel guide directories, is also part of the sales-promotion program. Central purchasing is available to all licensees through the wholly-owned Inn Keepers' Supply Company, which maintains a recently constructed warehouse and showroom facilities at its headquarters in Memphis. Also located there is a school for personnel training, which offers a three-week course to the licensee and his key employees. A regular inspection program is conducted by company personnel to assure conformity with the specifications and requirements placed on all licensees.

The company does not allow "no-vacancy" signs to be used, reviews the room rate structures carefully to see that rates (averaging $8.75) are adhered to, uses a 52-room minimum as a construction guide, and encourages "Coffee Host" service in the rooms, free kennels and children's playground, and the acceptance of American Express credit cards. The family plan—no charge for children under twelve— is a set policy. Licensees are expected to participate in the regional and annual meetings of operators, to have a voice in such considerations as the advertising and sales promotion budget and program. The company provides licensees with a standard accounting system and reviews their operating statements not only for control purposes, but also to assist with operating problems.

A new venture for the company is the production of "Holiday Inn Compacts," which are mobile or trailer-type room units that can be used in coordinated groups of 32 for quick installation of accommodations in likely areas. They are intended to provide minimum, yet adequate and comfortable, accommodations at moderate rates. A factory in Camden, Arkansas has been purchased to produce those units.

HOWARD JOHNSON'S MOTOR LODGES

The Howard Johnson Company, founded in 1925, now operates, franchises and supplies a highway restaurant chain which extends from New England down the entire East Coast and reaches to the Midwest, predominantly east of the Mississippi. As of October 15, 1962, there were 634 restaurant units operated under the Howard Johnson's name, 294 by the company and 340 by licensees. Twelve more are operated under the name "Red Coach Grill." The roadside restaurant business—most famous for its 28 flavors of ice cream—has exclusive rights to operate on either all or parts of eight major turnpikes or limited-access highways in the eastern United States.

In March, 1961, the present company was organized as the successor to the original enterprise, and in May of that year the members of the Johnson family sold 660,000 common shares to the public as a secondary issue. In March, 1962, an additional 370,000 shares were sold. The Johnson family retained 53.2 per cent control through the remaining shares.

The company extended its operation into the motor lodge field in 1954, and in October, 1962 its directory of licensed motor lodges listed 136 establishments located at, or adjacent to, Howard Johnson's Restaurants. They are all independently owned and are operated under a license agreement with the company. The licensee pays an initial fee of $10,000 and a continuing royalty of $8.50 per room per month, or 5 per cent of the guest room rentals and other business income agreed to under the license, whichever is larger. All Howard Johnson's Motor Lodges are associated with a Howard Johnson's Restaurant, but the license is for the motor lodge only and does not cover the restaurant, which may be retained as a separate operation.

The licensee must conform to approved plans and specifications as outlined by the company. Howard Johnson's also approves standards of operation and service for the establishment which are outlined in an architect's handbook and an operator's handbook compiled by the company. The company must also approve all signs, advertising and forms of publicity used by the licensee. Use of the name applies only to the premises covered in the license agreement. All changes or additions to the property must be approved by the company. The licensee is to be restricted in operation to the rental of guest rooms and services as stipulated, and must be properly insured.

In the event of sale, the first offer must be made to the company. The price is based either on the book value of the land, buildings and equipment, or on the fair market value, whichever is lower, without any amount considered for good will or "going-concern" value. Any successor to the licensee must be acceptable to the company, and in the event of cancellation by the company or owner, the lessee or other interest shall not operate a motor lodge, motel or hotel on the property without written consent from the company. This restriction runs for five years after cancellation or as long as a Howard Johnson's Restaurant is in operation in the immediate vicinity.

The cupola, orange tile roof of the gate lodge, and use of blue-green and orange colors, which are company trademarks, are specifically stipulated in the agreement. The licensee agrees to submit a monthly statement covering rooms rented and gross receipts, keep accurate records, and submit semi-annual and annual profit and loss statements and balance sheets, the latter to be certified by a certified public accountant.

The licensees receive assistance from the company with respect to determination of facilities as well as with architectural and operating problems. The basic plan is geared to 60 room units, and the construction cost is about $10,000 per unit. The average room rate is $10.50.

The company maintains a central purchasing organization through its 17 plants, commissaries and distribution centers. Such items as soap, matches, linens, etc., have been standardized to afford the benefits of volume purchasing. Howard Johnson's sponsors a national advertising program integrated with its restaurant operation from which the licensee benefits. A free TWX(R) advance registration system and distribution of motor lodge directories are also part of this program and are required as a cooperative function of all licensees.

RAMADA INN ROADSIDE HOTELS

The present Ramada Inns started out as a group of Flamingo Motor Hotels, established in 1952 in the states of Arizona, California and Texas. In December, 1958 this chain, with its distinctive Williamsburg architecture and white-columned porte-cochere entrances, became known as Ramada Inn Roadside Hotels.

Ramada, Inc. was incorporated in the State of Deleware in December, 1961, and became publicly owned in December, 1962, with the exchange of common stock for beneficial interests in the multiple partnerships and trusts of the constituent enterprises included under the name "Ramada Inn." The principal executive offices are located at 3801 East Van Buren Street, Phoenix, Arizona.

In December, 1962, forty-two roadside and resort properties were in operation, 25 company owned and 17 franchised, with a total of 4,490 rooms. Thirty-eight additional Ramada Inns were under construction, in financing or in planning, including both franchise operations and constituent companies. Ramada Inns range in size from 60 units to the 325-room "flagship" Ramada Inn in Phoenix, Arizona. They are equipped with full facilities in keeping with luxury-class motor hotels, and the company places emphasis on providing banquet and meeting facilities.

Franchise members are offered the assistance of the company's staff in the following ways:

1. Site evaluation. Assaying the potentional of the proposed location and providing guidance in acquiring it on the right basis.

2. Active participation in solving problems of architecture, engineering, construction and furnishings.

3. Preparation of data and information for loan sources and financing.

4. An organized buying plan to give the franchise holder the advantages of mass purchasing.

5. Counseled managerial and staff selections, followed by a complete training program.

6. A chain-wide teletype referral system of advance reservations combined with a program of outdoor and media advertising.

7. A continuous, coordinated advertising and publicity program using the most effective media, locally, regionally and nationally. Each Ramada operation contributes 5 cents per available room per day to cover the cost of this program.

8. Regular seminar sessions and a national convention of members.

9. A follow-through of assistance to the franchise holder during the entire life of the franchise. This includes a continuous review of operating results and occasional inspections.

The franchise applicant must present his personal and financial qualifications for the review and judgment of a franchise committee, consisting of members of the franchise division and the franchise development staff of the company. He must be able to show an adequate financial statement and agree to work in close cooperation with the other members and the executive offices of the company. He must also agree to maintain the established standards of quality and service of Ramada Inns.

The franchise fee in 1962 was $11,000 with an additional $1,500 fee charged to cover the costs involved in preliminary plans and specifications, including location research, renderings and the preparation of construction estimates. Upon completion of the motor hotel, a royalty of 10 cents per room per day, or 2.5 per cent of gross room sales, whichever is greater, becomes payable monthly to Ramada Inns.

THE TRAVELODGE CORPORATION

This company prefers that its co-owned operations be regarded as a network rather than a chain and uses the term "lodge" rather than motel or hotel in describing its properties. TraveLodge Center, opened in 1962 and located in El Cajon, California, houses the executive and administrative offices of the company, its facilities for volume purchasing of supplies, and a training school.

Starting with three lodges in 1946, it has expanded to more than 220 TraveLodges in the United States, 8 in Canada, 33 in Australia and one in southern France. The United States establishments are 19 to 125 rooms in size, averaging 41. The majority of lodges are located on the west coast—there are 97 in California alone—although the group has now spread through 34 states to the east coast and Florida. Most occupy convenient downtown locations.

The host is the managing partner in a joint venture with the company in the construction and operation of room facilities designed to appeal to both the business traveler and tourist at comparatively modest rates. The company arranges for the selection and leasing of the site, the architectural planning, construction and furnishing of the property and other service facilities. The managing partner provides a capital contribution based on a per-room cost estimate. The company then arranges for the mortgage and agrees to provide the additional funds necessary to complete the facilities involved. The manager-partner receives 10 per cent of the gross income to cover his salary and the cost of management help. He and the company each own a 50 per cent interest in the venture and profits are divided accordingly. All of the accounting is done in the company's main office.

The company has its own credit card system, but the TraveLodges also honor American Express, Carte Blanche, Diner's Club, Bankamericard, and Air Travel cards.

A free advance reservation service is available by telephone or TWX between TraveLodges, the payment being covered by a common advertising fund. This same fund provides for the printing and distribution of directories listing all establishments, including a description, photograph and rate schedule. Special area directories are also used in conjunction with the sales promotion program.

Where climatic conditions require it, lodges are air conditioned, and the majority have swimming pools. The partnership operation does not include restaurant facilities, although many of the lodges provide "courtesy coffee" or a Continental breakfast.

The company has compiled a manual of operations as a guide for the co-owner-managers. It also holds semi-annual conferences attended by key staff and partners in the joint ventures, where policies and information on developments in the business are discussed. The company has also worked out insurance programs for the group, including blanket-liability policies, multiple-location fire insurance plans and health, accident and group life plans for employees.

IMPERIAL '400' NATIONAL, INC.

This corporation also acts as a co-owner with motels operated as joint ventures. Organized and headquartered originally in Los Angeles, this company has recently moved its home office to Englewood Cliffs, New Jersey. The established policy of the company is to enter into a separate joint venture with the prospective partner-manager, the company arranging for the selection and leasing or purchase of the site, the architectural planning, construction and furnishing of the property and other services. The company agrees to provide the funds necessary over and above the capital contribution of the resident partner and the mortgage necessary to complete the unit which is the subject of the joint venture. The capital cash contribution of the partner-manager is approximately one-third of the estimated cost of the project and is set at $1,700 per motel unit.

The first motel was opened in Los Angeles on July 5, 1960; by January 31, 1962, there were 26 in operation, of which 25 were joint ventures and one was company owned. This number has increased to 60, most of which are located in the far western part of the country, with a few in the Midwest. The establishments are uniform in design and appearance and offer guest-room accommodations and attendant services, including restaurant or cocktail bar. Swimming pools are a standard facility, as are room telephones, air conditioning and television. Downtown locations are preferred, thus appealing to the commercial traveler as well as the tourist trade. About 10 per cent of the units have kitchen facilities available, complete with utensils.

The land is usually leased and the basis of land rental is set at 7 per cent net to the landowner based on an agreed valuation. Leases run from 54 to 99 years, and the landlord must agree to subjugate his lease rights to the mortgage.

The partnership agreement states that the partner-manager shall take over the daily operation, devoting full time to the project and providing at his own expense whatever personnel and assistance are necessary to operate the motel business office. For this he is allowed 10 per cent of the cash receipts from room rentals plus the use of living quarters on the premises.

Imperial will organize and open the motel for business, including publicity, advertising and announcements. After all current expenses, mortgage payments, taxes, insurance and capital replacements are provided for, the balance of income is divided equally between the company and the co-owner, both being considered equal partners in the venture. Three per cent of gross income is charged for cooperative advertising and sales promotion by the company, which with the fees for central office bookkeeping, accountants and auditing, are charged as an expense of the joint venture.

The partner must be married, thus providing the operation the benefit of a man-and-wife team. He is interviewed by an officer of the company and then also interviewed and passed on by a five-man co-owner approval board. Before the opening of his establishment the new partner spends two weeks at the training school provided for partner-participants in Hollywood, California. The new motel is already opened by the company staff and operating when the new partner arrives, and the maids and others are already instructed in the company's standard methods and procedures.

The co-owner's interest may not be sold or transferred without consent of the company. In the event of sale or dissolution of the joint venture the co-owner and company first receive sums equal to their original investment; the balance of the proceeds of sale are then divided equally.

19

Administration and Management

Efficiency of operation is best obtained by experienced management, which has already met and solved the problems involved in catering to the traveling public. Lacking this background, management must then be guided by the experiences of others in the business, gained by approaching them directly and studying published data related to operations or by hiring assistants with a background in the business. Otherwise, the inexperienced operator must hazard the chance of loss through mistakes in judgment.

Many excellent sources of information are available to the newcomer. The trade associations provide a means of direct contact with others in the business at their regional meetings and conventions, and the material in their bulletins and special studies is made available to members. The industry's referral and recommending organizations also afford this opportunity. The trade press is a prime source of information helpful to management.

The various motel and hotel associations sponsor many trade shows, short courses and training classes. Home study courses are available through the American Hotel Institute and several other recognized schools. Universities with courses in motel and hotel operation also afford some short course training and issue bulletins on special subjects of current interest. A number of colleges offer courses in hotel and motel operation, either in their schools of business administration or in separate schools devoted to the accommodations field. Among the best known are Cornell University, at Ithaca, New York; Denver

230

University; Florida State University, at Tallahasee; Michigan State University, at East Lansing; University of New Hampshire, at Durham; Oklahoma State University, at Clearwater; and Washington State University, at Pullman.

In operations of fewer than 40 units it is generally not feasible to plan for absentee ownership. This is not a rigid rule, of course; there are instances in which a motel of fewer units has provided an adequate living for the manager and a satisfactory profit for the investor. However, in smaller operations the living quarters provided constitute an important aspect of compensation to the operator, the amount of actual dollar profit being limited. These factors tend to make the smaller establishment more logically a direct operation rather than a pure real estate investment.

The operator of a small motel who has direct contact with his guests and attends to all the details of his operation is in a position to be most flexible in his policies and to need comparatively little assistance in carrying them out. Yet he, too, must operate efficiently to obtain the best results and can benefit greatly from the experiences of larger establishments. He should be guided by their methods and controls to the extent that they may be adapted profitably to his simpler operation. With a motel of from 12 to 24 rental units he may not need the help of records beyond a simple cash-receipts and disbursements book, a registration card form and a guest-account sheet, but it would help him to keep statistics on his rooms occupancy and average rate, for use not only as a current guide but also in the event of negotiations for a subsequent sale of the property. His monthly and annual operating figures will be a comparative guide, just as they are to the big operator.

Most small operators prepare their figures primarily for income tax purposes, whereas records and statistics always kept up to date can be useful to management in many ways if they are compiled intelligently and used as more than just a history of the past. The material outlined in this chapter and those that follow can be of as much benefit to the smaller operator as to the larger one, even though for practical purposes these subjects may be discussed in much greater detail than would apply to the simpler operation.

DETERMINING THE ROOM RATE

A number of factors enter into the determination of the rental rates to be charged for guest rooms. Rates must, first of all, be fitted to the pocketbook of the guest, for in the last analysis it is he who sets them, not the motel operator. Another consideration is that once established and publicized either through actual occupancy or advertising and promotional efforts, rates cannot be increased readily without affecting established guest patronage. The process of adjustment upward is ordinarily slow for this reason. Neither can a downward adjustment immediately recover the motel's position in the travel market, for the guest's reaction to the rate stays with him, and adverse word-of-mouth advertising may be hard to overcome without considerable sales promotion expense. Thus great care must be taken in setting room rates at levels that will not, by seeming out of line to current guests, have a negative effect on future patronage.

Although it is considered bad practice by some organizations to advertise rates on signs at the entrance or in the front office of the motel, it is considered good practice to list rate schedules in brochures and travel guides. Such printed advertising media are usually seen by the traveler well in advance of his stay at a motel and therefore are not readily used as rate-cutting weapons by competing establishments.

Rate-Cutting

It was established during the Depression that total guest patronage in an area does not necessarily increase because of lower room rates. In fact, the disastrous effects of rate-cuttting indulged in by the hotel industry during that period should serve as a warning to the motel man, who is now entering a period of intensive competition. The operator who initiates rate-cutting may see a temporary increase in occupancy, but nearby establishments will be forced to retaliate in kind, leveling occupancy and resulting in both depressed rates and profits generally.

The Approach

There are several approaches to determining rates, the most common based on the operator's judgment of what the guest is willing to pay for the type of accommodations and service afforded by the motel. Here, the rates do not necessarily bear any direct relationship to costs and the guides are the rates charged by similar establishments in comparable circumstances. A second method is to base rates on the costs of operation, allowing for a fair return on the investment. Actually both approaches should be reviewed in determining the rate schedule, and certainly the second approach additionally offers a sensible way to determine the economic feasibility of a new facility.

The Hubbart Formula

A formula for computing guest-room rates was developed for the American Hotel & Motel Association by its accounting consultants and named after Mr. Roy Hubbart, who was chairman of the committee in charge of the work. Actually, it had been used for years prior to its publication by the association in 1952.

Under the Hubbart Formula an estimate is made of the number of guest rooms to be sold in a normal year. Then a tabulation is made of the cost of operation, to which is added an amount representing the expected fair return on the investment, which total amount is then divided by the number of estimated occupied rooms to obtain the average rate that must be charged. Taking into account the risks of the business, a return of 10 per cent to 15 per cent on equity capital is considered by most investors to be a reasonable expectation. Rate computation under the Hubbart Formula is best explained by the accompanying illustration which uses a 30-room motel and a 120-room motor hotel as examples.

AVERAGE RATE COMPUTATION
Using Hubbart Formula

	30-Room Motel	*120-Room Motor Hotel*
Estimates of Annual Operating Costs		
Payroll—except catering dept.	$16,800	$105,000
Payroll taxes, etc.	1,250	8,000
Housekeeping	6,000	33,000
Telephone	3,500	19,000
Administrative and general	5,000	33,000
Advertising and promotion	3,600	18,000
Heat, light and power	3,500	25,000
Repairs and maintenance	3,000	20,000
Total operating expenses	$42,650	$261,000
Fixed Charges and Return on Capital		
Local property taxes	3,750	18,000
Insurance on property	700	3,750
Depreciation	14,500	90,000
Interest on borrowed capital	9,000	59,000
Return on equity investment	15,000	30,000
Total costs and expected profit	$85,600	$461,750

Deduct:
Income other than guest-room sales

Profit on catering operations	$ —	$ 85,000
Telephone sales	3,600	18,750
Store rentals and other income	4,000	15,000
Total credits	$ 7,600	$118,750

Amount to be provided by guest-room sales	$78,000	$343,000

Computation of rate necessary to cover

Total available rooms per year	10,950	43,800
Rooms based on 70% occupancy	7,665	30,660

Net costs divided by occupied rooms, which is average rate	$10.18	$11.19
Estimated double occupancy	50%	40%
Average rate per guest	$ 6.79	$ 7.99

Notes on values assumed and financing
Original cost of land, building and

and equipment	$300,000	$1,350,000
Borrowed capital at 6%	150,000	650,000
Debenture loan at 5%	—	400,000
Equity capital at 10%	150,000	—
Equity capital at 15%	—	200,000

Usually the basic rate is applied to the majority of rooms. The additional rate charged for double occupancy is most often the same for all rooms and is based on the cost of servicing the extra guest. It is normally about half again the basic single occupancy rate but in many instances is graduated for costlier accommodations. Suite rates may be set at a single price, whether single or double.

The range of rates, in keeping with the respective accommodations offered by the motel, is based on such factors as comparative amounts of living space, quality of furnishings, convenience of location, view, etc. It is well to remember that most statistics indicate that motels and hotels fill from the bottom up—that is, the lower-priced rooms sell first, and thus the average rate goes up as the occupancy increases.

The policies as to variations in rates from the established schedule and the services to be included in the rate must also be determined by management. It is not considered ethical practice to charge variable rates for the same accommodations based on management's appraisal of the guest and his need at the time of arrival. However, in certain sections of the country it is accepted practice to vary the rates from season to season and to charge different rates during certain local events which may cause all establishments to be temporarily crowded. It has long been accepted policy in motels to offer a special commercial rate for salesmen and others who may be repeat customers through the year. The "family plan," which was adopted by hotels to combat the competition of motels for the tourist trade, now has universal acceptance in almost all sections of the accommodations industry. Special rates are often given to government employees and others who are limited in their traveling budgets and to certain types of group business, such as airline employees, to attract additional patronage from these sources.

Management must also establish a policy regarding the payment of commissions to travel agencies for tourist and group business directed to its establishments. Some motels have arrangements with nearby industries and business establishments whereby rooms are rented to them over extended periods at reduced rates. Usually the agreement guarantees that the rooms will be available when needed but also provides that they can be rented to others when not needed. Special package deals for groups planning to hold meetings, conventions or special tours are not uncommon. In these arrangements guaranteed rates are usually charged, regardless of the type of room occupied.

Frequently a guest will desire the use of a room only during the day. The charge for such use is normally based on a "day rate," which is lower than the overnight rate. Day-use occupancy is not included in sales statistics unless the income derived is substantial enough to be of material influence on these statistics. In some operating statements the day-use sales are shown separately. Usually, however, they are included in total room sales.

The pricing of room accommodations at the most advantageous level is probably the operator's most important decision. Since room sales are a combination of occupancy level multiplied by rate he will naturally want to obtain as high a rate as will bring him the volume necessary for profitable operation. In practice, he will probably not fix his rates by any set formula, but will be guided by all of the considerations mentioned in this section and his judgment as to their application in his individual case.

20

The Front Office

The business office should be located so that the guest can register and make subsequent visits there without inconvenience to himself. Therefore, adjacent temporary parking should be provided and the approach to the office should not require the guest to pass through a lounge or lobby. It is not ordinarily considered good practice to go to the extent of registering the guest while he is still in his car, but many hotels and motor hotels have motor-entrance arrangements convenient to the registration desk, and the operators of many smaller establishments advocate meeting and greeting the prospective guest at his automobile.

FRONT OFFICE FUNCTIONS

The front office provides a place for guest registration and room sales, guest mail service, telephone calls and messages, reservations and referrals, and requests and complaints. It functions as a center for distributing information on the services of the motel, community tourist attractions and travel and road conditions and for directing bellmen, porters and services to guest rooms. Business transactions with the guest are also handled here and include keeping guests' accounts and transacting their payment, establishing credit standing, cashing checks, making change and providing a place for storing guests' valuables.

In large establishments these duties are performed by the room clerk, the mail-and-key clerk and the switchboard operator. The same jobs may be carried out in a smaller establishment by one person.

The hours of operation depend on the flow of guest traffic. The motor hotel will generally provide 24-hour front office coverage, which involves two day crews and a night man, who is responsible for making out the "night audit," which reviews and summarizes the day's transactions.

Salesmanship and the building of good guest relations by the front office staff is essential to successful operation. Although the guest is not "always right" the motel staff should always appear anxious to

View of the lobby of an Albert Pick Motel, East Lansing, Michigan, showing position of front desk, lounge area, vending machines.

Courtesy: Albert Pick Motels

please him. The staff should also show pride in the facilities and standards of service and, above all, be familiar with the merchandise offered. A basic objective is to sell the higher-priced rooms, but the guest's needs and capacity to pay should be judged fairly and can most often be quickly ascertained.

Reservations

Nowadays large numbers of referrals from one motel or hotel to another are obtained through chain, recommending, and franchise groups and the volume of business from those sources has reached the stage where advance reservations are an important consideration. The motel's policies in handling such reservations should be definitely outlined and maintained.

The hotel industry has long lived with the problem of unfulfilled reservations. Most often its bookings are made without advance payment or deposit. Experience has taught that allowance must be made for a percentage of "no-shows," but the problem is complicated by the fact that some guests will not leave as expected. Thus, there is always a danger of overbooking the establishment, a situation that is embarrassing and damaging to one's reputation.

Management must therefore use its judgement on whether to demand advance payment in connection with reservations. The usual practice is to advise the prospective guest that reservations will only be held until a specified hour, usually 6 p.m., unless an advance payment, deposit or guarantee is made through an associated motel, in which case the reservation will be held until arrival. Management should also specify the policy regarding refunds when reservations are cancelled. The prospective guest is often required to make the cancellation a certain number of hours prior to expected time of arrival in order to qualify for the refund.

Requests for reservations received by mail, telephone or TWX should be acknowledged in similar fashion. Reservations received by telephone or made on the premises are, of course, acknowledged orally. All reservations should be recorded immediately in a reservation file or book.

Referral associations and trade organizations offer their affiliates established methods for handling advance reservations. In most of these cooperative arrangements the motel receiving the reservation is expected to pay for the telephone call, telegram or TWX message, although some plans call for guest payment. Advance payment is often cleared through the referral organization's office. In some cases, however, remittances are made direct from one motel to another. The guest presents his receipt at the front office in all instances.

In the smaller establishments and where they are not a material item, advance reservations can be recorded in a small reservations book, with bookings listed by days. An effective method is to record each request on a 3- by 5-inch card showing the date the reservation was made, the date and time of expected arrival, name of guest or his party, his connection with any group or convention, the accommodations desired and the rate quoted. Cards for the current month are filed chronologically. Larger motor hotels facilitate the handling of reservations by means of a reservation rack, which also uses chronological filing. This rack can be in movable sections, making it possible to move individual sections to the front clerk's station so that he will have the bookings at hand a few days in advance, enabling him to make assignments without difficulty. Each day the morning clerk on duty will make notations on the current reservation cards or rack slips and on the room rack as to the assignments planned for the day.

Registration

All guests should be required to register, not only to provide a record of their arrival and control over room sales but because registration is a factor in maintaining the moral character of the motel. This requirement applies to the day-use occupant and the residential guest as well as to the regular transient or overnight guest. The guest usually signs for himself and his party, but in some instances of advance reservation, management may register for him prior to his arrival as a matter of convenience. Pre-registration and assignment are particularly helpful in the case of convention, tourist or other group arrivals. State law should be checked by management to ensure

---

REGISTRATION CARD

GUESTS WITHOUT BAGGAGE PLEASE PAY IN ADVANCE

Money, jewels and valuables must be deposited in the office safe, otherwise the proprietor will not be responsible for any loss.

Name _____

Street _____

City _____ State _____

Representing _____

Room	Rate	Arrive	Folio
		A. M: P. M:	
Date	No. in Party	Clerk	

Remarks

Form 35B   JOHN WILLY. INC., EVANSTON, ILL.

This stock form of registration card can double as an account card by using the reverse side.

Courtesy: John Willy, Inc.

compliance to regulations regarding registration and the length of time such records must be kept.

The registration sheet formerly used by hotels has now been almost completely supplanted by the use of a numbered registration card, which is more practical and also provides the protection of privacy to the guest. Because of ease in sorting registration cards, they can be used for later filing, facilitating the compilation of data on arrivals and departures. For cross reference the registration card and guest-

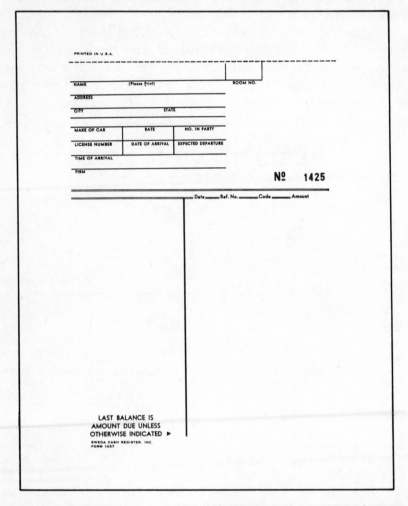

This form is both registration card and guest account card. Posted amounts are keyed with special code numbers that are explained on the bottom or reverse of the guest copy.

Courtesy: Monroe/Sweda

acount folio often carry the same number, and in some smaller operations, bookkeeping and control are further simplified by having the record of the guest's account on the reverse side of the registration card.

The registration card should be dated, include lines for writing in the name of the guest and the number of persons in his party, the guest's mailing address and business or group connection and the make and license number of his automobile. If the guest's handwriting is not legible, the clerk should ascertain the proper spelling and print that information on the card to make later reference easier. The card should also have spaces for room number and rate.

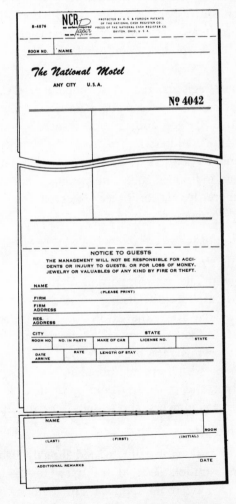

No carbon is required for this form that utilizes a specially-processed paper to provide duplicate copies of registration and guest accounts.

Courtesy: National Cash Register Company

The Room Rack

A room rack is not necessary for the small motel inasmuch as the status of room occupancy can be noted from the rack on which the room keys are kept. In larger operations the room rack is a convenience to the clerk and an essential part of the system of control on room sales. The rack should be located next to the registration section of the desk facing the clerk's position. It should be hidden from view to allow the clerk freedom in deciding room assignment and to protect the privacy of guests, who are listed on the rack.

The rack contains a slot or pocket for each guest-room unit in the motel. Each such space contains information as to the room's capacity, bath facilities, rate and other characteristics that will be helpful to the clerk in determining whether it is suitable for the guest's needs.

After the guest registers, the clerk prepares a rack slip indicating the name of each of the guests, the number of persons assigned to each room, the rate charged, and, in some instances, additional information such as mailing addresses. The rack slip is then placed in the assigned slot and stays there until the guest has checked out. The modern rack has indicators coded in various colors to show which rooms are temporarily out of order, reserved for later arrivals or not yet made up for guest occupancy.

The Information Rack

The information rack serves the key stations concerned with direct service to the guest. The most important of these stations is the front office, where this alphabetical listing of guests can be conveniently placed for use by the clerk, the cashier and the telephone operator. If the switchboard is located elsewhere, it should have its own information rack. Slips for this rack are made out at the same time room rack slips are prepared. Often, additional information slips are issued to the housekeeper and other key employees in order to keep them abreast of room assignments and enhance personalized service.

The Mail-and-Key Rack

A mail-and-key rack is usually located directly behind the clerk's station at the registration desk in full view of the guest. Its compartments, arranged by room number, are used for guest mail and messages and the deposit of room keys. The bottom row of this rack contains compartments alphabetically arranged to hold mail and messages addressed to guests who have not yet arrived or been assigned.

In some motels the room keys are not kept in the mail rack where they are on public view, and in a few modern front-office layouts even the mail is not readily visible, a light over the box signalling the presence of mail. Sometimes a name plate is located directly below the mail-and-key compartment so that the clerk may call the guest by name or check his identification when giving out the contents of his box.

Room Keys

Most motels keep two keys in the rack for each room. An auxiliary set is also usually kept in a locked compartment in another location in or near the front office. Room keys are sometimes a problem to the management of a motel; forgetful guests often take them along on departure or otherwise lose them. For that reason keys are usually tagged with the name and address of the motel as well as the identifying room number, the reverse side of the tag bearing instructions to drop the key in the mail, return postage guaranteed. It is good practice to post a sign in each guest room reminding the guest to leave his key at the desk upon departure and to have the cashier, bellman or car attendant politely ask the guest if he has turned in his key upon checking out. In smaller operations, when the guest has paid in advance he is frequently asked to leave his key in the room door upon departure.

Front Office Bookkeeping

If the volume of business warrants it, the handling of cash transactions and posting of guest accounts is placed in the hands of a front office cashier, whose station is next to that of the clerk at the front desk. The location should be reasonably protected by partitions so that the cashier can attend to her duties without interference or fear of loss though pilferage. The cashier should be provided a cash drawer in which to lock funds for making change, cashing checks and paying for such petty cash items as are designated by the management.

When the clerk has made out his rack slips the registration card is turned over to the cashier, who makes out a numbered guest-account sheet, establishing cross references, if necessary, and including such information as the date, room number and rate, guest's name and address. Bookkeeping is usually done by hand unless the motel is large enough to warrant machine accounting, usually restricted to establishments of 100 rooms or more with full facilities. A protected window is provided at the cashier's station for contact with the guest. Next to it should be sufficient counter space to place the necessary records and to handle cash.

DAILY BALANCE FORM

MONEY IN DRAWER			DATE			
COINS			WEATHER			
CURRENCY			NO. OF ROOMS OCCUPIED			
CHECKS			NO. OF GUESTS			
TOTAL						
TOTAL CASH REC'D (B)				RESET NUMBER		
OVER			TODAY			
			PREVIOUS			
SHORT			No. TOTALS RESET			

ADJUSTED DEPT. TOTALS	CORRECTIONS		DISTRIBUTION OF SALES
TOTAL SALES TODAY			
PREVIOUS SALES	OUTSTDG START OF DAY (ADD)	(D)	
SALES TO DATE	TOTAL	(A)	

MISC. CREDITS		
CASH REC'D ON ACC'T (ADD)		
WITHDRAWAL (ADD)		
TOTAL (SUBTRACT FROM A)		
OUTSTANDING END OF DAY (C)		
CASH REC'D ON ACC'T		
ADVANCE PAYMENTS (ADD)		
TOTAL CASH		
ADV. PAY REF. (SUBTRACT)		
TOTAL CASH IN DRAWER (B)		
ADVANCE PAYMENT BALANCE		
PREVIOUS BALANCE FOR MONTH		
ADVANCE PAYMENTS (ADD)		
TOTAL		
WITHDRAWAL (SUBTRACT)		
NEW BALANCE		

SWEDA CASH REGISTER, INC.
FORM 1104   PRINTED IN U.S.A.

Accumulated departmental charges and credits are printed out on this daily balance form during the night audit.

Courtesy: Monroe/Sweda

Guest accounts should be kept up to the minute, since the guest often leaves without prior notice. It is customary to ask the departing guest if any recent charges have been made that may not yet have been posted to his account. This posting is done during the day, before the sales records of the operating departments have been prepared and made available for checking. The control of guest transactions is therefore a part of the night clerk's duties; he prepares a transcript of the accounts and ties them up with the various departmental sales records and front office cash sheets.

The front office sales record for a small establishment usually consists of a cash book or sheet, and the guests are given a receipt or statement of their account prepared at departure. In the larger operations, the ledger sheet and the guest's statement of account are posted simultaneously.

Payment for Rooms and Services

In highway motels and those establishments located in smaller communities, advance payments are more the rule than in the resort, city and suburban motels. Places which cater to the tourist trade and to salesmen often find that when the traveler wishes to get an early start, he prefers advance payment. If payment is in advance the clerk is often required to mark the registration card accordingly. Naturally, the guest-account sheet and cashier's sheet will reflect the transaction.

The motor hotel with full facilities, in keeping with the policies of conventional hotels, usually allows the guest to pay upon departure unless there is some indication that he is a poor credit risk, perhaps because he is carrying "light baggage" or no luggage at all. In this case management must outline the policy and control procedure with respect to the accumulation of charges against the guest's account. If the guest's stay is prolonged he is most often expected to pay his bill at least weekly unless other credit arrangements have been made. In many circumstances of transient occupancy, the manager receives a list of three-day bills to review for credit purposes.

The entire credit policy of the motel is a matter to be determined by management. Many travelers are now accustomed to having credit extended to them upon properly establishing their credit status. This convenience allows the guest to sign his bill upon departure and have it sent to his home or business address for later payment. Patrons who are local residents are also often accustomed to signing their restaurant checks and being billed on a monthly basis. Most hotels have for years been developing their own credit systems and credit card identifications as a part of their sales promotion programs. The popularity of such credit card systems as American Express, Hilton's Carte Blanche, and Diner's Club has greatly increased this manner of doing business in recent years. Management must determine the extent to which these cards will be accepted for credit and whether the motel will pay the charges—usually from 4 to 6 per cent of the bill—made by these companies for their guarantee and collections service. The charges and accounts for persons of established credit who are not registered and living at the motel are kept in what is called the "city ledger." If the volume of such business warrants it, this ledger may be kept in the auditor's office, but it should always be available to the front office cashier.

There is an element of risk involved in cashing checks, accepting C.O.D. deliveries, and making cash advances from front office funds. The risk can be minimized if management sets limits on amounts and requires satisfactory identification. Many motels follow a policy of accepting checks only in payment of accounts, in which cases home addresses and auto licenses offer some protection against loss. The American Hotel & Motel Association has an arrangement with the Burns Detective Agency for the apprehension of bad-check passers, and in metropolitan centers hotels warn each other by Teletype about suspicious cases. If a motel issues its own credit cards, an effective way of checking the identity of the card holder is to have the motel records indicate his birth date, which can then be requested of the holder.

Mail, Messages and Forwarding Notices

Usually a space is provided in the front office area where incoming mail can be checked against the information rack, marked and distributed to the mail rack. If a departing guest leaves a forwarding address it should be noted in a card file so that mail for guests whose names do not appear on the current information rack may be checked against that record and also against the advance reservation file. If not marked "hold," the balance of mail received for persons not staying at the motel may be held for a specified number of days and then returned to the sender, in which case it is also advisable to note on the envelope that the addressee is not at the motel. The receipt of registered mail, telegrams and packages should be recorded in a book provided for that purpose, and notice of it should be sent to the guest's room or placed in his box so that he can stop at the desk and sign for such items. Time and date should be stamped on telegrams and messages.

If the guest is not available to receive an incoming telephone call, notification of the call, or the message, should be placed in his box and his room. Stock forms are available in all hotel stationery houses for that purpose as well as for recording outgoing calls made through the motel switchboard. Management should determine the basis of charges for outgoing telephone calls. There is usually a service charge in addition to the actual cost of the call. Service charges on interstate calls are currently restricted, and management should check with its local association to find the amount of service charge permitted.

Storage of Valuables

Management should check state laws governing responsibility for guests' effects and valuables and comply with the regulations regarding proper notice to guests in this regard. Provisions for safe storage of

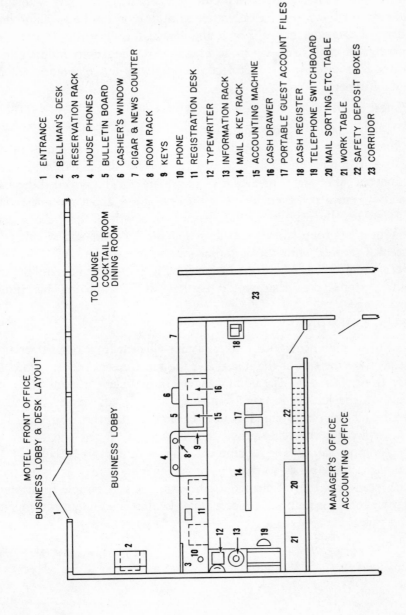

MOTEL FRONT OFFICE
BUSINESS LOBBY & DESK LAYOUT

TO LOUNGE
COCKTAIL ROOM
DINING ROOM

BUSINESS LOBBY

MANAGER'S OFFICE
ACCOUNTING OFFICE

1 ENTRANCE
2 BELLMAN'S DESK
3 RESERVATION RACK
4 HOUSE PHONES
5 BULLETIN BOARD
6 CASHIER'S WINDOW
7 CIGAR & NEWS COUNTER
8 ROOM RACK
9 KEYS
10 PHONE
11 REGISTRATION DESK
12 TYPEWRITER
13 INFORMATION RACK
14 MAIL & KEY RACK
15 ACCOUNTING MACHINE
16 CASH DRAWER
17 PORTABLE GUEST ACCOUNT FILES
18 CASH REGISTER
19 TELEPHONE SWITCHBOARD
20 MAIL SORTING, ETC. TABLE
21 WORK TABLE
22 SAFETY DEPOSIT BOXES
23 CORRIDOR

guest valuables is required, and the motel should post prominent notices to the effect that it will not be responsible for valuables unless they are deposited in the front office. The motel may provide special envelopes or safety deposit boxes for storage in a vault or safe. Valuables are returned to the guest only after identification has been established. Loss of baggage or valuables and damage to guests' property are matters of concern to everyone in the accommodations industry, and claims are often paid to protect the goodwill and reputation of the establishment.

Guest History

Many motels and most hotels compile a "guest history" record, used primarily as a reference for determining the guest's preferences in the event of return business. It is also useful for direct-mail and other promotional efforts. The extent of information to be recorded depends on how much management feels it should know about the guest. The history usually records the frequency and length of stay, the guest's business or group affiliation, the reason for his visits and whether he seemed satisfied with the accommodations and service. Additional information for this record might include the guest's credit standing and any personal data that would be helpful in attracting his future patronage.

Front Office Plan

The plan and equipment necessary for efficient front office operation depend on the size of the house and the functions to be performed by the front office staff. The best arrangement provides for items of equipment to be located near a counter or desk of convenient height to enable the guest to stand while registering and checking out. The centerpiece of the registration desk consists of a pen and a pad of registration cards. The equipment and working areas behind the counter should be set so that the prospective guest may easily identify the location of the various front office functions. A sample front office layout for a medium-sized motor hotel is illustrated on an accompanying page.

21

Housekeeping

Because the success or failure of a motel operation is determined primarily by the amount of income derived from guest-room sales, it is important that the patron be pleased with his accommodations. A bright, clean room is the best way to supplement a cordial welcome.

In a smaller motel the housekeeping duties are usually performed by the wife of the operating team, and the maintenance and repair functions are the responsibility of the husband. Motels of from 12 to 40 units require additional help, consisting of maids, cleaning women and a houseman or handyman. The functions of the housekeeping department in motor hotels are directed by a full-time housekeeper and staff. Whether the housekeeper also supervises the maintenance crew, yardman, gardener and laundry workers depends on the staff organization plan and is further influenced by the size and extent of the overall facilities. If maintenance and utilities are to be the responsibility of a full-time engineer or superintendent, he and his staff will cooperate with the housekeeping department.

The number of rooms assigned to each maid depends on the extent of her duties and the methods used, these in turn depending on the staff organization plan and the layouts of the rooms and other areas to be serviced. If the maid does the complete make-up of the room, including changing the linens, wiping and dusting furniture, sweeping, vacuuming, scouring of bathrooms, cleaning windows, removing trash and replacing room supplies she may average from 10 to 15 rooms per day, depending on the occupancy. If bath maids or cleaners are added to the staff, their assignments will be coordinated with those of the maids. The houseman assists with the heavier work, such as furniture moving, outside cleaning, wall and window washing, hall vacuuming, etc. He will also perform the janitorial duties of trash gathering and disposal and care of walks and grounds. In a larger motor hotel the care of the lounge, lobby, restaurant area and other public rooms may be assigned to a parlor maid and housemen. In those establishments where maids are assigned only the guest rooms themselves, the average assignment per maid may range from 16 to 18 rooms or more daily.

Additional personnel will be needed if the guest is to be offered turn-down service preparatory to retiring. This service is quite common in resorts and luxury motor hotels and in motels with studio-type rooms. Whether the evening maid will also lay out pajamas, nightgowns and slippers and provide related niceties of service is dependent on operating policy. Another aspect of policy has to do with the frequency of bed linen changes for non-transient guests. In such cases linen is usually changed every other day.

The equipment afforded the housekeeping staff has a direct influence on their efficiency, as does the distance they must go to replenish supplies and perform their duties. Factors influencing efficiency and labor costs include: the location of maids' and janitors' closets in relation to the guest-room area; the use of maids' carts for easier transport of supplies; the use of electric brooms and vacuum cleaners. New supplies are being developed constantly, and the motel operator and housekeeper should keep abreast of such advances in the field.

Proper training of personnel will result in a more effective operation and greater guest satisfaction. Up-to-date housekeeping methods are outlined in a number of manuals and texts available through national, state and local trade associations. These same organizations often provide short courses and correspondence courses on the subject. Another source of information is the trade press.

The day maids usually arrive for duty at 8 a.m. Sometimes their hours are staggered so that some start later than others and thus are able to cover late check-outs and changes. The work of making up and cleaning the rooms starts with those that have been vacated. If the guest is still in the room, it is good policy not to disturb him until later in the day. Some rooms have devices which indicate when a guest-room door is locked from the inside. In the event that a guest wishes to sleep late or be left alone, a "Do Not Disturb" sign is provided. In any instance, the maid should knock on the door before entering a room. Whenever possible, those rooms housing guests staying over should be done first and all rooms should be made up and ready for assignment by mid-afternoon.

Management will determine the check-out hour, which is usually based on average arrival and departure times. Check-out time in motels is usually between 3 p.m. and 6 p.m. Signs or cards notifying guests as to check-out time should be placed in the guest room and at the front desk. If the guest wishes to use the room beyond the posted time, management has the right to make an additional charge for such use.

It is the duty of the housekeeper to inform the front office when a room is made up and ready for assignment. In larger establishments the housekeeper also prepares a daily report on the room occupancy, based on the reports made by the maids after they have had an opportunity to check the occupancy in their sections. The housekeeper's daily report is used as a double check on room sales and is sent to the auditor's office to be compared with the clerk's or night auditor's report. It is then checked against the room rack in order to ensure that the rack properly indicates whether a room is occupied or vacant. Each guest-room number is listed on the housekeeper's report form and a space is provided to indicate the condition in which each room was found by the housekeeping staff. A code or symbols are used on this form to save space and time in preparing the report. A sample code would be to use the letter "O" for rooms still occupied, an "X" for rooms slept in but now vacated (no baggage in the room), a "V" for vacant or unoccupied rooms and an "M" or "Z" for rooms out of order. An afternoon maids' report may also be made up and sent to the front office as a check on the room rack. This is the report that usually catches the "sleepers," rooms for which the rack slips were not removed upon check-out, and the "skippers," rooms vacated by guests who did not pay their bills.

The maids' reports may be simple. They are often made on an ordinary scratch pad. It may be a better idea, however, to provide mimeographed or printed forms (specially designed to meet the needs of the house). Motel and hotel supply houses have standard forms that can be used for both the maids' and housekeeper's reports. These forms usually provide space in which to report maintenance needs, losses due to pilferage, and any unusual conditions found in the guest rooms which should be brought to the attention of management.

DIXIE GOVERNOR MOTEL
EAST HAZELCREST, ILLINOIS

DATE _____

HOUSEKEEPER'S REPORT

O – OCCUPIED
C. O. – CHECK OUT
V – VACANT - IN ORDER
S. O. – SLEEP OUT
O. O. O. – OUT OF ORDER

BUILDING - A				BUILDING - B			
ROOM NO.	REPORT	ROOM NO.	REPORT	ROOM NO.	REPORT	ROOM NO.	REPORT
101		301		119		319	
103		303		121		321	
105		305		123		323	
107		307		125		325	
109		309		127		327	
111		311		129		329	
115		315		131		331	
117		317		133		333	

BUILDING - C				BUILDING - D			
ROOM NO.	REPORT	ROOM NO.	REPORT	ROOM NO.	REPORT	ROOM NO.	REPORT
135		335		151		351	
137		337		153		353	

Typical daily housekeeper's report.

Courtesy: Sherway Press

The extent to which the housekeeper is involved in the handling of repairs and maintenance depends on the policy of the house and the size of the maintenance staff. It is not unusual for her to schedule and supervise painting and interior decorating, carpet replacement and similar work. Even if she is not directly responsible for repairs the work will be done in cooperation with her, and she will notify both management and the maintenance staff whenever the need is found for repairs on the motel premises. She or members of her supervisory staff should make regular inspections of the rooms, not only to judge the efficiency of the maids, but also to check the physical condition of each room and its contents. An inventory and check list on the items to be inspected should be prepared by management.

The control of house linens and uniforms is also the responsibility of the housekeeper and she should have adequate and convenient space for the handling of these items. The linen room usually adjoins the space occupied by the housekeeper's office and desk. Space for a seamstress to work is also often provided in that location.

Methods of linen and uniform control differ with the conditions in each house. It is generally conceded that physical control on a piece basis is the most practical method. For instance, every morning the linen room issues to each maid the number of sheets, pillow cases, towels, etc., needed for servicing the rooms in her section. The maids are then expected to return soiled or unused linens equal to the number issued. Uniforms are controlled by replacing clean for soiled, or new for old. The housekeeping department also keeps a record of the linens sent to and received from the laundry each day. It is particularly important to check the count and charges made by the laundry. Where the charge is on a per-pound basis, however, it is impractical to make a daily count of the pieces, and a check by count is made on an occasional test basis when discrepancies are suspected.

It is advisable to control linens, china, glassware, silver and uniforms by periodic inventory. With this method the losses are determined by comparing the latest count with previous inventories adjusted for new purchases. The size of the loss will reflect pilferage, the wear due to laundering, and the carelessness of employees. Since the value of these items mounts up, their care and control are important in keeping the cost of replacement in line.

Regular inventories are helpful in planning future purchases and determining the sufficiency of reserve stocks. In some instances a record of discards is kept as a check on the reasonableness of the losses indicated by inventory checks. If the regular inventories are not priced, as is often the case when they are not tied into the general books of account, the indicated losses will be a matter only of operating information, whereas, if priced, they may also be used by the auditor or bookkeeper to determine balance sheet valuations of assets.

If the motel operates its own laundry, the housekeeper usually supervises, although in the larger houses a laundry manager may be in charge. In any event the housekeeping and laundry personnel should operate in close cooperation. Whether it is advisable from a cost or service standpoint to have the motel do its own laundering and whether it should own or rent its linens and washable uniforms will depend upon many factors which management must take into consideration. Among these factors are the size of the house, the availability of space for laundry operations, the ability of management and staff to perform the necessary work involved and the way in which the prices and services of the local commercial laundry compare with the estimated costs of financing, housing, equipping, staffing and operating a laundry at the motel.

With its own laundry, the motel management will have direct control over the formulas and processes used, be able to schedule laundry operations to fit in with the needs of the motel and enjoy the advantages of a direct inventory control. It may be more practical, however, to have a commercial laundry take care of the motel's needs.

If arrangements with a commercial laundry include rental of linens, qualities and quantities should be carefully spelled out. Should management elect to purchase its own linens and send them out for laundering, care should be taken that they are returned on time and that no substitutions are made by the laundry.

A book* by L. A. Bradley, staff member of Iowa State University and laundry consultant of the American Hotel & Motel Association, describes in detail laundry processes, linen tests, equipment needs and the relative merits of the motel doing its own work or contracting with a commercial laundry. It is recommended to the reader who wishes to pursue this subject further.

For certain specialized services, outside contractors may be better equipped than motel personnel. Outside help is often sought for such jobs as painting, plumbing, electrical work, masonry, carpentry, landscaping and gardening, elevator and sign maintenance and machine repairs. Pest control, window washing, carpet installation and cleaning and interior decorating are usually best left in the hands of experts. The difference between professional service and less expert work can be quite telling in these areas, and the additional cost of a professional job is often justified.

*Guide for Good Laundry and Linen Services, New York: Ahrens Book Company, Inc. 1961.

22

Personnel

It is said that the personality of the manager can be gauged by the behavior of his employees and the atmosphere of the motel. Therefore, to achieve the friendly and efficient operation that will make the best impression it is essential that the manager take advantage of the tools afforded him to mold his staff. As it becomes necessary for the motel manager to delegate duties and responsibilities to others, many contacts with the guest are left to the employees; their contribution to successful public relations increases accordingly.

RECRUITMENT

It is advisable to take time to interview the job applicant and to have him fill out an application form. The application should list name, address, home telephone, history of employment and character references. Other, more personal, questions may be raised in the interview if necessary. Some knowledge of the applicant's family relationships and church affiliation, his sobriety and his reasons for leaving his last job may be revealing. References should be checked, even if there is no time to do so until after the applicant has been hired. If the employee is to be covered by a fidelity bond, the processing of the bonding company's form is also required, and the importance of references is increased.

Should the department head be responsible for the employee's performance, it is advisable to delegate the hiring to him, subject to management's approval. In some of the larger organizations, hiring,

255

training and other functions of employee relations are handled by a personnel manager and his staff, but in most motels and motor hotels the hiring is done by the manager and his department heads.

Attention must be paid to state and local laws regulating the hiring of minors, the use of women for certain jobs, wages and hours and health examinations. Employees must supply information for forms to be filed for withholding taxes and social security deductions. The employee's application is usually sent to the auditor's office with proper notations as to date of hiring, wages and other pertinent information. There, references are checked and the necessary information is added to the payroll records.

Job Descriptions and Specifications

It is quite helpful in building an organization to review the various positions to be filled and to put on paper a description of the duties and responsibilities of each job, specifying the attributes that will qualify the employee to fill it. By detailing such information and fitting it to the various jobs and positions in the motel, management can better establish the lines of authority. Such an analysis will also serve as the basis for subsequent training and for judging employee efficiency and value to the organization. The job description should cover what is to be done, the reason for doing it, how and when it is to be done and who is to do it. It will also indicate how the job may coordinate with the duties and responsibilities of others in the organization, and the extent of authority accorded to it.

Job specifications outline the necessary physical and mental requirements, skills and training; the hours and wage scales; the perquisites afforded, such as free meals, group insurance, and vacations. Also included are the possibilities for advancement, any bonus or profit-sharing arrangements and other incentives. In establishments with union contracts, job descriptions and specifications must be fitted to union regulations in order to avoid possible jurisdictional differences.

WORK STANDARDS AND PERFORMANCE

In gauging the efficiency of the staff it is best to establish standards of performance. These standards are based on several means of measurement, the most common being the ratio of labor cost to sales, determined by departments and for the motel as a whole; the amount of average daily sales per service employee; the number of rooms or meals serviced per employee, and the number of employees per available guest unit. Since the physical plant, service standards, staff organization and percentage of occupancy will vary from one operation to another, it is advisable to establish performance standards on the basis of direct experience. The guidance of general published statistics is helpful in setting up standards, but it must be kept in mind that the quotas or ratios shown in these studies should be adjusted to fit the specific conditions found in a given house. The time required to do a guest room and the number of guest rooms to be assigned per maid are the most common examples of widely applied production standards. It is obvious that they cannot be the same for all operations even under optimum conditions. However, statistics compiled for the entire direct operating staff can reveal much about employee efficiency. The need for a certain number of employees in the rooms and telephone departments can be gauged by the number of occupied rooms or the number of guests housed per day; the restaurant staff by the number of customers served per employee in each position; and the beverage staff by the average daily sales per employee.

Employees should be expected to adhere to established standards of deportment and grooming, often included in an instruction manual issued to the staff. Instructions may go so far as to prescribe the wording of greetings to the guest during the different service contacts. Standards should be reinforced by inspections conducted by supervisory personnel.

Training

A systematic and effective program of training and instruction is often the mark of an efficient operation. However, adherence to such a program is not an established policy in many motels, especially in the smaller establishments, and the result is a noticeably amateur performance by employees in many instances. To place a person on the job without first acquainting him with his duties, surroundings, relations with guests and other staff members and the tested methods and policies of the motel is to have him stumble through the job until he has had a chance to learn from experience, consuming time and effort and creating a bad impression on the guest as well.

On-the-job training is the usual method of breaking in a new employee, and that implies explaining the job to him and then allowing him to perform his duties under supervision. Direct supervision may be supplemented by equipping the employee with a manual outlining the house policies, facilities, and duties of each employee as taken from the job descriptions and specifications previously worked out. An orientation conference or lecture for new employees will be found most helpful. Then the new employee may be assigned to work as an assistant to an experienced member of the staff long enough to develop the confidence to carry on alone.

Other training methods utilizing off-duty time are also worthwhile. They can take the form of regular staff meetings, during which group discussions of problems and methods are led by the department head, always inviting the ideas and participation of those attending. Group instruction on the proper way to carry out assignments, which may involve a short-course program conducted at the motel by a qualified instructor, is another type of training often used. One point to be remembered is that such instruction should not be a "one-shot deal," but that repetition is often necessary to put certain points across and remind employees of important aspects of their jobs which may have been neglected.

Many organizations prefer to hire inexperienced help and to train them in their own methods, thus avoiding a reorientation that may involve much "unlearning."

Job instruction is often better related to the individual rather than the group, especially if the lesson is imparted at the time when the employee logically needs it. To win employee respect and accomplish maximum efficiency it is essential that the supervisor be capable of performing the duty himself and be able to impress upon those under him the importance and the benefits of doing the job well.

Education through home study courses, attendance at schools with courses in various phases of the motel and hotel business, and short-course sessions sponsored by local and national trade associations can also become a part of the training program. Motel operators often encourage staff members to take advantage of such instruction by providing tuition or paying transportation costs. Sometimes such financial assistance is given in the form of prizes for outstanding work performance.

The manager may conduct many of the staff meetings himself, or he may delegate that function to his department heads, but since management is primarily responsible for the training of employees he should keep in touch with the entire program. It is also desirable for management to have frequent meetings with department heads and key employees to discuss current problems, review past performance, exchange ideas, straighten out differences, and prepare for future events such as convention and meeting groups, banquets and parties.

Staff Morale

Morale—an employee's pride in the establishment and in his fellow workers—is a primary responsibility of management. Job security is a key factor here, of course, and an efficient organization will extend itself beyond the confines of the motel itself to see to the personal needs of its employees. On-the-job contentment is likely if the manager and his supervisory staff are cordial to employees and grant them proper recognition for their performance of duties. Presentation of badges or awards denoting length of service, sponsorship of bowling or softball teams, and the use of employees' names and pictures in publicity releases and promotional material are effective in promoting "esprit de corps."

A sense of personal security is further enhanced by such benefits as group life insurance and medical coverage. In addition, management may elect to provide for payroll advances or loans to cover illnesses or emergencies and may offer legal assistance when it is required. A personal interest can be demonstrated through the sending of Christmas cards, Christmas or Thanksgiving baskets to employees and their families. Often the best way to establish a good relationship with employees is an occasional private chat, where the employee may air his grievances and concerns.

Care should be taken to avoid creating jealousies through apparently preferential treatment of one employee over others. Furthermore, lines of authority should be followed; a department head's position may be weakened considerably if management deals directly with employees on matters that are logically in the supervisor's domain.

ORGANIZATION CHART

The extent of an organization and the lines of authority and responsibility for the operation of a motel are best illustrated and most easily understood if a chart is prepared showing the various positions and how they are related to the whole. Many of the questions relating to proper organization are answered in such a presentation. In a small operation it will be a very simple picture and can probably include each member of the staff by name as well as position. In some instances, employee interest in the chart is enhanced by placing his picture in the appropriate spot on the chart. In larger establishments the names and number of persons in each position are often omitted as a practical matter, but the types of jobs and their relationship to each other and to top management or ownership are shown.

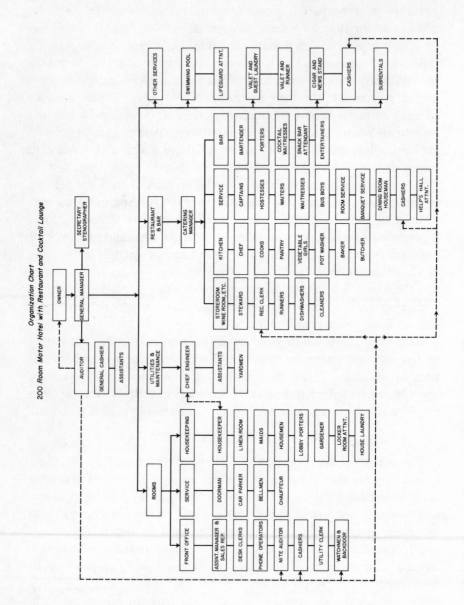

Organization Chart
200 Room Motor Hotel with Restaurant and Cocktail Lounge

A sample organization chart for a 200-room motor hotel doing a food and beverage volume averaging $1,650 per day is shown on an accompanying page. You will note that in this illustration the dotted line extending from the auditor's position indicates his direct responsibility to the owners as well as the employees responsible to him for income control purposes. The auditor in this instance also hires the various cashiers, but the manager has the ultimate responsibility and authority for the deportment and operational efficiency of all employees on the staff. Both the assistant manager and catering manager take part in sales solicitation and in making arrangements for conventions, meetings and banquets. In this chart the major operating departments are shown for clarity, and the need for cooperation between housekeeper and chief engineer on maintenance is illustrated. The direct responsibility of the department heads to the general manager and the assignment of responsibility for hiring employees in the various departments are also indicated.

23

Advertising Sales Promotion and Public Relations

Advertising, sales promotion and public relations programs are all tied together in an effort to bring the motel to the attention and consideration of the largest possible number of prospective patrons. To adapt the effective means and methods for accomplishing these ends, the motel operator should be acquainted with the fundamentals of merchandising. He should make an accurate appraisal of his market and have a knowledge of the various forms of advertising and the methods used in selling accommodations.

Most motel operators devise their own programs, guided to some extent by what they have observed others doing and by magazine articles. Seldom does a trade magazine fail to offer at least one article on the subject, usually submitted by, or written about, an operator who has found his program productive of increases in sales and income. Rarely does an association meeting omit a speaker or panel session discussing advertising and sales promotion. They are all success stories, for the failures are not bragged about either in published articles or by word of mouth. Nevertheless, both sources of information are very likely to provide some valuable suggestions relating to such a program.

Having a proper advertising and sales promotion program is important to the success of a project and for that reason it is advisable to seek the services of an expert, if sufficient funds are available to underwrite such a step. The engagement of an advertising consultant or agency should result in a more polished, professional job than that of a motel operator working part-time at the task. The professional will supply more than art work and copy. He should know the relative merits of the various media, be capable of channeling the message effectively, and be responsible for coordinating the advertising program with the sales and public relations program of his client's establishment.

In a smaller operation with only a limited number of guest units to sell, the amount devoted to advertising and promotion is usually more limited and the program is therefore more dependent on the operator's individual efforts. A few road signs, an entrance sign and direct mail are the most common advertising media in these circumstances. The funds applied to the program are commonly measured in relation to room sales, and although averages of the industry can be a guide to determining the proper level for such expenditures, the expected result on profits should be the primary factor in planning the program. In the 1962 study of motor hotels made by Horwath & Horwath, the establishments not operating a restaurant were shown to be spending $133 per available guest unit, or 4.7 per cent of room sales, and the projects operating restaurants were shown to be spending $148 per room, or 5.2 per cent of room sales, on advertising and sales promotion.

The first essential of any program is a good product. "Truth in advertising" has become an accepted principle, and fair value is therefore important in selling accommodations and service. The reputation of the motel is soon established with the public by the manner in which it satisfies the patronage generated by the advertising and selling program. Word-of-mouth advertising is most effective in establishing a reputation. Therefore it is essential that the guest speak well of the establishment after his stay, and the policies of the house should be pointed toward that end. Rate-gouging, unclean rooms, uncomfortable beds, poor food and lack of courtesy will soon offset the favorable effect of a sales and advertising program, no matter how well conceived. Unfavorable word-of-mouth advertising by travelers and people in the immediate community can do great harm to a motel. Overselling is dangerous for that reason, and care should be taken to see that the sales and advertising campaign properly represents the facilities and service afforded by the motel.

The business promotion program should merchandise the facilities to their greatest potential. The best prospect is one who is fully informed about the motel before he arrives. Therefore the campaign will concentrate on publicizing the name of the motel, its size and facilities, rate and price schedule, its location and directions for reaching it.

In planning a program it is best to start with a market study and determination of the type of guest that will use the facilities. Some of the questions to be answered by the study are: Where will these guests come from and why will they stop at the motel? How long will they stay, and what facilities other than rooms will meet their needs and attract them to the motel? The advertising and sales promotion program will then concentrate on the areas of greatest potential. Naturally, the timing of programs to coincide with local events and attractions, and with seasonal movements of tourists and sportsmen, is also important.

Road Signs

Because the motel industry received its original impetus from the tourist, road signs became a common medium for their advertising programs. Attractive signs placed at strategic intervals are used ex-

The entrance sign of the Glenwood Manor Motor House, Overland Park, Kansas, as it appears to the highway traveler.

Courtesy: Glenwood Manor Motor House

tensively, their messages including the name of the motel, a description of facilities and policies of service, and directions. Lighted or reflector-type signs are advisable, since a large number of motorists in search of accommodations remain on the highways after sundown.

Entrance sign, motor lobby and access to the rooms sections of Howard Johnson's Motor Lodge, Orlando, Florida, as seen from the highway.

Courtesy: Howard Johnson's Motor Lodges

The sign should be distinctive and well maintained. Many motels contract with professional road-sign companies on a rental basis, which includes maintenance.

It is likely that the most important road sign is the one at the entrance to the motel. If highway signs have already publicized the policies and services of the establishment, this sign can concentrate on identifying the motel for the traveler. Chain operations and referral organizations place much stress on their entrance signs, striving to make them as distinctive and impressive as possible. The brand name or trademark is a major element in calling the motorist's attention to the affiliation of a motel with a nationally-known group. Therefore, these groups have taken pains to combine design, size, marquee and color into an effective first impression. The entrance sign should be located at a point that will allow the traveler sufficient time to take the correct highway exit. Although it must be an attention-getter, the sign should complement the design of the entrance.

Travel Guides and Referral Groups

In recent years much of the business of motels has been derived from referrals from other establishments and from travel guides. Such sales promotion methods have received public acceptance and are generally appreciated as a convenience in travel. The amount of business so directed has steadily increased, particularly with the entry of chain and franchise group operations into the field. The large

group organizations conduct national advertising programs to augment their referral advantages, and the participating establishments
are asked to help meet the cost of such advertising, which cost may be
offset by making it less important for the participant to advertise
on his own. The operator's decision as to whether to participate in the
referral associations or seek a listing in travel guides should be made
after weighing the anticipated profits against the dues or subscription
costs. Another factor will be the extent to which his motel is compatible
with the image created by other members and the promotion sponsored
by the group.

Newspapers, Magazines, Trade Journals

Newspapers and magazines are not usually prime advertising media
for the individual motel operator. Newspapers are helpful, however,
in developing good community relations and in promoting local food
and beverage sales. Certain travel magazines and travel sections of
general publications are often used by resort projects or by individual
motels in connection with the promotion of special events. However,
such newspaper and magazine advertising is generally considered to be
too expensive for the individual operator unless it is a part of a
national campaign undertaken on a cooperative basis with other motels.
Advertising in trade journals has been found by some motel operators
to help promote referral business.

The use of due-bills in an advertising program, particularly in
selected small-town newspapers in an area surrounding the motel or
where registrations have indicated a guest potential, has recently
been activated by some operators. Such a program is a "trading in
kind," whereby the motel operator agrees to furnish accommodations
and service in return for advertising space in the newspaper. The
argument that the motelman is getting the advertising free because
he is furnishing accommodations that would otherwise not be used
is not correct, for he must still service the room and stand the cost
of its use. Therefore, if the value of the advertising does not measure
up to the value of the accommodations which are used in payment it
is best to forego any other advantage that may accrue. If these conditions are kept in mind the operator will be in a good position to
judge whether a due-bill arrangement will be to his advantage.

Publicity

Some of the best advertising comes from publicity stories, and the
motel's sales promotion program should include the channeling of
material with news interest to the press. Whenever possible the

motel operator should cooperate with the local press in obtaining pictures and interviews with visiting celebrities and in covering meetings or events of interest that take place on the premises. When newsmen realize that the motel operator is willing to aid them in gathering worthwhile story material, the chances are that they will show their appreciation by mentioning the establishment in their articles.

Direct Mail

Direct mail advertising is aimed mainly at previous guests in the hope of obtaining repeat business. The best prospective guest is the one who has already committed his patronage to the motel and has established his standing with it. The advantage of this type of promotion is that the message reaches the attention of a pre-selected prospect. As the title suggests, direct mail consists of letters, brochures, postal cards and other mailing pieces addressed to a particular party. The best list of addresses for a motel's direct-mail promotion is obtained from the records of previous guests. Such records as the guest-history file or registration cards are readily available for such use. Often the guest history reveals enough about the previous visits to enable management to put the message in a personal vein, making it more intimate and appealing. Other mailing lists are also used, such as those compiled by local tourist associations, lists of convention members and other groups about to visit the area, of persons in various income brackets or in nearby areas. Direct-mail material can also be sent to those people who have written to the motel for information and people who have been recommended by guests, business associates and employees.

The direct-mail advertising message may also be implemented by the guest who uses the motel's stationery and postal cards for his correspondence. Therefore it is advisable that those items be distinctive and attractive. They may carry a description of the motel and pictures of its facilities. Care should be taken to ensure that all descriptive copy and pictures accurately convey the character and reputation of the motel.

The brochure and postal cards should be colorful, designed to capture the interest of the recipient. They might feature a picture of the motel exterior and grounds, special shots of the swimming pool and recreational area, the ballroom or dining facility, and attractive views of the guest units. In the case of postal cards, many operators think it a good policy to inform the guest that the motel will pay for the cost of mailing.

The effectiveness of direct-mail promotion is largely dependent on the timing and the frequency of mailings. Christmas and birthday cards are good examples of mailing pieces which will keep the motel's name fresh in the minds of former guests. Direct-mail promotion can also be used to announce improvements and additions to the facilities and local events. Some operators find it a good idea to send guests thank-you notes for past patronage.

Radio and Television Advertising

Television advertising is generally considered too expensive a medium for motels and is usually undertaken only in cooperation with the local chamber of commerce or tourist association. Spot announcements on radio are used on occasion, care being taken to beam them at such times when the automobile traveler may be thinking of a place to stop. Announcements over smaller stations can be effective in resort areas and away from metropolitan centers, but it is important to ascertain whether the station's signal is strong enough to reach a worthwhile number of travelers.

Giveaway Items

Matchbook advertising is used almost universally in the accommodations industry. Attractive folders bearing the motel's message will find their way into the pockets and suitcases of departing guests; they may be distributed through nearby stores and service stations, and exchange distribution arrangements may be made with cooperating motels along the traveler's route. Regulations permitting, souvenir matchbooks may be used as mailing pieces. Countless other items are distributed by motels, including road maps, litter bags, key chains, bags for swimsuits and shoes, cocktail stirrers. Inexpensive souvenirs that reflect aspects of local interest are also popular giveaways. Naturally, all of these items should carry the name and location of the motel.

Ashtrays are often appropriated by guests. The souvenir appeal of this item may be enhanced by a novel and attractive design. Ballpoint pens, facial tissues, shoe cloths, glassine covers for sanitized drinking glasses, blotters and other guest supplies can also be made a part of the advertising program.

Travel Agencies

Travel agents charge a commission for business directed to an establishment. Therefore, the extent to which their services are used should depend on whether profits from the agency-directed patronage are sufficient to offset the fees involved. An important aspect of this question is whether occupancy would be at a high level even without the services of an agency. During slow periods and off-seasons additional profits may be available through tours and package deals coordinating bus, rail and airline services with accommodations. In such cases the services of a travel agency can be of great assistance.

Local Referrals

Automobile service stations are a frequent source of information for travelers seeking restaurants and overnight accommodations. In fact, many major oil companies have stressed in their advertising programs the availability of such travel services through their outlets. To gain the goodwill and cooperation of these referral sources, many motels have offered owners and employees complimentary meals or accommodations. Similar invitations are sometimes extended to selected personnel from nearby air terminals and to others in the community who are in a position to direct business to the motel.

Active participation in the local chamber of commerce, convention and tourist bureaus and civic clubs is an excellent way for management to make valuable contacts and develop goodwill on a local level. Furthermore, a motel's community-relations program should include support of local celebrations, civic affairs and sporting events. By establishing himself as a responsible citizen and civic leader, the motel operator will gain community respect and loyalty for his business.

Personal Selling

Many motel operators carry on a personal sales program, meeting with local businessmen, professional people and those engaged in government and social work. This personal solicitation may even extend to other parts of the country, where the motel operator will visit the headquarters of firms, institutions and other organizations whose representatives have reason to be in his area. If the motel has facilities for conventions, exhibits, meetings and banquets, it is essential that management embark on a personal sales program.

Internal Selling

Selling does not stop when the guest has registered. The effort made to encourage him to utilize the full facilities of the house and to satisfy him to the extent that he will be sufficiently impressed with the accommodations and services provided to want to return is just as important as the effort which resulted in his first visit. Courtesy and cordiality on the part of all employees are essential, but, in addition, those who have direct contact with the guest must be sales-minded. They are often in a position to offer a sales suggestion regarding services on the premises and should be schooled in what to say and when to say it.

Internal sales promotion can also take the form of proper directional signs placed in the public areas of the motel to make the guest aware of the many different activities and services offered for his comfort and pleasure. Printed matter, including brochures, can be distributed in the guest rooms and dining rooms as a part of the internal sales promotion program. Tent cards on the tables, and the menus, themselves, can be excellent means of getting the message across. A house directory in each guest room will serve to acquaint the guest with his surroundings, guide him to various facilities and suggest services that may otherwise escape his notice. Bulletin boards and colorful posters in the lounge or lobby and special advertising placed on the guest-room desk or dresser can be valuable internal sales promotion tools.

Many motels add unexpected niceties to their normal guest service. Pleasant touches in the guest room are an apple placed on the night table, a paperback book or magazine for evening reading, or a flower and morning paper to accompany breakfast served in the room.

24

Accounting Records and Controls

In business today it is no longer possible to conduct even the simplest operation without the help of some accounting records. For this reason it is advisable that the prospective owner or operator of a motel or motor hotel acquaint himself with the bookkeeping methods for recording and controlling transactions that are peculiar to this segment of the accommodations industry. These have been developed through the years by hotel accountants to cover the necessary bookkeeping functions in a manner best adapted to the needs of the motel and motor hotel.

The modern motel or motor hotel operator no longer looks at the figures compiled by the bookkeeper merely as a history of the past; instead, he puts them to use by having them fashioned into statements that he can easily read and interpret. They then become a guide and indicator of the effect of his operating policies and the effectiveness of his control of the business. Certain of the records keep him informed of the transactions which must be delegated to other members of his staff and which, for this reason, he cannot handle personally. Others are the means of summarizing the figures so that they can be transcribed into accounting statements for informing the operator, investors, lenders, trade creditors and other interested parties, of the financial status of the motel and the results of its operations. The reports to government agencies in connection with income taxes, payroll taxes and excise, sales and use taxes, which require the compilation of transactions, have made even the smallest operation cognizant of the importance of adequate records.

271

In the smaller motel operations, where room sales are the only major income factor, the records may be quite simple and are very likely kept on a cash basis. Often in these cases the owner-operator confines his records to a combination registration and guest-account card, a book in which cash receipts and payments are listed and a checkbook in which deposits and expenditures are recorded. Where the owner personally attends to all transactions, control functions are unnecessary, and he uses his records to assist his memory and to compile the totals needed for tax returns and statements which he might prepare for creditors, industry studies and for his own guidance in operation.

In a larger operation, complicated by the addition of such services as food and beverage sales and the delegation of responsibility and authority for handling certain transactions to others, the records serve as a control on these delegated transactions. A complete description of all methods of bookkeeping and control is beyond the scope of this book and therefore the text in this chapter will cover only the highlights pertaining to the phases that apply particularly to the motel and motor hotel business. The financial statements to be prepared from these records and the uniform systems of accounts for motels and motor hotels are covered in Chapter 25.

ACCOUNTING FUNCTIONS

The record-keeping functions of the bookkeeping staff can be grouped into three phases:

1. The recording of original transactions.

The forms and records in this phase are intended to be used at the time each financial transaction is made. They include the guest registration card, the restaurant check, the sales vouchers of minor departments, purchase invoices, time cards or books, requisition forms, bank checks, deposit slips, etc.

2. The listing and summarizing of transactions into logical categories.

In this phase transactions similar in nature are entered in records fashioned to enable the record-keeper to obtain the totals of each type of transaction in logical order. These forms include the receiving record, payroll sheet, transcript of the guest ledger, restaurant cashier's sheet, traffic sheets for telephone and other minor departments, the daily report of income and the following journals which are ordinarily termed "books of original entry":

Income or earnings journal
Allowance journal
Cash receipts book
Cash disbursements book
Purchase journal or voucher record
General journal, for entry of transactions not provided for in
the other journals mentioned.

The guest's account cards or sheets on which his charges, credits
and payments are recorded are kept in a subsidiary ledger. It may
also be more practical to keep a subsidiary accounts payable ledger,
especially if creditors are not paid the exact amount of their invoices
as they become due.

The general ledger, in which the totals from the journals are transcribed, or "posted," is the final depository of the accumulated transactions, containing an account for each type or category into which
the transactions are assembled to enable the bookkeeper to prepare
intelligent statements of financial condition and operating results.
In this ledger are indicated the following general areas covered by
a system of accounts:

Sales and income
Expenses
Assets
Liabilities
Net worth

3. The preparation of financial statements.

In this phase the figures accumulated in the records are again
transcribed onto statements fashioned to inform the reader of the
results compiled in the first two phases. Ordinarily they take the
form of a balance sheet and a profit-and-loss statement, but there may
be additional special statements made for the information of management on certain phases of operation, such as daily or periodic reports on food and beverage costs, payroll, etc., or monthly reports
on the status of accounts receivable. The balance sheet and profit-
and-loss statement are usually made monthly, and thus the records
are totaled, or "closed," once a month as a matter of practice.

Bookkeeping System Requirements

To cover the purposes for which it is devised, a complete bookkeeping system must provide the necessary forms, records and procedures for recording all transactions, include methods of controlling

these transactions and safeguarding the assets of the business, and provide the necessary data for reports to the owners, management, government agencies and others that may be required in the course of business.

The recording of transactions is basic and can be simplified by using standard forms and following the well-documented procedures outlined in any standard bookkeeping text.

The control procedures are somewhat more involved and depend on checks and balances used to avoid errors and to detect misappropriations and theft. Embezzlement has often been defined as a combination of temptation and opportunity, and this is the area in which control is important. The trusted employee who is left to his own devices is the one most apt to succumb to temptation; it is not fair to put a person in this position if it can be avoided. If it is possible to remove the temptation by a division of duties whereby more than one person is directly concerned with each transaction, the control system is strengthened, the opportunity for wrongdoing minimized.

The following examples indicate some of the most commonly used control features of a bookkeeping system:

1. The payments received through the mail should be recorded by someone other than the one in charge of accounts receivable.

2. All receipts should be turned in daily and banked intact.

3. Invoices for merchandise delivered should be given to someone other than the person receiving the merchandise. This "blind tally" method used in connection with a receiving record is quite effective.

4. Someone other than the storekeeper should take the periodic inventories, preferably someone from the auditor's office.

5. The daily housekeeper's report should be checked against the report on rooms occupied.

6. The payroll checks should be given out by someone other than the person who calculates wages and prepares checks.

7. The bank statement should be reconciled by a person who does not keep the records of the motel pertaining to banking transactions.

8. Cash register readings should be taken by someone other than than the clerk who acts as departmental cashier.

9. Each cashier should be provided with a fixed change fund (imprest fund) and a safe repository for it.

10. Quite often two signatures are required on any checks drawn on the motel's bank account.

The control duties cannot always be divided as completely as one would like, particularly in a small motel operation. It is then advisable that an independent check be made of the transactions by an outside auditor or accountant. An independent direct verification of the accounts receivable and payable, bank balances, house funds, inventories, and tests of other internal control features of the bookkeeping system should be a part of such outside examination.

The forms used in the bookkeeping system should be basically simple but complete enough to include all essential information. They should be controlled numerically to allow for the accounting of each transaction and to facilitate filing and cross reference, where necessary. Erasures and voided forms should be marked by someone with proper authority.

The books of account should also be simple but adequate for recording all transactions in satisfactory detail. In some circumstances it is advisable to use bound books for original entries so that continuity is not lost and pages are difficult to remove without detection. Examples of this are the cash receipts and disbursements journal, the purchase record, the general journal and inventory records. The general ledger and subsidiary records of accounts receivable and payable are frequently loose-leaf volumes, which allow for the insertion of new accounts and the removal of closed accounts to a permanent file.

There are a number of ready-made bookkeeping systems available for smaller motel operations that can be obtained from hotel stationery supply houses. However, because the accounting system is a vitally important implement contributing to successful operation, the larger motor hotels will find it advisable to have their systems installed by an experienced hotel accountant. He will fashion it to fit the needs of the establishment and will instruct the employees on their duties and responsibilities in connection with it.

Front Office Accounting

The registration of guests and the recording of guest's charges were discussed briefly in Chapter 20. However, since this is one place where the accounting methods differ slightly from those in a conventional mercantile business, it is believed advisable to outline the procedures and forms in more detail in this chapter on bookkeeping.

Because motel guests are accustomed to settling their bills at the time of departure, often without prior notice, it is necessary to keep the accounts receivable from guests up to the minute. These accounts are kept in a special ledger in the front office, it being the duty of the front office cashier to record the charges as they occur. They are kept in a loose-leaf file by room number for easy reference, preferably in a vertical box file equipped with guide cards to indicate the room numbers. It is necessary that arrangements be made to have the charges from the various department sent to the front office quickly so that they may be posted on the guest's bill. Thus, the posting is done before the controls are set up in proof of the correctness of the postings.

The guest ledger is designed so that the motel record and the guest's bill are posted simultaneously. In hand posting this is done with a carbon form or a double account form. For machine posting a heavier ledger paper is used for the account card so that the guest's bill and account card can easily be inserted to record the transaction on both forms with one operation.

THE ALLIS PRESS, K. C., MO. 27280

THE MORRIS INN
"On the Campus"
NOTRE DAME, INDIANA

N⁰   8

FROM FOLIO	TO FOLIO														
ITEMS															
BROUGHT FORWARD															
ROOM															
DINING ROOM															
ROOM SERVICE															
LOCAL PHONE															
LONG DISTANCE															
TELEGRAMS															
LAUNDRY															
VALET															
CASH ADVANCE															
NEWSTAND															
MISCELLANEOUS															
GOLF															
TRANSFERS															
TOTAL CHARGES															
CREDITS — CASH															
CREDITS — ALLOWANCES															
CREDITS — TRANSFERS															
TOTAL CREDITS															
BALANCE DUE															

Typical hand-posted seven-day guest account form.

Courtesy: The Allis Press

Most bills are rendered upon the departure of the guest; it is customary to render a weekly bill to transient guests who stay for longer periods. Therefore, the bill and ledger sheet are designed to cover a seven-day period.

In hand posting, the front office cashier must keep a record of her receipts and pay-outs. A sample form of the front office cash sheet is shown on an accompanying page. This form is completed by each watch; the net receipts shown on it should balance with the cash turned in. In machine posting the cash totals are automatically built up in the machine, which will print the totals of each watch without affecting the cash totals for the day.

In the case of local telephone charges, which may be numerous, it may be practical to accumulate them and post them in total at the end of the day. Automatic telephone dialing is now used in many motor hotels, and registers are placed in the front office for recording these charges. The machine ledger form has a space provided for this accumulation; in the case of hand posting, a form similar to the housekeeper's report illustrated in Chapter 21 is used.

Hand posting and transcript control are used in motels and motor hotels up to about 200 rooms in size. Machine posting can be used in smaller houses, but is more common in houses of over 100 rooms. In smaller establishments the posting machine has the sole advantage of producing a neat-looking record.

The Night Audit

It is obvious that proving the correctness of guest accounts cannot be accomplished effectively during the front office day shifts because of the necessity of catering to the guests and the continuous traffic of charge vouchers and other transactions which must be posted immediately to keep the guest accounts up to the minute. Therefore the work connected with this proof must be done at night when front office traffic is comparatively light. To be effective, this proof and control must be completed before the start of the following day. Therefore, proving the postings of the various departments to their traffic sheets and balancing the guest ledger are assigned to the clerk who usually comes on duty at 11 p.m. and stays until 7 a.m. He is called the "night auditor."

In hand posting, the night auditor will use a form called the "transcript of the guest ledger." Its purpose is to analyze the transactions by transcribing the accounts on a columnar sheet in such a

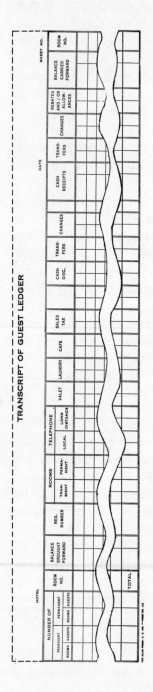

Guest accounts are listed on this transcript during the night audit.
Courtesy: Sherway Press

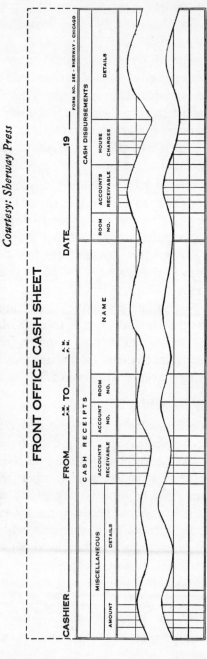

The standard form of front office cashier's report.
Courtesy: Sherway Press

manner that by using one line for each account the totals of the receivables at the beginning of day are shown. The charges from each department are entered in a separate column so that their totals can be checked against that department's report on such charges; the cash receipts, paid-outs and allowances are also shown in separate columns to agree with the front office cash sheets and allowance voucher records and the ending balance of the receivables.

The first duty of the night auditor is to complete the posting of guest accounts. Room charges are not posted until the end of the day and he will ordinarily start with them. If the telephone charges are accumulated he will at the same time make this posting, together with that of vouchers left unposted by the day clerk and any vouchers received before he is ready to close the accounts. (Usually midnight is the cut-off time on all charges, although it may be later if the restaurant is kept open beyond that hour.) He will then complete the accounts by totaling them and bringing the balance at the bottom of the day's column forward to the opening balance in the column for the following day.

As soon as the accounts are posted and totaled he copies them on the transcript form, using one line for each account. The transcript, when totaled and cross-footed, will show all transactions of the guest accounts for that night. To this must be added a transcribing of the accounts of guests who have departed that day, showing separately any accounts for departed guests who have arrived on the same day and are charged only for part-day use of the room. Up to this point all charges and credits to transient guest accounts have been determined. In order to tie the transcript totals to the departmental sales records it is necessary to add the charges and credits to the "city ledgers," which is usually done in total since it is impractical to transcribe these accounts in detail.

Now the transcript totals are compared with the various departmental sales records. In some instances the room charges are taken directly from the room rack and the other departmental sales are posted to the transcript from the vouchers, in which case errors in posting to the wrong account, missing accounts and clerical errors are often best noted by comparing the ending balances shown on the transcript with those shown on the ledger sheets. By this method, barring offsetting errors, the proof of the postings has been completed and the balances on the account cards or ledger sheets are proved to be correct.

To ease the work of the night auditor the room numbers are usually printed on the transcript sheets—a line for each room in the house. In some instances a column is also provided for the guest count in order that the night auditor's summary report may include a report on occupancy. Often the scheduled room rates are also included.

When a front office machine is used, it automatically totals each type of transaction, eliminating the necessity of preparing a transcript of the guest ledger. The machine also makes a tape record of each transaction posted, for reference in case of error. The night auditor clears the totals which are recorded on his machine balance report and, if the totals are the same as the total charges indicated on the sales records or tapes of the vouchers of each department, he knows all postings have been made. His next task is to make certain that the transactions are posted to the right account. He does this by first checking the room

DAILY CONTROL REPORT				
* Room Charges	1	₹23⌴ 139	1494.00	ROOM
* Tax	2	₹23⌴ 140	50.00	TAX
* Local Phone	3	₹23⌴ 141	11.00	PHON
* Long Distance	4	₹23⌴ 142	85.00	LGDS
* Bar & Rest.	5	₹23⌴ 143	400.00	REST
* Valet & Laundry	6	₹23⌴ 144	15.00	VALT
* Misc.	7	₹23⌴ 145	85.00	MISC
Total Sales	8	₹23⌴ 146	2140.00	BAL
	9			
* Payments	10	₹23⌴ 147	800.00	RC/A
Money to account for	11		800.10	
* Paid Out	12	₹23⌴ 148	18.39	PAID
Net Cash	13		781.61	
Actual Count	14		781.65	
Over Short	15		.04	
* Payments	16	₹23⌴ 149	800.00	RC/A
Other Advance Payments	(—)	85.00		
Local Advance Payments	(—)	50.00		
City Ledger Payments	(—)	65.00		
Guest Payments	(=)	600.00		

ACCOUNTS RECEIVABLE	Guest		City Ledger		Advance	
Balance Yesterday	1860	00	5650	00	550	00
Add: Charges Today	2140	00	150	00	XXXXX	XX
Add: Adv. Pay. Today	XXXXX	XX	XXXXX	XX	50	00
TOTAL	4000	00	5800	00	600	00
Deduct: Payments	600	00	65	00	XXXXX	XX
Deduct: Crs. Adv. Pay.	75	00	XXXXX	XX	75	00
Deduct: Chg. City Lg.	150	00	XXXXX	XX	XXXXX	XX
BALANCE TODAY	3175	00	5735	00	525	00

Weather_____   Temp._____

Signed_____

A sample night audit report prepared on the NCR Class 51 Register.
Courtesy: National Cash Register Company

number posted after each transaction on the ledger sheets as he is posting the room charges and then by examining the vouchers themselves to compare the room number printed by the machine with the room number written by the person preparing the voucher. The night auditor then takes an adding machine tape record of the guest ledger account balances to see that this total agrees with the ending balance total shown by the machine balance report.

The Auditing Office

Each morning the night auditor forwards his transcript, together with the departmental sales records, cash sheets, guest account cards that have been closed out, vouchers, register readings and tapes, to the auditing office where the income controller completes the verification of all transactions. The cash sales of the day, which are reported by the various departmental cashiers, are then combined with these charge totals on a daily report form to make up the total of the day's business.

A typical daily report form is illustrated on an accompanying page. Note that in addition to indicating the day's sales it is designed to carry other information of value to management, such as the sales for the month to date, the statistics on room occupancy, room rates, meals served, and comparisons with prior periods. Often, additional data such as the status of bank balances and accounts receivable are included on this form. This daily report becomes an integral part of the motel records, and a copy is kept in the auditor's office. The daily figures are in turn summarized in the income journal, which has one line for each day and columns coinciding with the revenue categories shown on the daily report.

Meanwhile the cash turn-ins of the front office and departmental cashiers are counted, checked to the cashier's reports and to the income controller's figures, after which the bank deposit is made up. For convenience, many motor hotels provide a slotted safety deposit box or safe in which the cashier may place her cash turn-ins and change fund when going off duty.

The auditing office, of course, handles the preparation of the payroll, starting with the time record and ending with the preparation of the payroll checks, payroll sheets and individual employee's record for tax purposes. It also checks and records the purchase and receipt of merchandise or services. Where the volume of purchases is heavy, good control would require a purchase order and a receiving slip, each to be validated and attached to the vendor's invoice.

All transactions are entered in the summary journals, which are totaled at the end of the month. The totals are transferred to a final record, the general ledger. In this ledger the monthly totals are accumulated for each category of sales, expenses, assets, liabilities and ownership or equity, and year-to-date totals are made. Since the business cycle of most enterprises is one year, the annual totals are the final summary from which financial statements are prepared; usually the books are ruled off at the end of each year.

DIXIE GOVERNOR MOTEL
DAILY REPORT

WEATHER_____ DAY_____ DATE_____ 19____

	TODAY	THIS MONTH TO DATE	LAST MONTH TO DATE	LAST YEAR MONTH TO DATE
ROOMS—TRANSIENT				
PERMANENT				
DAY USE				
POOL				
TOTAL				
PUBLIC ROOMS				
TELEPHONE—LOCAL				
LONG DISTANCE				
TELEGRAMS				
LAUNDRY				
VALET				
STORE RENTALS—RESTAURANT				
BARBER SHOP				
GIFT SHOP				
OTHERS—				
TOTAL EARNINGS				
RESTAURANT CHARGES				
TOTAL				

ROOM STATISTICS	TODAY	TOTAL TO DATE — THIS MONTH	LAST MONTH	LAST YEAR	ACCOUNTS RECEIVABLE	GUEST & CITY	ADVANCE PAYMENT
ROOMS - AVAILABLE					BALANCE YESTERDAY		
OCCUPIED					CHARGES		
VACANT					PAID OUTS		
COMPLIMENTARY					ADVANCE PAYMENTS		
OUT OF ORDER					TOTAL		
TOTAL ROOMS					CASH RECEIPTS		
NUMBER OF GUESTS					ALLOWANCES		
% OF OCCUPANCY	%	%	%	%	WITHDRAWALS		
% OF DOUBLE OCCUPANCY	%	%	%	%			
AVERAGE DAILY RATE PER OCCUPIED ROOM					TOTAL		
AVERAGE DAILY RATE PER GUEST					BALANCE TODAY		
NUMBER OF RESERVATIONS PER DAY					BANK BALANCE		
DID NOT ARRIVE					BALANCE YESTERDAY		
CANCELLED					DEPOSITS		
NET RESERVATIONS ARRIVALS					TOTAL		
PICK-UP					DISBURSEMENTS		
TOTAL					BALANCE TODAY		

REMARKS:_____

_____

SHERWAY - CHICAGO

A stock form of daily report may be adequate or a special form such as this may be designed.

Courtesy: Sherway Press

Duties of Employees

In the medium-size motor hotel with restaurant facilities the following employees would be involved in maintaining the accounting and control system:

Position	Duties
Room clerk	—Register guests.
	—Prepare guest accounts.
	—Post charges to guest accounts.
	—Prepare front office cash sheet.
	—Accept settlement upon check-out.

(If a front office cashier is on duty, she will perform the last three duties listed.)

Restaurant cashier	—Record settlement of checks.
	—Prepare summary record.
	—Prepare record of turn-in.
Night auditor	—Post room and local telephone charges to guest accounts.
	—Prepare room transcript or machine balance report.
	—Verify correctness of guest accounts.
Income controller	—Verify record of income.
	—Prepare daily report.
	—File account cards, income reports and vouchers.
General cashier	—Make deposits.
	—Verify cash turn-ins.
Clerk	—Prepare payroll records.
	—Record purchases.
	—Check receiving record.
	—Verify correctness of invoices.
Auditor	—Prepare summary journals.
	—Transfer totals to general ledger.
	—Prepare financial reports.

In addition, there may be a receiving clerk to check in the merchandise purchased, a storeroom man to handle the issues from the storeroom, wine-room, etc.; and a timekeeper or back-door man to control the receiving dock and employees' entrance.

The accounting office should be placed within a reasonable distance of the front desk, but it should be out of the general line of traffic of both guests and clerical employees so that greater control is possible. It should contain desks for the permanent staff plus at least one temporary desk for visitors. A general rule calls for approximately 100 square feet of work, storage and rest-room space for each full-time clerical employee. If a general cashier's position is used it would be advisable to provide a separate caged-in space for that employee as a safety measure.

Additional space will be required for the location of stations at which guests pay for restaurant, bar and other retail shop charges. These will vary in size, depending on the extent of required equipment. Normally, a cash register or other device upon which sales can be recorded would be used in the restaurant and the bar. Such a device would also be necessary for a busy shop in the lobby.

Equipment Requirements

Equipment needs for the accounting system will vary considerably, depending on the volume of business to be recorded and controlled. The following steps are to be covered in any complete accounting system:

1. The identification and recording of transactions in meaningful form.

2. The filing of these records in the proper category.

3. The performance of the required arithmetical functions.

4. The coordination of the various functions necessary to adequate control and verification.

5. The accumulation of totals and re-recording of transactions and statistics in permanent form.

6. The reporting of results.

Within the system are many points where machines or other devices may be used to speed up the bookkeeping. The actual need for such equipment will depend on the size and complexity of the operation; there is no fixed rule to indicate the point at which a machine should take over. Factors that will influence a decision on the matter are: the cost of replacing man-hours of labor, the increased detail made available for management; and the availability of trained machine operators.

Multi-purpose Forms. Time is saved with forms that can serve more than one purpose. Usually designed with carbon inserts or sensitized paper, they will produce documents for multiple use. An example is the guest-account statement and ledger form, which enables the clerk to record original transactions at one writing, providing a statement for the guest and a copy for the motel's permanent file. The autographic register provides more than one copy of a record by the use of a continuous carbonized form that is fed into the writing area by the turn of a wheel, providing a copy for the guest, one for the room rack and a control copy for auditing purposes.

Cash Register. This is a machine that is used to record and accumulate transactions by categories so that totals can be obtained readily. Many of these machines make the amount of each charge visible to the customer so that he is able to check on the correctness of the transaction. A number of machines also issue a receipt form to the patron. Checking machines print the amount of the transaction

KEY ARRANGEMENT

ROW 10	AMOUNT KEYS					ROW 2	ROW 1
ADVANCE PAYMENT	$900	$90	$9	90	9	ROOM CHARGE	CRED. BAL. PICK UP
SERVICE	$800	$80	$8	80	8	TAX	
TELEGRAM	$700	$70	$7	70	7	LOCAL PHONE	SUB TOTAL
GUEST C B	$600	$60	$6	60	6	LONG DISTANCE	
GARAGE	$500	$50	$5	50	5	RESTAURANT BAR	PREVIOUS BALANCE
MEETING ROOM	$400	$40	$4	40	4	VALET LAUNDRY	ROOM NUMBER
SWIMMING POOL	$300	$30	$3	30	3	MISC. CHARGE	
C.O.D.	$200	$20	$2	20	2	PAID OUT	NEW BALANCE
MISC.	$100	$10	$1	10	1	PAYMENT ON ACCT.	

Designed especially for the motel or motor hotel, this Monroe/Sweda machine serves as cash register as well as front office posting machine.

Courtesy: Monroe/Sweda

on a check as the sale is entered. These machines have a keyboard to denote the various categories and totals recorded, one or more printing stations and one or more drawers in which change funds and receipts are kept. Cash registers vary greatly in their functions and should be purchased to fit the job for which they are intended.

Pegboard. This is a device which, when used with the proper forms, enables the operator to enter a transaction on several forms simultaneously. A good example is its application to the payroll, in which the payroll check, payroll record and employee's earning record can be prepared in one writing.

Front Office Posting Machine. This is a special-purpose electrically operated machine developed for use in motels and hotels. It is used to post charges and credits to guests' accounts and at the same time to total automatically the guest's bill and accumulate the various transactions in their proper categories so that a summary of the day's postings can be obtained by depressing the proper total-keys. It also prints each transaction and total on a tape for audit and checking purposes.

Adding Machine. This is a listing device that accumulates the total figures entered on it through a keyboard. Most adding machines also provide a tape on which the entries and totals are recorded. They are available in either manual or electric models.

Calculator. This machine is used for multiplication and division as well as addition and subtraction and is a considerable time-saver where percentages and similar calculations are frequently made. It does not print on a tape or form, the answer being read from a register.

Bookkeeping Machine. This is a machine which resembles a typewriter and may, in fact, have a standard typewriter keyboard in addition to facilities for accumulating totals of transactions entered on it. The more complex machines automatically perform certain arithmetic functions and will produce summary records. In its simplest form this machine performs the same functions as a pegboard, enabling the operator to enter a transaction on several forms in one typing operation.

Automatic Data-Processing Equipment. Automatic data-processing machines have not yet been developed to the point where their application to an operation as small as a motel or motor hotel is practical, although there are some applications in hotels in connection with guest reservations, and it appears that a "break-through" for more complete use is imminent. A wide variety of devices will perform the various functions of record-keeping automatically. They are able to interpret information fed to them on such machine-language media as punched cards and tape. Calculations which are time-consuming when done by ordinary machine methods or by hand are performed in seconds by these calculators and the storage of information seems inexhaustible. However, before considering the use of automatic data-processing equipment it is advisable to seek professional advice and assistance. The cost of this equipment, most of which is available on a rental or service basis, is still beyond the means of the motel and motor hotel operator.

FOOD AND BEVERAGE COST ACCOUNTING

The motel or motor hotel operation which includes a food and beverage department is confronted with control procedures that differ from ordinary accounting methods. Because the net profit or loss result in this department depends largely on the ratio of commodity costs to sales, attention is centered on the merchandise costs of food and beverages. If the manager knows the ratios of food, beverage and payroll costs, he can make a reasonably accurate estimate of departmental profits. Since food and beverage costs tend to vary with sales volume, market prices and availability of supply, it is necessary to control these costs closely. In addition, the type of merchandise handled is subject to spoilage, pilferage and misuse to an extent that makes it advisable to keep currently informed on the effectiveness of operational policies in this department.

The purpose of this section is to outline the procedures necessary for a minimum system of food and beverage cost control. If the restaurant operation is large and complex, a more detailed and extensive system would be needed—one that could best be installed specifically for that operation only with professional assistance. However, there are certain basic daily records of sales, costs and ratios of costs to sales which should be kept by all operators.

Every system of food and beverage cost control includes several functions that are essentially those of management. Proper procedures for the purchasing, receiving, storing, issuing and preparation of the merchandise for resale must be adhered to in order for the control system to be effective. The daily and periodic reports of the fluctuations in costs serve to alert management to adverse situations requiring attention before they become so serious that severe losses result. Before describing the cost-control forms and procedures, we shall outline the other functions, since they form the basis of an effective system.

Purchasing

The buying of food and beverages is frequently handled by the manager in the motel or small motor hotel. This important function should never be reduced to the mere placing of orders, but should be done on the basis of proper specifications as to size, quality and quantitites of merchandise to be purchased. The general goal is to obtain the desired quality for the lowest available price; therefore, competitive bids should be obtained before orders are placed.

Certain cuts and grades of meat and sizes of containers for foodstuffs are more economical than others for each operation. The manager, with the help of his chef, should stipulate specifications for each item so that the bids obtained are meaningful. Certain brands and varieties of alcoholic beverages are more popular in one part of the country than in another, and the buyer must know the preferences in his area in order to do an effective purchasing job. Proper methods for the purchase of the correct raw materials should assure the most desirable product for resale.

Receiving

Unless the exact items and quantities ordered are received, the most knowledgeable purchasing will have little effectiveness. All goods ordered must be checked for quantity and quality at the time of delivery to assure proper protection at this vulnerable point.

The receiving function, to be properly carried out, requires, first, an adequate area in which the carrier can unload; second, an accurate method of checking quantity by weight and measure; and, third, a person who knows the purchasing specifications as to size and quality. The receiving function should be the responsibility of an individual who is trustworthy and able to recognize faulty merchandise easily and quickly. An accurate scale, large enough to handle the majority of normal delivery weights, should be easily accessible, and its accuracy should be tested periodically. Standard receiving record forms can be readily obtained from any printer of hotel forms. The receiver should be required to make a record of all items received upon delivery and after verification of quality and quantity. Since there are occasional differences between the billed and received weights, frequent periods when no differences are reported by the receiving clerk usually indicate a laxity in the receiving function.

Storing and Issuing

Adequate floor, shelf and bin space, under control to insure maintenance of the correct temperature and to prevent pilferage, should be available for all merchandise received. Immediately after goods have been checked in, they should be sent to the proper storage room. There are two good reasons for such prompt action: it keeps the receiving area from being tied up by in-transit items; and it assures that proper climate and security controls are provided.

The storage areas should be laid out logically, and a storeroom inventory book in which all items are listed by commodity classifications should be set up. Inventories should be taken at the end of each month. It is a wise practice to maintain a perpetual inventory record of the contents of the liquor storeroom so that the periodic physical inventory can be checked. All storage areas should be kept locked when not attended.

Merchandise should be removed from stores only upon written requisition. Like receiving, the issuing procedure should be under the control of one person, if possible. Proper advance planning in the food and beverage departments should reduce the number of separate requisitions required daily, making it possible to issue merchandise only at prescribed hours, thus freeing the storeroom man for diversified duties at other hours.

Preparation

Ideally, food and beverage products should be prepared to individual order so that there is little waste and loss of quality. Since this is feasible only with a very limited menu, it is necessary that production controls be instituted. A reasonable estimate of the probable demand for a menu item can be made, provided that adequate records of past production and sales are available. Although the forecasting of requirements can be time-consuming, the manager and chef can make close estimates based on experience. It is better to run out of an item occasionally than to over-prepare.

Advance preparation of alcoholic drinks is normally illegal. Before such a procedure is followed, it would be wise to check local beverage control laws.

Food Cost Control Forms and Procedures

The simplest form of regular food cost report is one that compares daily food purchases with sales and can be kept by the manager or an accounting office clerk. A columnar sheet with the following headings should be used:

Column Number	Column Heading	Section Heading
1	Date	
2	Today	
3	To date	Food sales
4	Today	
5	To date	Food purchases
6	Today	
7	To date	Food cost ratio

There will be wide daily fluctuations in the relationship between food sales and food purchases; however, the to-date totals will form a pattern that can be informative and valuable. The monthly totals, after adjustments for opening and closing inventories, will present a picture of the actual food cost, before any credit for meals to employees.

A more accurate daily cost can be obtained by basing the calculations on issues from the storerooms, plus those purchases that are charged directly to the preparation departments. Assuming that the in-process inventories are normally more or less the same, the fluctuations in daily cost under this procedure should be minor.

The form previously described would be expanded to contain columns for computing food cost; that is, storeroom issue, direct purchases and a total column. It will be necessary to maintain an accurate record of issues, pricing each requisition on a uniform "first-in, first-out" basis. The total of direct purchases can be obtained from the receiving record, where the items sent directly to preparation areas should be kept separately. The necessary forms are standard and may be obtained from most hotel supply houses.

Further Breakdowns

Additional detail and closer control may be obtained by breaking down the direct food purchases and storeroom issues by categories. One of the most effective procedures is a 12-category listing, which separates the items into readily identifiable groups:

Meats	Butter
Fish	Eggs
Poultry	Coffee & tea
Fruits	Ice cream
Vegetables	Baked goods
Milk and cream	Staples

The categories "fruits" and "vegetables" include fresh, frozen and canned products; and "staples" includes flour, sugar, salt, cheese, condiments, etc.

A clear pattern of the ratios of the categories to the total sales dollar can soon be established. Thereafter, fluctuations in the individual ratios will show where the total cost ratio may be out of line, so that immediate investigation can be directed to the proper category and prompt corrective action taken.

Beverage Cost Control

Unlike many food items, a major portion of the beverage purchases can be kept in storage without risk of spoilage. For that reason, purchases are usually less frequent and in larger quantities. A daily cost report based on purchases would therefore show severe fluctuations and would not be of value.

Beverage cost control is based upon issues from the stockroom to the bar. A par stock is frequently set up for the bar. However, items other than alcoholic beverages must be considered, such as mixers and the food products used in mixing drinks. Some examples of the latter are lemons, oranges and other fruit; milk and eggs. Columns should therefore be provided in the control form for issues from the stock room and for issues from food stores. Columns for listing the total cost today and to-date, sales today and to-date, and cost ratios today and to-date will also be required.

There are other, more complex and more effective types of beverage control systems in use. For example, a retail sales value control can be established. This is frequently employed to control temporary bar set-ups for functions. The retail sales value of the issues is established on the basis of size and prices of drinks. The bartender must return the equivalent in cash and closing inventory when the party is over. Another form of daily cost system requires a detailed analysis of sales by category and is based upon standard recipes and conversion values. Such systems should be attempted only where there are sufficient qualified employees available to keep the detailed records required, and should be set up under the guidance of professionals who are familiar with the procedures and standards necessary for proper control.

Even the smallest restaurant and/or bar operation requires a good cost control system. Efficient procedures for buying, storing and issuing merchandise should be followed. In more complex operations, the maintenance of detailed daily food and beverage cost reports is imperative for intelligent management, and in these cases professional help should be sought before attempting to set up such a system.

25

Financial Statements

Just as an artist uses his paints and brushes to portray the scene before him on his canvas, the accountant uses figures and statement forms to present a picture of the financial condition and operating results of a business. The artistry of the accountant is reflected in the clarity and ease with which his statements can be read and digested by the persons for whom they are prepared. The trend toward the elimination of technical terminology in such statements is recognition of the fact that persons not versed in accounting realize the need for an understanding of the subject.

A person need not have training in bookkeeping methods and accounting to be able to read a motel statement if it is properly drawn up and its purpose clearly explained. The reader should, however, have some knowledge of the more common statement forms in order to recognize the basis on which they are prepared and to comprehend the information they convey.

For this reason it is advisable that anyone intending to enter the motel or motor hotel business familiarize himself with these financial statements and learn how they can be put to use. The financial statements in this chapter should serve as evidence of their ease of interpretation and the quick understandings they yield.

It is possible to cover only the highlights of the financial statements in this chapter. For those interested in continuing their education in accounting for motels and motor hotels, there are a number of books and pamphlets available. Among these are:

The Uniform System of Accounts for Hotels. This uniform classification of accounts and suggested forms for financial statements for hotels was first published by the New York City Hotel Association in 1926. The 1962 edition, which is the sixth revised edition, is distributed by the National Association of Hotel Accountants.

The Uniform System of Accounts for Motels, Motor Hotels and Small Hotels. This booklet contains a similar classification and suggests financial statements, simplified for use by smaller properties. It was published by the American Hotel & Motel Association in 1962 and is also distributed through the National Association of Hotel Accountants.

Uniform Classification of Accounts for Motels, Motor Hotels, or Highway Lodges. This booklet was published by the "Tourist Court Journal" in 1960 and is endorsed by the American Motor Hotel Association.

All three booklets, prepared by accountants experienced in the field of transient accommodations, have a common goal—to fashion the financial statements so that they tell clearly the motel story and provide data from which experience factors may be developed that will benefit the motel business as a whole. There are no major differences between them with respect to the form of operating statements they recommend, and they give the motel and motor hotel business a common ground for comparison, enabling motelmen to speak the same language in discussing their financial and operating problems and offering them a wide field for comparison with the operating results of the motel and motor hotel business generally. (Examples are those studies shown in Appendix A.)

The classifications as outlined in these booklets can, of course, be expanded or contracted to meet the desires of the individual, since they are adaptable to all sizes and types of motels and motor hotels. The interest in uniformity centers on the operating figures—particularly those which lend themselves to comparison. For this reason care was taken to avoid any arbitrary divisions of income or expense figures that might spark honest differences of opinion as to how such divisions should be made.

In the case of a motel having several income-producing departments, the uniform classification of accounts provides for the direct payroll and expenses of each department to be deducted from its income, resulting in a "departmental profit," which, in effect, is each department's profit contribution toward covering overhead expenses, fixed charges, etc. Such overhead items as administrative and general expenses, advertising and business promotion, utilities repairs and maintenance, apply to all departments and it is difficult to allocate them on a departmental basis. Therefore, these overhead expenses should be shown as unallocated deductions from income in the uniform statement presentation.

The statement illustrations used in this chapter have been compiled from figures representing typical operations. They are not a means of measuring all types of operations in the field with respect to operating efficiency and financial soundness. They are intended only to illustrate the more common statement forms and might be regarded as reasonable expectations for the facilities outlined under reasonably good management.

Many persons not familiar with bookkeeping have difficulty in understanding a transaction that is not reflected in cash, and it is often more practical for a small motel operation to keep its records and prepare its statements on that basis. However, the books of most of the medium-size and larger motels are kept on the accrual basis of accounting, which means that the transactions are recorded when they are made rather than when they are paid. This method allows a more detailed portrayal of inventories, receivables, payables and accruals, as well as a more accurate apportionment of fixed charges. The statements presented here are based on this system.

The statements cover two distinct operations, one a 120-room motor hotel with a food and beverage operation, the other a 30-room motel with no dining room or bar.

120-ROOM MOTEL

This motor hotel has completed its third full year of operation. The original costs for the facilities are outlined as follows:

	Cost per room	Total Cost
Land	$ 833.33	$ 100,000
Building	8,000.00	960,000
Pool	200.00	24,000
Furniture and fixtures	2,066.67	248,000
Total	$11,100.00	$1,332,000

The major stockholder and promoter put up $50,000 and the land, obtained a $650,000 first-mortgage 6 per cent loan and sold $500,000 in 5 per cent debentures in a package deal with $50,000 of common stock.

BALANCE SHEET—EXHIBIT A

The balance sheet is a statement showing the financial position of the enterprise at a given moment. Since the motel and motor hotel business is continuously active and each transaction, however small, changes the picture of its financial condition just as a moving picture portrays a continuing story, the balance sheet has been aptly described as a "still picture" taken from that movie at the moment of the last transaction on the date for which the statement is prepared. This statement is divided into three basic parts, as follows:

1. Assets, or what is owned by the enterprise.
2. Liabilities, or what is owed by the enterprise.
3. Net worth or capital, representing the value of the owner's equity in the enterprise.

One major division of the assets is called "current assets," the cash, marketable securities and other liquid items such as receivables, inventories and prepaid expenses which are soon to be consumed or converted into cash in the ordinary course of business.

Liabilities are likewise divided into those that are current and those that are not. With respect to liabilities the word "current" generally means that payment is due within a year. If the current assets exceed the current liabilities by a good margin the cash position of the enterprise is said to be fluid, since the cash and other assets quickly and easily converted into cash are on hand to meet the liabilities that are due. This excess of current assets over current liabilities is called "working capital," and the ratio of current assets to current liabilities is called the "current ratio." The current ratio is of interest to the motel's creditors as an indication of the ability of the motel to meet its obligations on time and to maintain a good credit standing.

In Exhibit A the current assets totaled $119,550 and current liabilities were $82,200. This is a working-capital ratio of 1.45 to 1, which is an unusually fluid condition and would be regarded as a very good current position for a motor hotel. In fact, it is not unusual to find a motel or motor hotel well able to meet its obligations as they come due with a current ratio of 1 to 1 or less. This is one of the distinguishing characteristics of a motel balance sheet as compared to that of a manufacturing or mercantile company. It is possible because the motel income is largely on a cash basis, and there are no large sums tied up in receivables or inventories as there are in other types of business. The $30,000 of accounts receivable shown in Exhibit A represents 3.6 per cent of total sales, or about 13 days of average income. Moreover, the funds represented by inventories of food, beverages and supplies, prepaid expenses and house funds are offset by the trade creditors' accounts and accrued expenses. Therefore the current cash coming in can be used to pay last month's bills—if the motel is operating on a profitable basis. However, if business is bad it does not take long to reach the point where obligations and expenses cannot be paid currently and credit is impaired.

The second significant characteristic of a motel or motor hotel balance sheet is that by far the bulk of the value of the assets is represented in the physical plant; in this instance 88 per cent of the total assets are fixed assets—land, building and equipment. These assets have relatively long lives and the liabilities which were involved in their purchase have a similar long-term status and are shown below the current line in the statement, except, of course, the amount of principal due within the coming year, which is included with the current liabilities.

Exhibit A shows that in the three years of operation the owners have been able to pay the first mortgage requirements, which are an 8.5 per cent constant, payable monthly, including principal and interest, and the interest plus $125,000 of the principal on the debenture issue. In addition they have spent $45,000 to date for additions to furniture and equipment and have been able to build to their excellent cash position.

Because a major portion of the investment in a motel or motor hotel is tied up in long-lived property improvements, depreciation is a material factor in computing net earnings. This very factor has attracted many tax-conscious investors. In the example reviewed here the company has taken advantage of the 1954 Federal Income Tax Act by using the declining balance method of accelerated depreciation. This has reduced taxable earnings in these early years of operation, releasing funds for reduction of fixed indebtedness. Had the project been less profitable it would have been unable to take advantage of this saving.

The reader will note that the profit for the current year was only $37,400, whereas principal payments on the mortgage and debenture bonds amounted to $93,250. The apparent disparity between these figures is often a source of puzzlement to those not familiar with accounting statements. They know that most businesses generate "cash flow," but they cannot readily see the relationship between cash flow, profits, debt amortization and other changes reflected in the periodic balance sheets of the enterprise. These matters are best explained to them in a third statement, "Source and Application of Funds." The following illustration of this statement shows the funds that were produced by operations and the purposes for which they were expended in the current year:

Funds derived from

Operations—As shown in Exhibit B		$ 37,400
Add back:		
Operating charges that do not require funds		
Depreciation	$90,080	
Loan and organization expenses	5,320	
Total non-cash expenses		95,400
Total funds derived		$132,800

Funds applied to

Principal payment on first mortgage	$ 18,250
Principal payments on debenture bonds	75,000
Additions to furniture, fixtures and equipment	15,000
Increase in working capital	24,550
Total funds applied	$132,800

There was a carry-over loss resulting from the first year of operations and the expenses prior to opening which accounts for a retained earnings figure to date of only $11,565. Because of this loss there was no income tax until the last year. The balance sheet now indicates that continued operating profits will enable the owners to build up their equity in the property and, if desired, pay dividends on the common shares. The original net worth, created at the time of the organization of the enterprise, is shown as capital stock in the corporate form of business used in the illustration.

The balance sheet, or as it is sometimes called, the "statement of financial condition," is a major source of information to those concerned with the financing of a business venture. Bankers, holders or mortgages or other loans, vendors and others who may provide goods, services or money to an enterprise will be interested in knowing how secure their debt may be. Investors are likewise interested in the values represented by their investment. The business analyst will want to check the following revealing relationships:

1. Current position. Is the enterprise able to meet its obligations as they come due? What is the relationship of current assets to current liabilities?

2. Equity investment. What is the ratio of long-term debt to capital stock (invested capital)? In Exhibit A it is about 4.5 to 1, which indicates a "thin" equity. The first mortgage holder is further protected by the fact that the debenture bonds are secondary to his claim.

3. Ratio of long-term debt to value of fixed assets. Would a sale of the property realize enough to retire the debt and leave a balance for equity investors?

In this case the amount of the first mortgage was slightly less than 50 per cent of the original cost of land, building and equipment and is indicated to be quite secure. The debenture bonds, however, have a high risk factor. They were very likely purchased by local civic-minded

Exhibit A

Assets as at December 31, 1962

Current assets

Cash			
House funds	$ 5,000		
On deposit	50,000	$ 55,000	
Accounts receivable	$ 30,000		
Less reserve for doubtful accounts	1,500	28,500	
Inventories			
Food	$ 3,000		
Beverages	2,750		
Supplies	1,800	7,550	
Marketable securities		25,000	
Prepaid insurance, licenses, etc.		3,000	
Utility deposits		500	
Total current assets			$ 119,550
Fixed assets — at cost less depreciation			
Land		$100,000	
Building	$960,000		
Less — reserve for depreciation	162,640	797,360	
Swimming pool	$ 24,000		
Less — reserve for depreciation	7,925	16,075	
Furniture, fixtures and equipment			
Original cost	$248,000		
Additions	45,000		
Total	$293,000		
Less — reserve for depreciation	129,465	163,535	
China, glass, linen, silver		21,030	
Total fixed assets			1,098,000
Deferred charges			
Organization, mortgage and franchise costs			30,140
Total assets			$1,247,690

Exhibit A (*cont*)

Liabilities and Capital as at December 31, 1962

Current liabilities

Accounts payable — trade	$ 15,000	
Notes payable — equipment	7,500	
Taxes collected		
State sales tax	1,095	
Federal withholding and social		
security taxes	3,125	
Accrued local taxes	12,000	
Accrued payroll	8,000	
Accrued Federal income tax	14,500	
Other accrued expenses	1,180	
Mortgage payable — due within one year	19,350	
Deposits on parties and exchange		
reservations	450	
Total current liabilities		$ 82,200
Long-term indebtedness		
First mortgage 6% loan — dated		
December 31, 1959		
(Original amount $650,000)	$598,275	
Less amount due 1963	19,350	578,925
Debenture bonds — 5%		375,000
Capital		
Common stock — 2,000 shares at		
$100.00 par value	$200,000	
Retained earnings	11,565	
Total capital		211,565
Total liabilities and capital		$1,247,690

persons whose incentive was development of the area and the possibility of an increase in equity from the common stock which was included in the package deal constituting their investment.

The balance sheet will indicate to management the ratio of accounts receivable to total sales as well as the aging of the receivables, both barometers of the efficiency of credit and collection policies. The inventory turnover figure is also of interest to management as an indication of whether excess capital is tied up in the supply of merchandise on hand.

PROFIT AND LOSS STATEMENT—EXHIBITS B AND B-1

The profit-and-loss statement is a financial analysis of operating results for a specific period of time. The terminology used in the headings and the form of the statements are in accord with the suggestions made in the uniform-system-of-accounts booklets.

In Exhibit B the operating statement is shown in summary form in order to align the figures for the current year and the previous year in columns that will give an easy means of comparison. The theories on which this form is based are:

1. That the major source of income in a motel or motor hotel is room sales.

2. That other departmental operations are supplemental and have a lower profit potential.

3. That except for the food and beverage department the payroll and other operating expenses apply to the entire operation and in many instances are not departmentalized. These operating expenses are broken down into their major groupings in order to give an intelligent picture of how each expense item influences the final result.

4. That the "house profit" figure, which is the net result after deducting from sales the operating expenses controllable by management, is the dividing point between the results for which management is responsible and the costs chargeable to operations which are the responsibility of ownership and reflect the manner in which the project was purchased and financed.

5. That it is to the point of house profit that the reader of the operating statement can benefit from comparisons of the figures on a motel or motor hotel project with the figures of prior periods or those of other, similar enterprises. Insurance, local taxes, interest, depreciation and income taxes are so influenced by the wide variances in financial structures that comparisons other than those made with prior operating periods of the same project are of little practical value.

Financial analysis of operations is usually best aided by comparisons; these comparisons become a guide in judging the efficiency of an operation. Since very few such projects are exactly the same size or type, comparisons are made easier when the figures are broken down into a common denominator, such as the ratios of each element of operation to room sales or the costs per available room unit for the period under review. In each instance the figures of comparison are centered on the basic element of motel operation—room sales.

The fixed charges—property insurance, local taxes, interest and depreciation—are deducted from house profits in logical order. First to be deducted are insurance and taxes, leaving as a profit figure the amount available to meet obligations involved in financing the project. Next, interest charges are deducted, indicating the amount of profit left for depreciation, income taxes and net income available to the equity owners, in this case the stockholders.

Exhibit B is a form recommended to show the major elements of operation in comparison form. Exhibit B-1 shows the same operating figures for the current year in another form. The reader will note that in Exhibit B the departmental profit from the food and beverage operation is included in the sales and income figure and that the telephone operation, except for payroll, is listed under "other income." The form for the operating statement illustrated in Exhibit B-1 is recommended by the uniform system of accounts for motel operations requiring separate statements for each income-producing department. This provides a picture of the profit contribution from any department prior to deduction of overhead expenses and fixed charges. Although the form does not lend itself to easy side-by-side comparison of figures, it does show how the various major elements of operation influence the final result.

These two forms are commonly used in portraying operating results, and the choice of one over the other depends on the information desired by management, owners and others for whom the figures are prepared.

Sales Statistics—Schedule B-1

To additionally analyze and judge the results of major department incomes, supplementary statistics may be compiled. These are illustrated in Schedule B-1. (Note that this schedule lists 125 rooms. Five of these rooms were allocated for use by manager and staff and therefore are not available for guest rental.)

In the food department, statistics are usually based on a meal count, which when divided into sales yields the average check per person, giving in turn an idea of the price structure of the menu. A further breakdown provided here is that of dining room sales into meal periods. It is interesting to note the extent to which the establishment has augmented its income through the sale of banquets and parties, also shown separately.

The nature of beverage sales makes it nearly impossible to determine the number of persons served or the amount of the average check. The usual gauge of sales in this department is the average daily volume as compared to food sales, which in this case is 33.86 per cent. This is a good ratio and indicates that the cocktail lounge has gained popular acceptance.

Exhibits B and B-1 are summary statements of revenues, expenses and net income. The details of the items that comprise each total figure are usually shown in supporting schedules for each department and category

Exhibit B

	Amounts		Ratios to Room Sales		Annual Amounts Per Room	
	This Year	Last Year	This Year	Last Year	This Year	Last Year
Sales and income						
Room sales	$368,100	$338,420	100.00%	100.00%	$3,067.50	$2,820.17
Restaurant operating profit	86,850	82,050	23.59	24.25	723.75	683.75
Other income — net	16,200	12,330	4.40	3.64	135.00	102.75
Total sales and income	$471,150	$432,800	127.99%	127.89%	$3,926.25	$3,606.67
Operating expenses						
Payroll — rooms	$ 58,500	$ 55,000	15.89%	16.25%	$ 487.50	$ 458.33
— telephone	8,350	8,125	2.27	2.40	69.59	67.71
— administrative	25,400	25,000	6.90	7.39	211.67	208.33
— utilities and maintenance	12,650	10,025	3.44	2.96	105.41	83.55
Total payroll (except restaurant)	$104,900	$ 98,150	28.50%	29.00%	$ 874.17	$ 817.92
Payroll taxes, etc.	7,950	6,750	2.16	2.00	66.25	56.25
Housekeeping expense	33,500	32,500	9.10	9.60	279.16	270.83
Administrative expense	32,750	28,000	8.90	8.27	272.92	233.33
Advertising and promotion	18,000	16,925	4.88	5.00	150.00	141.04
Heat, light and power	24,500	23,750	6.66	7.02	204.17	197.92
Repairs and maintenance	21,000	19,200	5.70	5.68	175.00	160.00
Total operating expenses	$242,600	$225,275	65.90%	66.57%	$2,021.67	$1,877.29
House Profit	$228,550	$207,525	62.09%	61.32%	$1,904.58	$1,729.38

Exhibit B (cont)

	Amounts		Ratios to Room Sales		Annual Amounts Per Room	
	This Year	Last Year	This Year	Last Year	This Year	Last Year
Insurance and local taxes						
Insurance on property	$ 3,750	$ 3,750	1.02%	1.11%	$ 31.25	$ 31.25
Real estate and personal property taxes	18,000	18,000	4.89	5.32	150.00	150.00
Total taxes and insurance	$ 21,750	$ 21,750	5.91%	6.43%	$ 181.25	$ 181.25
Profit before interest	$206,800	$185,775	56.18%	54.89%	$1,723.33	$1,548.13
Interest						
First mortgage	$ 37,000	$ 38,025	10.05%	11.24%	$ 308.33	$ 316.88
Debentures	22,500	25,000	6.11	7.38	187.50	208.33
Total interest	$ 59,500	$ 63,025	16.16%	18.62%	$ 495.83	$ 525.21
Profit before depreciation	$147,300	$122,750	40.02%	36.27%	$1,227.50	$1,022.92
Depreciation and amortization						
Depreciation						
Building	$ 50,895	$ 54,145	13.83%	16.00%	$ 424.12	$ 451.21
Swimming pool	2,300	2,625	.62	.78	19.17	21.87
Furniture and equipment	36,885	42,980	10.02	12.70	307.38	358.17
Loan and organization expense	5,320	5,320	1.45	1.57	44.33	44.33
Total depreciation, etc.	$ 95,400	$105,070	25.92%	31.05%	$ 795.00	$ 875.58
Profit before income taxes	$ 51,900	$ 17,680	14.10%	5.22%	$ 432.50	$ 147.34
Provision for income taxes	14,500		3.94		120.83	
Net profit to surplus	$ 37,400	$ 17,680	10.16%	5.22%	$ 311.67	$ 147.34

Exhibit B-1

Departmental revenue and income	Sales	Cost of Sales	Payroll and Related Expenses	Other Expenses	Profit (or Loss)
Rooms	$368,100		$ 62,935	$ 33,500	$271,665
Food	327,800	$143,600	134,720	39,030	86,850
Beverages	111,000	34,600			
Telephone	19,230	18,850	8,980		(8,600)
Other income	6,820				6,820
Departmental totals and gross operating income	$832,950	$197,050	$206,635	$ 72,530	$356,735
Deductions from income					
Administrative and general			$ 27,352	$ 32,750	
Advertising, sales promotion				18,000	
Utilities			13,610	24,500	
Repairs and maintenance				21,000	
Total deductions			$ 40,935	$ 96,250	$137,185
Total house revenue, expense and profit	$832,950	$197,050	$247,570	$168,780	$219,550
Rentals from leased space					9,000
Gross operating profit					$228,550
Capital expenses					
Insurance and local taxes				$ 21,750	
Interest				59,500	
Depreciation				90,080	
Loan and organization expense amortization				5,320	
Total capital expenses					176,650
Net profit before income taxes					$ 51,900
Provision for income taxes					14,500
Net profit for period					$ 37,400

Schedule B-1

Rooms Statistics		*This Year*		*Last Year*
Total rooms in hotel		125		125
Deduct rooms not for rent		5		5
Total rooms for rent		120		120
Available guest rooms per year		43,920		43,800
Rooms occupied		34,596		32,666
Number of guests		54,056		54,471
Room sales		$368,100		$338,420
Average daily room sales		$1,005		$927
Percentage occupancy		78.77%		74.58%
Percentage double occupancy		56.25%		66.75%
Average rate per occupied room		$10.64		$10.36
Average rate per guest		$6.81		$6.21

Food Statistics

		This Year		Last Year
Seating capacity				
Dining room		100		100
Banquet rooms		250		250

Food Sales	*Daily*	*Annual*	*Daily*	*Annual*
Dining room — Breakfast	$ 50.06	$ 18,320	$ 47.51	$ 17,340
— Lunch	275.41	100,800	291.98	106,575
— Dinner	320.16	117,180	325.03	118,635
Total	$645.63	$236,300	$664.52	$242,550
Banquets and parties	250.00	91,500	230.00	83,950
Total food sales	$895.63	$327,800	$894.52	$326,500
Ratio to room sales		89.05%		96.48%
Persons served				
Dining room — Breakfast	100	36,640	95	34,680
— Lunch	197	72,000	201	73,500
— Dinner	183	66,960	185	67,406
Total	480	175,600	481	175,586
Banquets and parties	125	45,750	115	41,975
Total persons served	605	221,350	596	217,561
Average check per person				
Dining room — Breakfast		$ .50		$ .50
— Lunch		1.40		1.45
— Dinner		1.75		1.76
Total		$1.35		$1.38
Banquets and parties		2.00		2.00
Total food sales		$1.48		$1.50

Beverage Statistics	*Daily*	*Annual*	*Daily*	*Annual*
Sales — Cocktail Lounge/Bar	$240.78	$ 88,125	$246.50	$ 89,975
Banquets and parties	62.50	22,875	59.80	21,825
Total beverage sales	$303.28	$111,000	$306.30	$111,800
Ratio to food sales		33.86%		34.24%

of expense. These are outlined in detail in the uniform-system booklets which are recommended as a reference guide for readers interested in pursuing the subject of motel and motor hotel statements beyond the treatment allotted to them in this text.

30-ROOM MOTEL

This establishment offers only room accommodations and limited service, but insofar as room operations are concerned there is no material difference between its statement and that of the 120-room motor hotel. It is owner-operated, has no food and beverage department and is in its fifth full year of operation. The original investment is outlined as follows:

	Cost per room	Total Cost
Land	$ 1,000	$ 30,000
Building	7,000	210,000
Pool	333	10,000
Furniture and fixtures	1,667	50,000
Total	$10,000	$300,000

Land and swimming pool costs are higher per room than are those for the 120-room motor hotel because there are fewer guest-room units in proportion to the land area and pool costs. On the other hand, the building and equipment costs are lower per unit because there is no catering facility or need for public space.

The original loan was for $125,000, or 50 per cent of the land and building values. Except for a personal bank loan, the owner supplied the entire equity capital. Because the owner feels that it serves his income tax situation best, he uses the straight-line method of depreciation.

BALANCE SHEET—EXHIBIT C

A comparatively small amount is needed for current working funds since the sales and income are virtually on a cash basis and no funds are tied up in inventories. The owner therefore finds it practical to charge all supplies to expense as they are purchased and keeps no inventory accounts.

Because the bank loan, equipment notes and mortgage payments due within the coming year, totaling $14,575, are included in current liabilities, the ratio of current assets to current liabilities is .52 to 1. Yet the $7,425 on deposit is more than sufficient to pay current trade creditors and accrued expenses. Furthermore, the profit picture shown

Exhibit C

Current assets
Cash

House funds	$ 200		
Funds on deposit — (bank account)	7,425	$ 7,625	
Accounts receivable		1,500	
Prepaid insurance, licenses, etc.		1,250	
Utility deposit		250	
Total current assets			$ 10,625

Fixed assets — at cost
    less depreciation

Land		$ 30,000	
Building	$210,000		
Less reserve for depreciation	33,600	176,400	
Swimming pool	$ 10,000		
Less reserve for depreciation	3,335	6,665	
Furniture and equipment			
Original cost	$ 50,000		
Additions	6,000		
Total	$ 56,000		
Less — reserve for depreciation	20,850	35,150	
Total fixed assets			248,215
Total assets			$258,840

Liabilities and Capital

Current liabilities

Accounts payable	$ 2,200	
Equipment notes (due in current year)	3,000	
Bank loan	4,000	
Taxes collected (withholding and social security)	500	
Accrued payroll	750	
Accrued local taxes	2,000	
Accrued interest	150	
Other accrued expenses	350	
Mortgage payment (due in current year)	7,575	
Total current liabilities		$ 20,525

Long-term liabilities

First mortgage 6% — (Originally $150,000)	$123,750		
Less — current amount due	7,575	$116,175	
Equipment notes — due after one year		3,000	
Total long-term liabilities			119,175

Proprietor's equity

Balance at beginning of year	$111,000		
Add — profit (see Exhibit D)	18,140	$129,140	
Deduct — withdrawals		10,000	
Net proprietor's equity			$119,140
Total liabilities and capital			$258,840

Exhibit D

	Amounts		Ratios to Room Sales		Annual Amounts Per Room	
	This Year	*Last Year*	*This Year*	*Last Year*	*This Year*	*Last Year*
Sales and income						
Room sales	$85,000	$80,000	100.00%	100.00%	$2,833.34	$2,666.67
Telephone	3,565	3,200	4.19	4.00	118.83	106.66
Other income	4,000	3,750	4.71	4.69	133.33	125.00
Total sales and income	$92,565	$86,950	108.90%	108.69%	$3,085.50	$2,898.33
Operating expenses						
Payroll	$18,000	$16,800	21.18%	21.00%	$ 600.00	$ 560.00
Payroll taxes, etc.	1,525	1,300	1.79	1.63	50.83	43.33
Housekeeping	6,450	6,000	7.59	7.50	215.00	200.00
Telephone cost	3,565	3,300	4.19	4.13	118.83	110.00
Administrative expenses	5,500	5,450	6.47	6.81	183.34	181.67
Advertising and promotion	4,000	3,600	4.71	4.50	133.33	120.00
Heat, light and power	3,825	3,600	4.50	4.50	127.50	120.00
Repairs and maintenance	3,750	3,250	4.41	4.06	125.00	108.33
Total operating expenses	$46,615	$43,300	54.84%	54.13%	$1,553.83	$1,443.33
House Profit	$45,950	$43,650	54.06%	54.56%	$1,531.67	$1,455.00

Exhibit D (cont)

	Amounts		Ratios to Room Sales		Annual Amounts Per Room	
	This Year	Last Year	This Year	Last Year	This Year	Last Year
Insurance and local taxes						
Insurance on property	$ 900	$ 900	1.06%	1.13%	$ 30.00	$ 30.00
Real estate and personal property taxes	4,000	4,000	4.71	5.00	133.34	133.34
Total insurance and taxes	$ 4,900	$ 4,900	5.77%	6.13%	$ 163.34	$ 163.34
Profit before interest	$41,050	$38,750	48.29%	48.43%	$1,368.33	$1,291.66
Interest						
First mortgage	$ 7,425	$ 7,850	8.74%	9.81%	$ 247.50	$ 261.66
Notes	900	1,020	1.05	1.27	30.00	34.00
Total interest	$ 8,325	$ 8,870	9.79%	11.08%	$ 277.50	$ 295.66
Profit before depreciation	$32,725	$29,880	38.50%	37.35%	$1,090.83	$ 996.00
Depreciation						
Building and improvements	$ 9,235	$ 9,235	10.87%	11.54%	$ 307.83	$ 307.83
Furniture and fixtures	5,350	5,200	6.29	6.50	178.33	173.33
Total depreciation	$14,585	$14,435	17.16%	18.04%	$ 486.16	$ 481.16
Profit before income tax	$18,140	$15,445	21.34%	19.31%	$ 604.67	$ 514.84

Statistics	This Year	Last Year
Available guest rooms	30	30
Available rooms per year	10,980	10,950
Rooms occupied	8,095	7,955
Number of guests	12,871	13,364

	This Year	Last Year
Percentage of occupancy	73.72%	72.65%
Percentage of double occupancy	59.00	68.00
Average rate per occupied room	$10.50	$10.06
Average rate per guest	$6.60	$5.99
Average daily room sales	$232.24	$219.18

in Exhibit D indicates that the owner can meet his other obligations from the cash which will be generated in anticipated future rentals. This illustrates the condition wherein a motel can operate as a going concern and meet its obligations currently with a small bank balance and an actual deficiency in working capital. However, the reader is again warned that this is only possible with a profitable operation and that a cash reserve for a bad year or dull season is advisable if a good credit standing is to be maintained. This situation is more often found in the smaller motels, where the effect of credit cards is not substantial enough to tie up working funds, and room sales are almost immediately reflected in the funds on deposit.

The fixed assets in this instance comprise almost 96 per cent of the total assets involved in the enterprise.

Because the proprietor has other interests and investments and the income from this project is only a part of the earnings included in his personal tax returns, no provision for income taxes is included in this balance sheet.

The proportion of equity capital and borrowed funds is about 50-50 and the first mortgage is still about 50 per cent of the value of the fixed assets, both measures indicating sound financing. The liberal loan terms give evidence of the owner's reputation for integrity.

The proprietor's equity increased $8,140 in the past year, due to the fact that the owner made cash withdrawals of $10,000, whereas the net profit before income taxes was $18,140.

PROFIT AND LOSS STATEMENT—EXHIBIT D

The summary form of the statement of revenues, expenses and net income in this example is set up in the same fashion as Exhibit B. The current year's operations are again compared with the results of the previous year in amount, ratios to room sales and annual amounts per room.

Room sales statistics, shown at the bottom of the exhibit, indicate that the average rate per occupied room is comparable to that of the 120-room motor hotel. This suggests that room accommodations in these projects are similar in quality. However, operating expenses, as measured both in ratio to room sales and as annual costs per room, are lower for the smaller establishment. This can probably be attributed to the absence of overhead expenses involved in a food and beverage department and to the fact that the owner-operator is in a better position to control costs personally.

House profit is about 54 per cent of room sales, compared with more than 60 per cent for the motor hotel. House profit per available room in the motel is $1500; for the motor hotel, $1800. The income from the latter's catering department is the decisive factor.

Although statistics on insurance, local taxes, interest, depreciation and net profit are included for both operations, the reader is reminded that these figures are best used in comparing operating periods of an individual project, and will not yield significant information when applied to other establishments. For example, the fixed costs for the motel are far lower per room than those of the motor hotel. This is due to the lesser costs per room involved in building and equipping the smaller project, the proportions of borrowed money to equity capital for the two operations and the different methods used for calculating depreciation.

The rate of return on the equity investment was 16.5 per cent before income tax, compared with an 18.7 per cent return on the capital stock investment in the motor hotel. Based on earnings, both percentages indicate a good investment.

Appendix A

Motor Hotel Operations in 1962

(from "The Horwath Accountant," Vol. 43, No. 5)

For our seventh annual study of motor hotel operations, we have expanded the coverage to 100 and have adhered to the following definition of "motor hotels" established in previous studies: accommodations which, in general, have unique physical attributes and locations enabling them to cater especially to the needs of motorists and which also offer conventional hotel services, such as 24-hour front desk operation, room telephones, guest laundry, valet, etc., and restaurant facilities either on the premises or nearby. The average size of the 100 carefully selected motor hotels was 134 rooms, the range being from 33 to 402 rooms. All sections of the country are represented in the sampling, and the types of operation contributing data cover the full range from highway to center-city, including some types, such as airport motor hotels, which meet special needs.

The gross revenue of the 13,370 units included in the 100 operations exceeded $71,500,000 in 1962 and was about 7 per cent greater than in 1961. Some relatively new motor hotels were added to the sampling this year. In fact, of all the operations covered, 5 were slightly under two years old, while 6 were over 10 years of age. The average age of the motor hotels in the entire group was 5 years.

BASES OF STATISTICS

The motor hotels supplying data for our study have been divided into two categories—"no operated restaurant" and "restaurant operated." Of the motor hotels in the "no operated restaurant" category, 52 per cent had restaurants on the premises operated by other parties under a lease arrangement. The restaurant lease income has been shown separately in order to permit comparisons of the operating results of those motor hotels with the data for fully integrated facilities.

Since the study was expanded this year to include 100 motor hotels, it has been necessary to compute new averages for 1961. The new 1961 figures shown in the study are for the same motor hotels for which 1962 statistics are given.

Averages are shown on three bases: annual amounts per available room, ratios to room sales and, where appropriate, ratios to total sales. The first of the aforementioned bases has received wide acceptance among motor hotel operators, and the other two have long been used in the hotel industry for comparing operating results.

313

PROFITS

The 1962 average house profits, or profits before any fixed charges of the property, are compared with the 1961 results as follows:

	Annual House Profit Per Room	
	1962	1961
No operated restaurant	$1,354	$1,454
Restaurant operated	1,604	1,574

From the information on fixed charges provided by the motor hotels, we prepared the following analysis:

	No Operated Restaurant		Restaurant Operated	
	1962	1961	1962	1961
Fixed charges				
Rent	$ 833	$ 938	$ 756	$ 821
Property insurance	22	22	20	26
Property taxes	159	136	156	135
Interest	209	202	254	261
Depreciation	330	323	487	487
Total fixed charges	$1,112	$1,101	$1,291	$1,358

The reduction in the average rent per room noted in last year's study was again apparent. Property taxes were higher than a year ago, as was the case in each of the preceding studies. Other fixed charges showed relatively minor fluctuations.

A comparison of net profits after deduction of fixed charges but before income taxes follows:

	No Operated Restaurant		Restaurant Operated	
	1962	1961	1962	1961
Net profit before income taxes				
Per room	$242	$353	$317	$231
Ratio to room sales	8.4%	12.2%	11.0%	8.2%
Ratio to total sales	7.7%	11.2%	5.3%	4.0%

For the second time since we have compiled net profit, those motor hotels operating restaurants showed better profits than those leasing or without restaurants. The drop in house profit per room in the latter category was carried through to a 30 per cent drop in net profit before taxes. A decrease in income and an increase in expenses were jointly responsible for the decline in operating result.

THE SALES DOLLAR

The motor hotels that operated restaurants reported a 4.7 per cent rise in total revenue per available room, as shown in the following schedule: (Amounts and ratios are averages of those reporting income from the various sources and therefore do not add to 100 per cent.)

	Amounts Per Room		Per Cent	
	1962	*1961*	*1962*	*1961*
Restaurant operated				
Guest room rentals	$2,891	$2,817	48.0%	49.0%
Public room rentals	28*	28*	.4*	.5*
Food	2,126	1,971	35.3	34.3
Beverages	815*	794*	12.9*	13.2*
Restaurant other income	24*	8*	.4*	.2*
Other income (gross)	309*	287*	5.1*	4.9*
Total	$6,022	$5,749	100.0%	100.0%

*Average only of those motor hotels reporting income from public rooms, beverage sales, restaurant other income and/or other income (gross).

The portion of the revenue dollar derived from room sales declined for the first time since we began these annual studies. Food and beverage sales per unit rose nearly 6½ per cent in 1962, with an 8 per cent rise in food sales contributing the major portion of the increase.

In the properties without restaurants or with leased facilities, total revenue per available room was slightly less than 1 per cent below the 1961 average. Although room sales have always predominated in this group, restaurant rental income has provided an increasingly smaller portion of the revenue dollar. In fact, since 1958, that source has shown a 62 per cent decrease, although room revenues have declined only slightly more than 4½ per cent. A breakdown of total revenue per room in this group follows:

	Amounts Per Room	
	1962	*1961*
No operated restaurant		
Guest room rentals	$2,867	$2,885
Public room rentals	11*	6*
Restaurant rental income	127*	130*
Other income (gross)	247*	230*
Total	$3,144	$3,162

*Average only of those motor hotels having rental income from public rooms, leased restaurants and/or other income (gross).

OCCUPANCY AND RATES

The average annual occupancies of the motor hotels showed only slight changes in 1962 from 1961. In the "no operated restaurant" category, the average was 72.03 per cent, slightly higher than the 71.59 per cent in the same operations last year. However, the motor hotels that operated restaurants showed a slight drop in occupancy, from 71.09 per cent a year ago to 70.72 per cent.

The average room rate showed a pattern that was the reverse of the occupancy pattern. A 3 per cent rise in average rates in the "operated restaurant" category accompanied the decline in occupancy, whereas a 1 per cent drop in room rate went with the slight increase in occupancies in those major hotels without restaurants or with leased food and beverage facilities.

The ratio of double occupancy was again lower in both categories. The decline, which has been consistent in our studies, showed a substantial drop in the year under review. A comparison follows:

	Percentage of Double Occupancy	
	1962	*1961*
No operated restaurants	61.49%	67.41%
Operated restaurants	44.76	48.63
Total	48%	53%

RESTAURANT OPERATIONS

The continued good showing of the restaurant profits indicated the presence of sound management policy and excellent controls.

In order to point up the methods used to maintain consistently good profits in the face of rising labor costs, we have included data on restaurant operations for 1958 along with data for 1962 and 1961 in the following comparative analysis:

	Ratios to Total Food and Beverage Sales		
	1962	*1961*	*1958*
Sales			
Food	75.8%	74.8%	74.5%
Beverages	24.2	25.2	25.5
Total sales	100.0%	100.0%	100.0%
Cost of goods sold			
Food (before credit for employees' meals) *	42.5%	42.7%	45.0%
Beverages*	30.4	30.5	31.5
Total cost of sales	39.5%	39.6%	41.6%
Gross profit	60.5%	60.4%	58.4%
Other income	.4	.1	
Total gross profit and other income	60.9%	60.5%	58.4%

	Ratios to Total Food and Beverage Sales		
(Cont.)			
	1962	1961	1958
Operating expenses			
Payroll	30.3%	30.3%	29.0%
Payroll taxes and employee benefits	3.1	2.8	1.9
Total	33.4%	33.1%	30.9%
Music and entertainment**	1.5		
Laundry	1.5	1.6	1.8
China, glassware, silver and linen	1.7	1.9	1.6
Cleaning and cleaning supplies	.9	1.0	.8
Paper supplies	.6	.6	.6
Menus, printing and stationery	.5	.5	.6
Miscellaneous	2.7	3.9	3.4
Total operating expenses	42.8%	42.6%	39.7%
Restaurant departmental profit	18.1%	17.9%	18.7%

*Ratios are based on individual departmental sales.
**Included in "Miscellaneous" in 1961 and 1958.

In the five-year period, payroll and related expenses have risen 8 per cent, and other expenses have increased nearly 7 per cent. The cost of sales has been reduced, however, by 5 per cent. Therefore, the decline in departmental profit was only 3 per cent. The restaurant operating results for motor hotels continue to be much better than those for conventional hotels.

The level of the annual sales per restaurant seat has become a fairly common measure of success of a restaurant operation. The average and ranges for the motor hotels with operated restaurants in the 1962 study group follow:

	Low	Average	High
Number of seats			
Restaurant and banquet	29	278	2,000
Bar	8	72	225
Food sales per restaurant seat	$372	$1,202	$4,606
Total sales per seat in restaurant and bar	$531	$1,336	$4,478

The annual food and beverage sales per restaurant employee were $9,241 in 1962. That is a daily average of slightly over $25, which is quite high. The combination of high productivity and good control and supervision have produced consistently good food and beverage profits in motor hotels.

OPERATING EXPENSES

The operating cost per available room exclusive of the restaurant operation increased in 1962 for the motor hotels represented in our study. The increase was 5 per cent in each category, with nearly all expenses showing rises over

1961. Payroll and related expenses were up almost 7½ per cent in the "no operated restaurant" category and over 5½ per cent in the "restaurant operated" category. The following schedule shows that the number of employees for every 10 rooms did not increase in 1962, indicating that the rise in payroll was due to higher wages:

| | *Number for Every 10 Rooms* | | | |
| | 1962 | | | 1961 |
Category	Low	Average	High	Average
Rooms or housekeeping (Front office clerks, maids, bellmen, etc.)	.8	1.6	2.7	1.7
Other (Administrative, maintenance, telephone, etc.)	.1	.8	2.1	1.0

The reductions in the number of employees may have been due to decreases in extra labor. They indicated a high degree of control over payroll requirements, and in view of the increase in revenues, management was to be highly commended for achieving them, provided they did not cause a reduction in services required by the guest.

Although motor hotels were able to check the steady rise in the most of operations in 1961, they did not fare so well in 1962, as the following table shows. Drops did occur in some operating expense ratios, however, of which the building category in repairs and maintenance is an example. Reductions in that area may have been justified in view of the relative newness of many of the motor hotels; on the other hand, postponement of necessary maintenance is usually false economy.

One expense item previously included in miscellaneous advertising expenses is now being shown separately. It is radio and television. That item averaged .1 of 1 per cent of room sales in 1962 in the motor hotels in the "no operated restaurant" category and .2 of 1 per cent in those with operated restaurants.

From the supplementary expense data supplied by a majority of the motor hotels, we prepared the following analysis of the ratios to room sales of the major items of expense in each category:

| | *No Operated Restaurant* | | *Restaurant Operated* | |
	1962	1961	1962	1961
Housekeeping				
Laundry	4.0%	4.0%	3.4%	3.5%
Linen and glassware	1.2	1.1	1.3	1.4
Cleaning supplies	.8	.7	.9	.8
Guest soap, paper and other supplies	1.3	1.2	1.3	1.5
Miscellaneous	1.4	1.2	1.9	1.9
Total housekeeping	8.7%	8.2%	8.8%	9.1%

(Cont.)	No Operated Restaurant		Restaurant Operated	
	1962	1961	1962	1961
Administrative				
Licenses and dues	.3%	.2%	.3%	.3%
Printing and stationery, postage and office supplies	.9	.7	1.1	.9
Management fee	2.6	2.8	2.2	2.1
Liability and other general insurance	.5	.6	.8	.9
Travel and entertainment	.4	.5	.8	.7
Accounting and legal fees	.8	.9	.8	.8
Miscellaneous	1.4	1.4	2.7	2.5
Total administrative	6.9%	7.1%	8.7%	8.2%
Advertising				
Printed matter, direct mail, etc.	.6%	.5%	.6%	.5%
Franchise fee	.8	.6	.1	.1
Signs	2.2	1.8	1.4	1.4
Radio and television	.1		.2	
Newspapers and magazines	2.0	1.3	1.1	1.1
Miscellaneous	.6	1.6	2.1	2.2
Total advertising	6.3%	5.8%	5.5%	5.3%
Heat, light and power				
Electricity	2.6%	2.5%	3.8%	3.7%
Fuel	1.6	1.5	1.6	1.6
Water	.5	.5	.8	.8
Miscellaneous	.8	.8	.7	.7
Total heat, light and power	5.5%	5.3%	6.9%	6.8%
Repairs and maintenance				
Building	.6%	.8%	.8%	.9%
Grounds	.4	.4	.7	.7
Swimming pool	.2	.2	.1	.2
Furnishings	.4	.3	.5	.7
Equipment	1.9	1.4	2.2	2.1
Painting and decorating	.4	.4	.6	.5
Miscellaneous	.1	.5	.1	.2
Total repairs and maintenance	4.0%	4.0%	5.0%	5.3%

Although the foregoing totals are the averages only of those motor hotels supplying detailed data and thus do not tie in exactly with the summary covering the operating results for the entire sampling, the trend of expenses is the same in both cases.

BALANCE SHEET RATIOS

We were provided with the information on total investment in land, building and equipment by a sufficient number of the motor hotels with leased or operated restaurants to enable us to compile the following summary:

	Cost Per Room (Before Depreciation) Leased or Operated Restaurant
Land	$ 754
Building	8,083
Swimming pool	145
Furniture and fixtures	2,184
Total investment per room	$11,095

Such information available for establishments without restaurants was too meager to provide useful averages. We have noted a definite trend toward construction of restaurants in all new motor hotels, either to be leased or operated. Therefore, data on the average investment in motor hotels without food and beverage facilities of any kind are perhaps of little value.

Other balance sheet ratios that were computed from the information available included:

Accounts receivable	
Increase over 1961	9%
Average amount per room	$164
Ratio to total sales	3%
Number of times average daily sales	11
Food inventory	
Increase over 1961	10%
Annual turnover	36.6 times

Summaries of Operations

	Annual Amounts per Room			
	No Operated Restaurant		Restaurant Operated	
	1962	1961	1962	1961
Income				
Guest room rentals	$2,867	$2,885	$2,891	$2,817
Public room rentals	11*	6*	28*	28*
Restaurant				
Operating profit			508	473
Lease income	127*	130*		
Other income (net)	64	60	79	61
Total	$2,991	$3,014	$3,496	$3,370
Operating expenses				
Payroll	$ 714	$ 667	$ 783	$ 750
Payroll taxes and employee benefits	63	57	78	65
Total	$ 777	$ 724	$ 861	$ 815
Housekeeping	256	248	270	268
Administrative	193	197	253	227
Advertising	148	136	165	152
Heat, light and power	152	147	199	192
Repairs and maintenance	111	108	144	142
Total	$1,637	$1,560	$1,892	$1,796
House profit (before taxes, interest, depreciation, etc.)	$1,354	$1,454	$1,604	$1,574
Percentage of occupancy	72.03%	71.59%	70.72%	71.09%
Average rate per occupied room	$10.91	$11.04	$11.20	$10.86
Ratio to total sales including restaurant rental income and other income				
Payroll (including restaurant)	22.7%	21.1%	27.1%	26.9%
Payroll taxes and employee benefits	2.0	1.8	2.7	2.4
Total	24.7%	22.9%	29.8%	29.3%
Administrative expenses	6.1%	6.2%	4.2%	4.0%
Advertising	4.7	4.3	2.7	2.6
Heat, light and power	4.8	4.7	3.3	3.3
Repairs and maintenance	3.5	3.4	2.4	2.5
House profit	43.1	46.0	26.6	27.4

*Average only of those motor hotels having rental income from public rooms and/or leased restaurants.

Summaries (cont)

	Ratios to Room Sales			
	No Operated Restaurant		Restaurant Operated	
	1962	1961	1962	1961
Income				
Guest room rentals	100.0%	100.0%	100.0%	100.0%
Public room rentals	.3*	.1*	1.0*	1.0*
Restaurant				
Operating profit			17.6	16.8
Lease income	5.2*	5.3*		
Other income (net)	2.2	2.1	2.7	2.2
Total	104.3%	104.4%	120.9%	119.6%
Operating expenses				
Payroll	24.9%	23.1%	27.1%	26.6%
Payroll taxes and employee benefits	2.2	2.0	2.7	2.3
Total	27.1%	25.1%	29.8%	28.9%
Housekeeping	8.9	8.6	9.3	9.5
Administrative	6.7	6.8	8.7	8.1
Advertising	5.2	4.7	5.7	5.4
Heat, light and power	5.3	5.1	6.9	6.8
Repairs and maintenance	3.9	3.7	5.0	5.0
Total	57.1%	54.0%	65.4%	63.7%
House profit (before taxes, interest, depreciation, etc.)	47.2%	50.4%	55.5%	55.9%

*Average only of those motor hotels having rental income from public rooms and/or leased restaurants.

SUMMARY

The net profit, before interest, depreciation and income taxes, was 9.5 per cent of the average investment in motor hotels that operated restaurants in 1962. It was approximately 8 per cent in those that did not operate restaurants. Results were not as good in 1962 in the latter category, primarily because of slight declines in revenue and an increase in expenses. A rise in room rates apparently offset the effect of increases in costs in the "restaurant operated" category, making it possible for those motor hotels to show a slight improvement in operating results. There are two patterns that we believe are somewhat disturbing:

1. Some motor hotels may have fallen into the habit of using automatic room rate increases to counteract the effect of rising costs. Greater operating efficiency is a much better answer.
2. Some motor hotels have tended to reduce maintenance when business is poor and other costs are increasing. That is false economy.

Despite the existence of the disturbing patterns just mentioned, the showing of the motor hotels was still quite impressive in 1962.

Appendix B

A Checklist on Purchase and Sale of Motel and Motor Hotel Properties

Because there is no standard form or formula that can easily be adapted to a purchase or lease agreement involving a motel or motor hotel operation, it is advisable that the parties review all its aspects and contingencies and prepare a preliminary checklist as a guide to the final signed draft. The terms of such an agreement are limited only by the ability of the parties to bargain with each other, and there are no set rules as to the obligations or duties of either party.

It is good business to secure competent legal advice in the preparation of the agreement, particularly to see that none of its terms are in conflict with federal, state or local laws and regulations, and also to see that the intent is properly worded to guard against later misinterpretation. It is also wise to seek the counsel of someone familiar with sale or lease contracts as they pertain to motel and motor hotel operations to advise on the practical application of the contract. An accountant should advise on the technical aspects pertaining to the verifications and determination of the values involved, and should review the income tax factors.

As in all legal documents, the simplest form is best, but general terms often serve to complicate and create legal technicalities through their vagueness, just as involved contracts often present too impractical and restrictive an interpretation. Both extremes invite future trouble and possible costly litigation.

The following checklist is intended as a guide on the items that are most often considered and covered in preparing a purchase and sale agreement applied to a motel or motor hotel. However, the reader is warned that it does not cover all contingencies and conditions that may arise. For instance, references to legal descriptions of the property, the financial form and responsibility of the parties involved, the description of the many types of liabilities to be assumed or transferred, and the warranties of the seller and buyer are purposely omitted, these being the responsibility of legal counsel. If the transaction is made through the purchase of a corporation's capital stock the problems connected with transfer of assets and obligations become simplified to the extent that they are based on the verification of the corporation's balance sheet.

The wide variety now found in properties of this type, from the small motel which offers only rooms to the more elaborate motor hotel with many operated departments and services would make it impossible to prepare a checklist complete in all respects. Therefore this list is presented as a starting guide on which to pattern—by amplification or omission—the points to be covered in preparing a purchase or sale agreement on a specific property.

CHECKLIST

We have assumed that the buyer has made a physical inspection of the property and is satisfied with its condition, has examined the books and records of the seller or certified statements as to financial condition and prior operating results and has made calculations of future earnings in justification of the purchase price. We have also assumed that the purchase price and general financial terms of the sale have been determined to the satisfaction of both buyer and seller.

A. *Date of Sale and Settlement Date*
  1. *On what date will purchaser take possession?*
Because most accounting records and statements are prepared on a monthly basis it would be advisable to have the purchaser take possession on the first of the month, thus expediting such accounting problems as may be involved in the transfer of receivables, inventories, and the allocation of prorations on licenses, taxes, insurance, utility charges, payroll, etc., which are usually a normal procedure at the close of each month.
  2. *What is the hour of closing?*
Normally the guest-room rentals apply to the day when the guest starts his overnight stay. Thus if the agreement states that all income is to be applied at the close of the normal business day, the question of apportionment of room rentals is simplified, whereas if a definite hour, such as midnight, is mentioned, this apportionment requires a more complicated definition. All income rentals are ordinarily apportioned through the night preceding the effective date in motels and hotels.
The same problem occurs in late functions and parties, which may extend to late hours of the morning and involve inventories of food, beverages and other salable items of these departments. Normally the entire sales of the function, up to late dining room or cocktail bar closing, are considered to be income of the day on which such operations commence.
  3. *What is the basis and time of final settlement?*
As a practical matter the time of final payment is usually postponed until all values involved are determined, the necessary transfers of licenses and operating contracts are effected and proper notification is given to third parties. Thus, buyer and seller agree to date of possession and start of buyer's operations, which may differ from the date the purchaser receives actual title as well as the date when he makes his final payment. Determination of these dates should be specified in the agreement. The agreement should also state whether the sale is for cash, or what obligations are to be assumed by the purchaser as part of the purchase price.

B. *What Assets Are Included in The Sale?*

1. *House funds*

If the seller retains the house funds, the purchaser must be prepared to furnish replacements for them. In practical application these funds are usually turned over to the purchaser by actual count, who then remits to the seller in the amount so determined. The seller will eliminate all non-cash items included in these funds, such as paid-out slips, petty cash expense vouchers, etc. Any cash shortages or overages will be adjusted by agreement at the time of transfer.

2. *Transferable deposits*

Utility, license, or tax deposits, etc., which are transferable will be transferred to the name of the purchaser and will be paid for by him. This may also apply to certain lease deposits, investment securities in civic projects, cooperatives, local associations or clubs, in which case their value should be determined and the transfer effected, paid for by the purchaser.

3. *Receivables*

(*a*) If sold to the Purchaser. Agreement should be reached on their collectible value and detailed trial balances drawn to determine their amount at the time of transfer. Seller should guarantee their validity.

(*b*) If retained by Seller. It is usually more practical for the purchaser to collect the existing receivables in the ordinary course of business so as not to inconvenience the guest and patron, and to remit such collections to the seller as they are made. The regular billing methods of the seller must be reviewed and prorations made of all accounts involving monthly or weekly rentals for permanent guests, stores and concessions. Trial balances of the accounts at the date of closing will determine the amounts involved. The usual manner of handling guest and city ledger accounts is to mark the folio balances with a distinctive color or sign for convenience in apportioning the collections. Buyer and seller must agree on apportionment of percentage rentals from sub-tenants and concessions if the rental date differs from the date of sale.

The parties must then agree on how collections are to be applied, whether first to the seller's old balance or to the buyer's current account, in which case the seller is credited only when the opening balance is reduced or paid up. They must also agree on the intervals of remittance of collections made by the buyer and by what date the seller will attempt to complete his own collection efforts. The buyer usually agrees to use due diligence in collection in the ordinary course of business, but assumes no responsibility for losses in collection of the seller's accounts. Therefore the seller must have the right to review collections subsequent to the closing date and to supplement the buyer's collection efforts in a reasonable manner.

At the date of closing, advance deposits on reservations, credit balances on accounts receivable and sub-tenants' security deposits should be listed and their disposition determined. If the buyer is to assume responsibility for them, the seller will credit them to the purchase price.

A list of all permanent guests, sub-tenants and concessions should indicate the name, space involved, rental and other terms of the lease or concession, with an agreement made between buyer and seller on the terms involved. A list of all advance deposits on rooms, functions, and related services should be compiled by the seller and agreement made with the buyer as to the terms in connection with any future sales commitments or reservations.

4. *Inventories*

(a) Buyer and seller must agree on the nature and extent of inventories for merchandise, supplies and equipment. They should also agree on who will price, extend and determine the values involved. Both parties should have representatives present at the time of count, and, to avoid later argument, it is advisable to provide copies for initialing by both representatives.

(b) Buyer and seller must agree on the date and time for inventories. Food, beverage and supplies inventories located in a storeroom can best be taken at the time the storeroom is closed on the seller's business day. If receiving sheets are in use they will serve as reference.

The producing inventory of food already issued and the beverage inventory at the bar is best taken in the morning of the effective date of sale prior to the start of operations. Buyer and seller should agree on what items will be included and how they will be priced. For instance, will prepared foods be included and will bar inventories include opened bottles? (Laws pertaining to the sale of liquor in bulk and opened bottles should be investigated.)

Supplies inventories are usually restricted to items in the controlled storeroom and otherwise stored in unbroken packages. It is customary to consider that supplies already issued to the housekeeper, engineer, front office and other service departments, to guest rooms, dining rooms, etc., are the seller's expense. However, supplies in maids' or janitors' closets, linen room, front office, administrative offices, engine room and maintenance shops may be considered material enough to warrant valuation in the sale, in which case buyer and seller must agree on how these values will be determined.

(c) Buyer and seller must agree on the pricing of the inventories. Usually inventories are priced at the seller's cost, but it is best to have a specific agreement.

(d) Buyer and seller should agree on what values will be placed on unused upholstery and drapery materials, carpets, fuel, garage or filling station supplies, paints, carpenters' and engineers' supplies that are on hand.

(e) Buyer and seller should agree on the values to be placed on linens, china, glassware, silver, uniforms and utensils. Ordinarily this operating equipment is included in the sale price as a part of the furniture, fixtures and equipment to the extent that it is in actual use. A separate valuation of these items is restricted to reserve stocks on hand in unbroken packages. If the items in use are inventoried separately, their value is usually placed at one-half of the cost based on current replacement.

(f) Buyer and seller should agree on the disposition of all obsolete or unusable items which remain in storage. They will not ordinarily be included in the inventory value to be paid for by the buyer.

Arrangements may be made for the buyer to purchase only selected inventory items, leaving the seller to dispose of the balance.

5. *Prepaid expenses and deferred charges*

(*a*) The seller should compile a complete list of all existing insurance coverage. The agreement should state which policies are to be transferred to the buyer and how their premiums are to be apportioned. The buyer should consider replacement of non-transferable policies, arranging at the same time for a review of the coverage by an insurance broker or advisor.

The liability of the seller for workmen's compensation, products liability, etc., on which premiums are based on sales volume or payroll should be determined in the event that these policies are transferred to the purchaser. (Ordinarily new policies are required or are found to be more practical.)

The buyer should arrange for the transfer of the State Unemployment Insurance credit and the seller's rate classification in states where this is allowed.

(*b*) The buyer will need a complete list of all existing service contracts, such as elevator maintenance, office equipment maintenance, television and air-conditioning maintenance, road signs, etc. If contracts are transferable, an agreement must be reached on apportionment with notification sent to the contractors involved.

(*c*) Similar arrangements are necessary for all licenses and permits.

6. *Fixed assets*

(*a*) The title to the property and its legal description should be determined by legal counsel, who will also review any zoning problems, easements, or other restrictions placed on it. It may also be advisable to have a surveyor check the property boundaries. If the sale involves leased property, the terms of the lease and its transferability will also be a matter for review by legal counsel.

(*b*) An examination of the physical condition of the buildings, pool and parking area by a competent engineer and motel operator is advisable if the purchaser is to accept the property "as is" without warranty from the seller. Plans and blueprints should be made available to the buyer for use in future maintenance. The attorney will check with local fire and building inspection units for possible building code violations.

(*c*) Seller should list any items of furniture, fixtures and equipment not included in the sale; their removal date should be stipulated in the agreement. The same applies to any personal items owned by resident guests and subtenants.

Rented equipment must also be listed. Copies of the rental agreement should be furnished to the buyer, and the lessor should be notified of the impending sale.

If the seller is to retain space on the property after the sale for office use or otherwise, the terms of such use should be outlined in the agreement.

7. *Liabilities*

(*a*) The seller should request final statements from all purveyors and others with whom he has been doing business. It would facilitate the transfer if a detailed list of such creditors and the amounts due them were made available to the buyer, not only to allocate these costs between buyer and seller, but also to inform the buyer of sources of supplies and services.

(b) The seller should furnish a detailed list of all commitments, to be either cancelled or taken over by the buyer, with notification to the contracting party of the transfer and intended disposition of the remaining commitment. Commonly the buyer considers it advantageous to continue contracts for such items as linens, soap, book matches, printing and stationery.

(c) If the seller has made contracts with newspapers and other publications on a "due-bill" basis, whereby the motel furnishes guest rooms and other services as payment, the terms and unused balance of these contracts should be listed. Buyer and seller will agree on their cancellation or continuance and the seller will notify the contracting publication.

(d) The seller will either arrange for a final statement on all utilities or agree with the buyer on the apportionment and payment of the invoices rendered in the ordinary course of business. Utility companies should be notified of the sale and arrangements should be made to transfer any utility deposits to the buyer.

(e) The parties should agree on the apportionment of local taxes and arrange for proper adjustment if the amount of such taxes can not be determined at the closing date. The seller should give a warranty that all such taxes are currently paid, that there are no outstanding tax liens on the property of which the buyer has not been notified. Should the sale involve stock rather than property, the buyer and seller should agree on their respective responsibilities as to franchise and income taxes for past periods which are not determinable at the date of sale and are subject to future examinations. (Costs of litigation also figure in this agreement.) All taxing bodies should be notified of the sale by the seller.

(f) The seller should furnish a complete list of employees and a description of their employment and compensation. Buyer and seller will agree on the apportionment of payroll if payment dates differ from the closing date. Usually the salaries and wages of the night employees are the expense of the seller for the periods of service which start on the date prior to closing.

Buyer and seller will agree on the apportionment of vacation pay. The amount may either be determined as at the closing date or the buyer may agree to assume the burden when the vacation period arrives.

Should the seller hold a union contract, the union should be notified of the sale and arrangements made for the buyer to assume the existing responsibilities. This contract should be made available to the buyer, and the settlement of any existing disputes over funds in connection with employee benefits should be effected. The responsibility for payment of any retroactive wage adjustments should also be decided between buyer and seller.

If the buyer desires the continuance of group insurance or similar employee benefits currently in effect, the parties involved should be notified and the transfers made, with the costs apportioned as at the closing date.

If the seller has any bonus or percentage arrangements with employees which the buyer may wish to continue, the parties should also agree on the apportionment of the payments involved if they cover periods other than at the date of closing.

(g) Should property hold an agreement with a franchise or referral group which the buyer intends to continue, the seller should notify the company or association in order that the necessary transfer arrangements may be made. Buyer and seller will agree on the apportionment of dues, fees and costs involved in this transfer.

The seller should also supply a list of trade associations, civic clubs and other organizations in which membership is held, notifying them of the sale and reaching agreement with the buyer on the transfer and apportionment of dues, payment of transfer fees and other costs involved. Similar arrangements should be made with respect to subscriptions to trade periodicals and related publications.

(h) The seller should furnish the buyer with trust indentures and other evidence and data on any equipment installment contracts, mortgages, loans, or similar obligations to be assumed by the buyer. The creditor should be notified of the sale by the seller so that arrangements may be made for the transfer of primary responsibility for the outstanding debt. Adjustment for prepaid or accrued interest will be made as of the date of closing and any deposits with trustees will be transferred to the credit of the buyer.

(i) The seller will furnish a detailed list of all contract commitments and contingencies involving such items as mechanics' liens, lawsuits, damage claims or disputed liabilities and will reach agreement with the buyer on their dispositions.

(j) Buyer and seller should agree on who is to pay brokerage fees, revenue stamps, recording and registration fees, filing fees on mortgages and related fees.

8. *Baggage and safety deposit boxes*
   (a) The seller will furnish a list of all baggage and personal belongings checked or left in the care of the motel, which list will be acknowledged by the buyer upon taking possession of the property, after which time their care becomes the buyer's responsibility. Buyer and seller will agree on the length of time any "hold" baggage retained by the seller as security for unpaid accounts will be stored for him. (Usually no more than six months is allowed for its disposal by the seller.)
   (b) Responsibility for contents in safety deposit boxes becomes the joint concern of both buyer and seller at the date of closing. Therefore they should make a joint inventory of the boxes in use and the seller should notify all boxholders of the sale, requesting the removal of contents or transfer of responsibility through a new agreement with the buyer in accordance with the terms on which the box is rented or assigned. Both buyer and seller should have representatives present when these boxes are opened and contents verified.

9. *Accounting records, correspondence, guest history,*
   sales promotion records
   Buyer and seller should agree on the extent to which the records of the seller will be made available to the buyer for convenience in conducting the business through the period of transfer. The guest folios, registration cards, cashiers' sheets, receiving forms, issue requisitions, payroll records

and similar items are usually continued by the buyer as a matter of convenience. Past records are also valuable to him. Whether the seller's general books, purchase records and details on accounts payable are retained by the new owner depends on the circumstances and relationships of the parties to the sale.

Of additional benefit to the buyer are general correspondence, guest history records, record of future reservations and bookings as well as the general lists, brochures and other advertising matter. Buyer and seller should agree on the extent to which these items will be left on the premises and the responsibility of the buyer for their care while they remain in his possession.

SUMMARY

It should be obvious to the reader that this list does not cover all possible contingencies. However, the major items which are often of concern are included. The extent to which they are covered in the purchase agreement depends on the nature of the property and individuals involved. The best advice is to prepare your own list prior to negotiations and to obtain competent counsel and assistance in preparing the agreement and in implementing the transaction.

Appendix C

A Checklist on Leases of Motel and Motor Hotel Properties

The following list, like its counterpart in Appendix B, is not all-inclusive. No set pattern exists in all leasing agreements; terms differ with each property and the bargaining powers of the parties involved. Many of the items in Appendix B apply to leasing as well as to purchasing; moreover, the advice that the agreement be drawn up by a competent attorney is equally appropriate to this discussion.

Concessions in connection with a lease transaction are made both ways, depending on how anxious the tenant is to obtain the right to operate the property and how concerned the landlord may be to obtain management. Both are partners, in effect, and the best deal is one which gives the lessee adequate compensation for his efforts and the lessor maximum return on his investment.

CHECKLIST

We have assumed that the tenant is satisfied as to the physical aspects, past performance, and future possibilities of the property and that both tenant and landlord have agreed to the rental terms.

A. *Parties*

1. If the lease is made with an individual as tenant and is assignable to a corporation, the extent of the remaining personal responsibility of the assignor should be specified. The proper designation and responsibility of the parties to the lease should be reviewed by the attorney. If the assignment is to a corporation, which is a legal entity, the sale of its stock can also affect the transfer of the company contracts and assets; if specific individual responsibilities are a factor in the lease it should be drawn in a manner that will not jeopardize the landlord in this respect.

2. If the personal services of the manager are a requirement, he will become a third party to the agreement and the terms under which the lease may be continued or cancelled if he resigns, becomes incapacitated or dies should be definitely outlined. In this instance it is also advisable that the landlord require the tenant to carry insurance coverage on the person so designated.

331

B. *Term*

The lease will specify the date and time of possession, the time period to be covered and the number, length and terms of any extensions in time.

In a sale or transfer of a lease the comments made under item A in the purchase and sale checklist apply. If the lease is for a new property it should state the period to be allowed the landlord to make the property available for operation and the date or time the tenant must take possession and begin operations. Usually the rental starts with the first day of operation. The length or term of the lease may also start with that date, although often the two dates do not coincide.

Ordinarily a motel or motor hotel lease would be for a long term, the initial period usually being from 20 to 25 years or longer. However, 10-year leases with extension provisions are not uncommon, landlord and tenants agreeing that at some later period conditions may change, necessitating a revision of the terms. The option for extensions is usually left to the tenant, the rental being specified as continuing on the same terms. However, there are also leases which provide for a change in rental values or other considerations to be agreed upon between landlord and tenant prior to the extension period.

C. *Property Leased*

Most motel leases cover land and buildings, with the tenant providing the furnishings and working capital necessary for operation. If the lease is for the land only, with the tenant constructing and equipping the facilities, provision should be made to have the landlord subjugate his lease to the mortgage loan required to finance the project. Usually these land leases are long-term, running from 50 to 99 years. The rental is based on a normal investment return to the landowner and is usually on a "net lease" basis, in which case the tenant in addition to the cash rental pays all taxes, assessments and other operating costs.

If the leased property includes furniture and fixtures it is advisable to have an inventory of such equipment prepared and attached as an exhibit to the lease document. It is also necessary that the lease outline the tenant's responsibility as to replacements and renewals of equipment. The usual stipulation is that the tenant agrees to maintain and return the property "in the same condition, amount and quality as he has received it, ordinary wear and tear excepted."

As a practical matter it is best for the tenant to furnish such operating equipment as linens, china, glassware, silver, utensils and uniforms, since these items are of shorter life, subject to pilferage and more in the nature of operating supplies. The uniform system of accounts recommends this, charging the expense of replacing these items directly to the operating departments rather than as a depreciation item.

If the tenant owns the furniture and equipment the lease should provide for its disposition at the end of the lease term, either by removal from the property or by sale to the landlord or new tenant. Usually the landlord will want to buy the furniture in order to keep his property productive. The lease should then state the basis on which he can acquire it. Some leases quote a flat sum, while others stipulate that the basis should be the book value (cost less depreciation) at expiration. This latter provision disregards flucuations in market value—especially over a long term of 20 or 30 years. The provision that appears fair at the time the lease is drawn may be a definite disadvantage when the lease expires. A more favorable provision would call for the purchaser to pay the fair value as determined by competent appraisers.

In connection with a new project the landlord and tenant should agree on the plans and specifications. The tenant should be allowed the right to have a representative at the property during construction to protect his interests. If the tenant desires changes that involve additional costs, the parties should agree on who is to pay them.

In earlier leases the landlord usually paid the real estate taxes and insurance on the building and agreed to keep the exterior in good repair. The tenant furnished the hotel and gave a chattel mortgage on the furnishings to the landlord as a guarantee of the lease. The current trend has been to the "net lease," which relieves the landlord of all operating expenditures except those connected with his financing costs. Some leases provide for a division between landlord and tenant of any increase in real estate taxes during the life of the agreement.

D. *Rentals*
1. *Fixed rentals*
The fixed rental, based on a fair return to the landlord, gives the owner little reason to take any active interest in the operation beyond seeing that the rent is paid, the property well maintained and the operation conducted on a respectable plane. This fixed rental arrangement more nearly approaches an ordinary real estate lease transaction in nature.

It is essential that the fixed rental be an amount that the operator can pay under conditions that may prevail over the life of the lease; if it is too high it must either be adjusted by abatement or deferral, or the lease may be cancelled. Naturally it is difficult to foresee these conditions at the outset, and therefore adjustments are usually made as the need arises. No attempt is made in the original document to outline the basis for such adjustments.

2. *Percentage rentals*
The percentage rental has two major forms. Both types normally call for a fixed minimum rental sufficient to give the landlord income to pay his loan obligations, taxes and other necessary expenses, plus a return on his investment. The tenant should expect the landlord to adjust the return on his investment downward in determining the minimum rental in return for the opportunity to participate through the percentage clause in any increased sales volume or profits generated by the operation. This minimum is often based on an arbitrary figure that the tenant can be confident of meeting. If a minimum guarantee is made it is often advisable for the tenant to request additionally a maximum rental clause. Of course the landlord looks upon the percentage rental as a hedge against inflation and may resist this proposal.

In both percentage rental bases the landlord takes the position of being a partner in the business of the tenant and should require the tenant to provide him with statements of account for the items on which the rental is based, preferably certified to by a public accountant. He should also have access to the books and records of the tenant on a reasonable basis. It will simplify the matter of definition of sales and profits if reference is made to the published uniform system of accounts as recommended by industry trade associations.

(*a*) The most common percentage arrangement is based on sales or gross income as defined in the uniform system of accounts. Many attorneys use the term "gross receipts," which is often confusing if the operator's records are kept on an accrual basis. However, some provision should be made for deducting uncollected accounts, the usual method being to allow a credit for accounts actually written off. The lease usually calls for a minimum rental payable monthly in advance, and an additional percentage based on sales in excess of the amount on which the minimum rests, adjusted annually. Payment of the percentage rental may be required after a reasonable determining period—usually 30 days if monthly payments are made, or 40 to 60 days if payment is annual.

The typical percentage rental basis is 25 per cent of room sales. However, the figure fluctuates with local conditions, depending on the profit potential of the property and other lease requirements. Percentages for food and beverage sales average 5 per cent and from 5 per cent to 15 per cent, respectively. In many instances where the food operation is considered an accommodation service to the guest, no percentage rental is applied to restaurant sales.

A percentage rental based on total sales, although sometimes used, has its dangers. The tenant is apt to regard the precentage as applying equally to food, beverage and other sales as it does to room sales. He would be reluctant to pay 10 per cent on food, but would like to have a lease calling for 10 per cent on room sales. His operations may be adversely influenced by this attitude.

Store rentals and concession income are often included on the same basis as guest room rentals, but telephone sales, laundry, valet and other income items are excluded from the percentage calculations since their profit potential is small.

Several leases call for an acceleration in rental percentage, based on increased sales volume. There is a danger present in this arrangment which becomes evident if maximum percentages fall out of line with normal operating figures, acting as a squeeze on the tenant, who is forced to meet the higher costs of labor, commodities and service that often accompany increased business. Although it is true that higher occupancies result in higher profit ratios, the attempt of the landlord to participate in these higher profits through accelerated rental percentages often backfires when the lessee finds it necessary to adjust rates and prices to cover increased operating expenses.

The lease should be specific on what allowances, complimentary rooms, meals and other services are to be allowed as deductions from gross sales. In the uniform system of accounts for hotels the term "net sales" would normally apply as the basic figure for determining the percentage rental. These allowances are best left to the tenant's decision since they are ordinarily controlled by his policy of operation. The lease may specify rooms, meals, etc., for the staff and motel use, not to be included in sales, although it is often taken for granted that these items will not be considered in calculating percentage rentals.

(b) The second percentage rental arrangement is based on a division of profits. In this instance the landlord becomes a full partner in the business. What is meant by "profits" should be very carefully defined in the lease. Much confusion and misunderstanding can be avoided by linking the definition to the terms used in the uniform system of accounts recommended by the trade associations. Attorneys often use the term "receipts and disbursements" when they actually are referring to "income and expenses" and the lease should state whether the profit is to be figured on the accrual or cash basis. In our opinion, the accrual basis is preferable and not as vulnerable to manipulation, but in smaller operations the cash basis is often more practical.

The lease should specifically cover such items as the maximum salary allowed the tenant as an operating expense deduction in computing rent and at what point the rental participation should be calculated. For example, the rental division is usually calculated before deducting the tenant's income taxes and in some instances before interest on the tenant's obligations. In other cases the division may be made before depreciation but after deducting any of the tenant's capital expenditures for replacements and improvements to the property. Some agreements specify definite amounts to be paid to landlord and tenant after which the remaining profit is divided between them. There is no guide as to the percentage division. Some leases specify amounts to be spent on advertising and promotion, repairs and maintenance, etc., which may affect the rental calculation.

It is evident that his type of rental calculation follows no set formula and is truly a bargaining process between landlord and tenant, intended to give each a rightful share of the proceeds of operation.

E. *Security*

It is customary for the tenant to buy the furniture and pledge it as security for the rent in compliance with the lease provisions. If the leased property includes the furnishings, the lessee normally provides a deposit in cash or securities as a guarantee, either under an escrow agreement with a provision that it be returned when the lease expires, or that it be applied against the last year's rental. The landlord must pay income tax on a cash deposit so applied in the year he receives it.

In rare instances the tenant agrees to furnish only the necessary working capital, making the agreement a management contract in the form of a lease. The landlord thus takes more of a chance on the financial responsibility and operating ability of the tenant and may require that the tenant restrict himself on drawings or dividends and maintain a specific equity investment and working capital position.

F. *Upkeep and Maintenance*

Regardless of whether the property is rented furnished or unfurnished the lease should provide the landlord reasonable protection against a tenant's "milking" the property by increasing his own profits at the expense of necessary repairs, maintenance and replacements. A general provision that the tenant must maintain the property in good condition should be supplemented by an additional clause stipulating that if the lessee spends less than a fixed minimum amount or percentage of income for repairs, maintenance, and replacements he must pay the difference between his actual expenditures and this minimum as additional rent unless the landlord consents to its application in some other manner. In order to adjust such expenditures between years it may be specified that this excess be placed in reserve for future expenditures on the property.

The uniform system of accounts classification of expenses should serve as the guide in defining repairs and maintenance costs. Replacements of linens, china, glassware, silver, utensils and uniforms may be classified by some individuals as expenditures to be included under this clause, whereas it is customary to consider these replacement items as direct operating expenses, not as repairs and maintenance.

Another vaguely worded clause often found in leases calls for the landlord to pay for all exterior maintenance, with the tenant being responsible for maintaining the interior. This is liable to misinterpretation, especially when it comes to major elevator, plumbing, or other building equipment repairs in later years.

The lease should prohibit the tenant from pledging to a third party without the landlord's consent any of the new furnishings and equipment he buys to replace the old, possibly impairing the value of the furniture and equipment serving as security for the lease.

Not infrequently an operator leases a property in need of much rehabilitation and improvement on the condition that he will make the necessary expenditures within a specified time. The landlord may accept these expenditures in lieu of a guarantee deposit upon presentation of proof that the expenditures have been made. In the event that the length of the lease or rental concession does not afford the operator a reasonable time to recover his costs, the lease should contain a provision for compensating him for his investment should the agreement not be renewed. It is often possible for landlord and tenant to establish this division of expenditures at the outset.

G. *Other Provisions*

1. *Arbitration*

The lease should contain a provision whereby differences of opinion as to its interpretation can be settled by arbitration. A common arrangement is to have each party appoint a representative. They in turn will choose a third party to decide on a basis for settlement. Often a person in a specific public office, public accounting firm, or financial institution is named as arbitrator.

2. *Structural alterations*

The lessee should not have the right to make any material structural alterations to the property without written consent of the owner. Obviously the owner is interested in how such changes may influence the property value and the original basis of the rent.

3. *Insurance*

The lease should enumerate the kinds and amounts of insurance to be carried on the property and its operating risks and should further specify who is responsible for payment. The lease should also call for coverage to be reviewed periodically and adjusted to appraisal values and other factors determining its adequacy. The lease should provide for the use and disposition of any sums resulting from claims collected on these policies, and usually stipulates that policies covering the landlord's property and interests, if paid for by the tenant, be deposited with the landlord or his agent.

4. *Concessions in rental during business interruptions*

The lease should cover the eventuality of total or partial damage by fire or other hazard, outlining the concession in rental during the period the property is not operative and the responsibility for repairing such damage.

5. *Termination before expiration of lease*

The lease should cover the rights of landlord and tenant in the event of insolvency or a forced closing due to governmental regulations or emergency restrictions. It should also state the rights of landlord and tenant in case of default on the lease provisions.

6. *Sub-leases*

The lease should describe the conditions under which the lease may be sold or transferred or any portion of it subleased. The landlord may choose to lease only the guest-rooms section, retaining the store rentals, catering department, garage or other facilities for himself or for assignment to separate tenants. In such cases each lease should specifically outline the right of ingress and egress, access to driveways and storage areas, etc., and arrangements regarding heat, light, water and other service costs and charges.

7. *General*

The lease should contain clauses regarding the proper conduct of the business within the law; the payment of all taxes, liens and utility charges; the rights to the use of the name of the motel or motor hotel; the rights of heirs and assigns; the rights of the landlord with respect to inspection of the premises and to possession in case of termination of the lease. These and related items common to the motel lease are sometime referred to as "boiler plate" by attorneys and follow a fairly well-established pattern in their phraseology.

H. *Leasehold value*

The prospective lessee taking over an existing property should be given the opportunity to examine operating statements for the prior two or three years to assist him in estimating the profit possibilities. The present management is aware of the bad points of the property that reflect themselves in higher-than-normal costs; it is up to the new tenants to discover them. Have adequate expenditures been made for repairs and replacements, for advertising and bad accounts? Do not forget that the cost of contemplated improvements adds to the tenant's capital investment—on which he should expect a return.

In the purchase and sale of an existing lease the value over and above the value of the assets taken over is an intangible factor which must be based on the profit potential. Comparative rentals of similar properties are not a prime determining factor, although they may evince interest in the possibilities of the particular project. It is not unreasonable that the amount paid for a motel leasehold and the assets included therewith would bring a higher return than the ordinary investment in real estate. A basis of 12 per cent to 15 per cent earning on the entire investment, plus a return of the original values in the remaining period of the lease or earlier, plus adequate compensation for management, is not considered to be out of line. Some real estate brokers use a yardstick of value based on three times the average earning before depreciation and income taxes. However, this must be tested in each case and adjusted to fit the circumstances. The remaining length of the lease, the physical condition of the property, and the reputation of the project must all be a part of the consideration along with its profit probabilities.

Neither are existing book values of leaseholds a particularly good guide; the basis for their determination should be carefully reviewed if they are to be used at all. Situations exist where these leasehold values have been set up to offset corporate stock issued to the original promoter of the project, in which cases they bear no relationship to real values.

For income tax purposes it is often advisable to have a high value for the furniture, furnishings and equipment and a low value for the leasehold, since the former can be depreciated over a comparatively short period while the latter must be written off over the life of the lease.

An owner may enter into a leasing agreement even though he remains hopeful of selling the property. In these circumstances the lessee should be provided with some protection, generally in the form of a guarantee that he will have the option of purchasing the property by matching the highest bona fide bid. Furthermore, whether or not he buys the property, he should have adequate compensation for any improvement expenditure to the property as well as for the present value of anticipated profits that would accrue to him during the remainder of the lease period. It is best to outline these last two items in specific amounts to apply to each year of the unexpired term of the lease, thus avoiding controversy at the time of sale.

Index